HERBERT VON KARAJAN

Acknowledgements

The author wishes to thank Herbert von Karajan for the generous amount of time and energy he contributed to this project; Deutsche Grammophon for making so much of Maestro von Karajan's recorded music available; the National Archives, and especially Amy Schmidt for her able guidance through that immense jungle of invaluable documents; The Berlin Document Center; Günther and Georgia Schatzdorfer for making life in Austria both understandable and enjoyable; Oliver Rathkolb for sharing his wealth of historical knowledge; Seiji Ozawa, Todd Perry, Tom Morris, and Bill Brunnel of the Boston Symphony Orchestra; Alan Balter, a fine young conductor, for the insights about his craft; Tom Wallace at W. W. Norton for thoughtful editing; Bryan van Sweringen for translation and commiseration; Jane Scheuerman for cheerfully processing the words; Georgina Oliver and Sunday Fellows for additional research; all the singers, musicians, and conductors who took time to talk about their work and express their views; and the various agents, students, and lovers of music who shared their perceptions with me.

Herbert von Karajan

A Biographical Portrait

Roger Vaughan

Weidenfeld & Nicolson
London

For Kippy

The author wishes to thank the following for giving him permission to quote from
copyrighted material:

Elisabeth Schwarzkopf, excerpted from *On and Off the Record:
A Memoir of Walter Legge*, copyright © 1982 Musical Adviser
Establishment, reprinted with permission of Charles Scribner's
Sons. *Opera on Record*, edited by Alan Blyth, Hutchinson, London
1979; Harper & Row, New York 1982; reprinted with permission
of A. M. Heath & Company, Limited. *Putting the Record Straight*,
by John Culshaw, copyright © 1981 by Martin Secker & Warburg,
Ltd., reprinted by permission of Viking Penguin Inc. Andrew
Porter for material which appeared in *The New Yorker*.

First published in Great Britain in 1986 by
George Weidenfeld & Nicolson Limited
91 Clapham High Street
London SW4 7TA

This paperback edition published by
George Weidenfeld & Nicolson Limited 1990

ISBN 0 297 81052 9

Printed and bound in Great Britain by
The Guernsey Press Co. Ltd.,
Guernsey, Channel Islands.

Contents

Illustrations

The Biographical Portrait

A Foreword

There are two kinds of biographies. In one, the subject is deceased.
Through letters, personal papers, books, and other tangible research,
and by interviewing people who knew the subject, the biographer
reconstructs as clear a picture as possible of the subject's life and
personality. Such a biography is objective, scholarly work, a job for
historians. The advantage of such a work is that nothing, however
heinous, need be held back. The subject is dead, after all. All can be
revealed.

In the second type the subject is living, which is first of all a great
advantage. Nothing can replace the value of a face-to-face encounter
with a person one hopes to portray. Of course the disadvantages pile
up on the other side of the scale, sometimes creating an uncomfortable
feeling of imbalance. Personal papers and letters are still locked away.
Friends, even enemies, are reluctant to speak frankly about a person
wo·thy of biographical treatment. Such a person usually has considerable power. His recriminations strike deep. In addition, there are
certain boundaries of decency that must be observed. The living biography, best described as a "biographical portrait" given that it is
incomplete, is a journalistic undertaking. The journalist long ago decided that whatever the disadvantages, having his subjects alive was
more to his liking.

This book is a biographical portrait. Because close collaboration—
a relationship—between the subject and the writer is implied by such
a book, it is important to know how the book came to be. That story
is often relegated to the book jacket, or left out. It shouldn't be. It is
difficult for a biographical portrait not to be personal, since objectivity

tends to diminish as familiarity grows. The "how" of it provides critical insight: it reveals the point of view.

It is important to know, therefore, that I met Herbert von Karajan as a sailor. In 1981 I went to St. Tropez in the south of France to write an article for *Sail* magazine about consultant Gary Jobson teaching Karajan the intricacies of his 77-foot "maxi" sailboat. In preparation for our visit, Jobson sent Karajan the book I wrote about the 1979 Fastnet Race, *One Man's Voyage*, during which a violent storm claimed fifteen lives. In a letter to Jobson, Karajan wrote: "Thank you for the book by Mr. Vaughan. I find it simply marvelous, please tell him of my admiration. The precision of his report, and what is more, his short biography of Mr. [John] Kilroy, is a masterwork of writing. I wish I had somebody who does the same for me." In the first five minutes I spent with Karajan, he repeated his wishes.

One of my initial worries was that I am neither musician nor musicologist, music historian nor music critic. Working acquaintance with at least one of these music subdivisions seemed essential for tackling the biography of a man who has been called the world's greatest living conductor; a prodigy at four and a half (piano), a man with some 800 recordings to his credit, and, since 1955, music director (for life) of the Berlin Philharmonic Orchestra, an ensemble generally acclaimed as one of the world's best. But I quickly learned that no one with such credentials would have the faintest hope of approaching Karajan. He does not generally trust people in the music business, and he would be more likely to engage Liberace as guest soloist than even consider scholarly arm wrestling with a professional music person of any persuasion.

Karajan has been a conductor since he was eighteen, a music director since he was twenty. He has conducted many of the major symphonies a hundred times and has polished an opera repertoire of fifty or more pieces over fifty-five years. He has always conducted without a score. The longest, most complex operas reside in their entirety in his heart and memory. Even in his younger days he didn't read reviews, and he went home directly from the podium after concerts, seeking solitude, not comradeship. By the age of seventy-three (in 1981) his ego had become blinding, colossal. He doesn't argue, he doesn't discuss. He dictates. He has a particular approach to music making that he is certain is right. He would eat musical pretenders for breakfast.

So I am lucky to be a sailor. Karajan relates to sailors, fliers, outdoor people. At heart he is a man of the mountains, happiest when surrounded by nature at its most imposing. His houses are located amid breathtaking mountain vistas in St. Moritz, Switzerland, and Anif, near Salzburg, Austria, and on the edge of the Mediterranean Sea. He has a cottage in the forest outside Vienna. As a child he learned that trust was what one held for the person climbing ahead on the rope. All his life he has climbed, skied, sailed, driven fast cars and motorcycles, and flown airplanes. Most of his close acquaintances have come from those pursuits, not music.

But one couldn't approach Karajan without at least a modicum of musical understanding, and I am lucky there as well. I began the piano at age nine. When I was eleven I asked my father if he would obtain the sheet music for a current popular song, "Tonight We Love." He came home with music that was known by a number, by a composer whose name I couldn't pronounce. "Tonight We Love" was a theme stolen directly from the First Piano Concerto of Peter Ilyich Tchaikovsky, a piece that remains one of my favorites.

I stuck with lessons for five years, complete with the horror of recitals at the local Women's Club Hall, then drifted towards jazz on my own, thanks to natural rhythm and a good ear. In college I took music courses and discovered the pleasure of listening to a symphony while I followed along in the score.

I have been a music lover and occasional player all my life. I first wrote about music in 1978, when I covered the Boston Symphony's hundredth anniversary. That led to my accompanying the Boston Symphony to China in 1979. The best part of that association was getting to know music director Seiji Ozawa, a charming and talented man who was, and is, a student of Herbert von Karajan.

So it was with amazement and considerable pleasure that I found myself, in October 1982, sitting in New York's Carnegie Hall for all rehearsals and four concerts by the Berlin Philharmonic Orchestra, Herbert von Karajan, music director.

OXFORD, MARYLAND
March 1985

I
Triumph in New York

October 1982

Carnegie Hall had been sold out for six months. The Berlin Philharmonic hadn't played in New York for six years, and just the rumor of their visit had been sufficient to overheat the ticket office switchboard. Herbert von Karajan and the Berlin Philharmonic, living, breathing, making music together for twenty-seven years. Inseparable. A latter-day phenomenon in a time when very little lasts for twenty-seven years. When the posters announcing their four New York concerts had been put in the frames outside the hall, the little black and white "sold out" stickers were already attached. The advertised prices topped out at $35 per concert. Scalpers were having a field day in the $200 to $300 range. It was New York's ticket of the week, maybe the month. It was the music ticket of the year.

Inside the hall, there was a problem. Herbert von Karajan had stopped rehearsal after only a few bars of Stravinsky's *Apollo* and had turned on his stool, peering into the semi-darkness of the nearly empty hall for a lieutenant with whom he could confer. A man ran quickly toward the elevated stage, then another, and another. They craned their necks in order to speak with Karajan, who towered above them on his high perch.

The problem was a noise. Herbert von Karajan had heard a noise, and he didn't like it. He held up a hand. The group fell silent, listening. "There it is ... you hear it?" Karajan said, smiling the way a father might to encourage his child's dawning comprehension of the obvious. It was faint, ever so faint, but yes, they heard it. What could be done? They would look into it. Karajan said he wouldn't complain if the noise was in pitch, but it wasn't. The lieutenants laughed. He said he supposed nothing could be done about the sporadic rumble of the subway. With nervous laughter, the group of lieutenants supposed not. Karajan wanted to know when the subway was built, when the hall was built. He suspected bad planning. Then he spun on his stool back toward the orchestra, gaining their attention and dispatching the lieutenants with that single gesture. "So!" he said to the players, raising his baton and mumbling a comment in German that made them chuckle. Rehearsal continued, not that it was terribly necessary. Stravinsky's *Apollo* is a showcase for the string sections, a familiar piece for seasoned players. After the trans-Atlantic flight, Karajan was just working out the travel kinks.

Karajan looked good for a man of seventy-three who was supposed to be in constant pain from a deteriorating back condition. He walked with difficulty, pulling his right leg after him stiffly, and with obvious effort. But in front of the orchestra he seemed rested, relaxed, younger than his years. Alert. He is a handsome man. His heavily lined, aristo-cratic face reflects his Greek heritage. His slightly olive skin is smoother than a man of his age deserves. His hair is gray, almost white, and is brushed back from his face in a manner that makes him appear to have just finished a ski run. He is not a large man, around five-foot six in built-up shoes, and he is compact, gathered, from a lifetime of sports. He currently fights off the increasingly inevitable paunch with rigorous attention to diet inspired by a degree of vanity that is unusual in a man of his age. "Dashing," Karajan has often been called in the past. Somehow, at seventy-three, the description still applies.

As is his habit when he begins a rehearsal, he turned and scanned the seats as he conducted, making eye contact with each of the dozen or so people in attendance, nodding the slightest of nods, making sure there were no uninvited intruders, counting the house. His rehearsal attire had been upgraded a bit from the tired jogging suits he habi-tually wears when at home in the Grosse Festspielhaus in Salzburg. He wore dark flannel pants and a black cashmere turtleneck with the sleeves pushed up to the elbows. On his feet were a pair of black, kangaroo-leather, high-cut shoes that are custom-made for him by the Adidas Company of Austria.

At the break, Karajan received a report on the noise. It was a pump in the basement of the hall that moves water to a holding tank on the roof, from whence it is dispensed to a hundred and forty apartments on the upper floors of the building. Mr. McCree, the hall's manager, said Karajan heard it the minute he walked on stage. McCree said he had never heard it before, probably because he had been living in

New York too long and was inured to noise. It was agreed that the pump would be turned off for all rehearsals, and of course for concerts. McCree said he hoped the hall wouldn't run out of water.

As for the subway, not even Herbert von Karajan could do anything about that. Not in New York, anyway. If the scene had been Austria, where Karajan is considered something of a natural resource—a national hero—and if Austria had subways, and if the subways ran under the hall (which would be unlikely), he could have stopped them during concert hours, no doubt about it. Certainly in Salzburg, and probably in Vienna, where people still speak about the "Karajan years," when he commanded the Vienna State Opera, with the same grim tone one might use when referring to war. Possibly also in Berlin, where he has been in charge of musical fortunes for nearly thirty years, and most definitely in Japan, where he is all but deified.

Max Rudolph, the well-known conductor and teacher, has said that conductors have a right to feel important: "They represent the masters, after all." Most conductors, the good ones at least, manage to reinforce their importance with considerable amounts of power. Power seems to go with the profession. Consider this: in a hall there is an orchestra of a hundred players who are chatting, tuning their instruments, drumming, playing phrases, telling jokes, and there are two thousand people getting seated, arranging their coats, flipping through programs, waving at friends, talking, coughing. One person enters and the hall immediately becomes quiet. He raises a small white stick and there is dead silence, followed by noise of the most complex sort rendered in pleasurable sound. Instant order from chaos. Such a response to one's presence is more than any mortal can be expected to bear without effect. The ego, which must be immense as a prerequisite for even entering the profession, is further enlarged. Delusions rush in. Depending on the basic nature and stability of the individual, a conductor's self-image can get more or less out of hand.

Karajan was born close enough to the purple to expect a certain amount of natural submission from others. The "von" in his name is a family title—Knight of the Holy Roman Empire—which was conferred upon his great-grandfather Georg Johann Karajannis by Duke Friedrich August von Sachsen for his work in the textile industry. Karajan's father, a noted physician, inherited the title. Titles are illegal in Austria today, but those families who have them continue to use them without hindrance, a contradiction which is a good example of the Austrian way.

Karajan's authoritarian stance seems to have been inborn, along with the musical talent that enabled him to play a Mozart rondo, in concert, when he was six. Power is not something Karajan has had trouble getting used to.

Karajan's power is worth study because he represents the end of a certain era of conductors. The last of the dinosaurs, he has been called. Today's younger conductors spread themselves thin, employing jet travel to make international careers guest conducting, rather than building power bases at home the way Karajan did in Berlin (and Salzburg and Vienna). The emancipation (through organization and unionization) of orchestra players in the last twenty years has served to bring conductors down somewhat from the dictatorial heights. Former Boston Symphony Orchestra Music Director Erich Leinsdorf recalls in his book, *The Composer's Advocate*, that when he first arrived in the United States in 1937, "a musician at the Radio City Music Hall would recognize that he was being given notice if the conductor raised two fingers of his left hand while continuing to beat time with his right. It meant the unfortunate person had two weeks of employment left." And gone are the days when any conductor had the option to record nearly any piece for the first, or even the third time. When Karajan began cutting records in 1937, the libraries were very thin. When he recorded a symphony, chances were it was the *only* version available. He also had the vision—"the nose," as he says—to estimate the vast potential of the recording industry. Not only did he record enthusiastically on wax masters when his contemporaries shunned the frustrating task, but he was also in the forefront of each major step in the development of electronic recording: the long-playing record, stereo, quadrophonic sound, and now compact (laser) discs.

Karajan's power was far-reaching in the late 1950s and '60s. Simultaneously, he was music director of the Berlin Philharmonic; artistic advisor of La Scala; artistic director of the Salzburg Festival; artistic director of the Vienna State Opera; and music director of the London Philharmonia Orchestra. "General Music Director of Europe," he was called, and with good reason. Everyone wanted a piece of Karajan in those days, and that was fine with him. The lean postwar years had left their scars. His hunger was deep, his ambition great, his musical mission burning. He was fifty years old, having already served a long apprenticeship in small theaters in Germany. He was ready. He consciously sought power, mainly for his own security. "Early in my career," he says, "I saw a man fired out-of-hand. It was unjustified. I hate injustice and situations that can overpower me, that are out of my control. I said to myself then, 'this must never happen to me.'"

For ten years his life was a mad dash from city to city—Milan,

Vienna, Berlin, Salzburg, and London—with foreign tours, guest appearances, and a recording schedule that resulted in twenty records a year. His superstar was ascending, and it was accompanied by super-human effort. But it was enough to tax even his remarkable organizational abilities. He held important meetings in airports, between flights. When he conducted in Berlin, he insisted the concert end in time for him to rush from the podium to his car and make the 10:40 overnight train to Vienna that left from the Zoo station.

Ultimately he decided he didn't like being an administrator (those he administered got mighty weary of it as well, by all accounts), so he pulled back to his Berlin Philharmonic base, stopped guest conducting, and cleverly reduced the scope of his responsibilities without diminishing the range of his power.

Now he has the additional leverage of age. As Donal Henehan of the *New York Times* wrote upon observing Karajan's reception in New York, "it would seem he has passed over into the Saintly sphere that leading conductors seem to inhabit by right as they reach elderhood." Elderhood, for conductors, is a time when the talent, the accomplishment—the power—becomes hopelessly entangled with the myth. The result is a mystique unlike that attached to any other profession.

The old age reached by so many conductors can be explained in part by the excellent exercise the continuous waving of their arms affords the cardiovascular system. But the rest is more obscure. Except for the rare actor or actress, no one but conductors *perform* with regularity into their eighties. One is simply not used to seeing such aged and still effective performers. This is a phenomenon in itself, and it is touching, compelling. Other artists of advanced years work in private, and their work is more tangible. Unlike music, one can see it, feel it. Music is ethereal, mercurial, a mystery in itself. And exactly what the conductor does up there, that is elusive too. Hence the confusion, the emotional anxiety that a great conductor generates in his waning years. The response to him, and to his music, becomes more and more governed by emotion. A saintly sphere indeed. Or more precisely, since Karajan will never qualify for sainthood, a sphere of idolatry.

A conversation I witnessed between a young German conductor and a former Viennese music critic on the subject of Karajan is pertinent. A few years ago, Karajan was scheduled to conduct Haydn's *Creation* at Goldene Hall, stately home of the Musikfreunde (Friends of Music) in Vienna. Karajan had to cancel and another conductor was engaged. As a result of the change, the hall was only half full.

Young German conductor: "That's absurd. I love Karajan, but he's temperamentally unsuited to conduct Haydn. The replacement conductor is better with Haydn."

Viennese critic: "People don't go to hear Haydn, they go to see Karajan conduct."

A third party: "How strange. One expects the Musikfreunde audience to be the most educated in the world."

Viennese critic: "That says nothing about Vienna and the Musikfreunde—it says something about the rest of the world."

Later on the former Viennese critic suggested, only partly in jest, that if a stereo system were set up in a hall, people would pay to watch Karajan conduct it.

Idol or not, Herbert von Karajan wouldn't try to change the schedule of New York's subways. His view of life may be Olympian, but he is also a very pragmatic man. Preparation, organization, and especially control are at the heart of his heavily disciplined method of operation. He knows when to hold back. When talking about his approach to various pursuits—music, flying, skiing—he will often use the cat as example. "Watch a cat," he says, "and you will see that a cat never jumps until he is sure he can make it. He studies the situation, then either jumps or doesn't. But you never see him miss once he jumps." Those who keep cats will spot the flaw here: cats do miss. Not often, but they do miss. Thus, Karajan is like the cat.

The fits of rage and the tantrums that seem a tradition among highly strung music personalities, particularly sopranos, tenors, and conductors, are not part of Karajan's repertoire. Such outbursts are not his style. He would consider them a waste of time and energy. Inefficient. He is an Austrian, after all. Once, in Salzburg, he arrived at the Festspielhaus with the usual five minutes to spare before a concert and was informed that the organ was out of commission. Repairmen had worked on the instrument all afternoon to no avail. The evening's program was Brahms's *German Requiem*, a piece in which the organ is featured. Karajan was momentarily startled at the news—he had assumed the repairmen would succeed—then he shrugged. "So, the organ is broken. I will tell the audience they will have to hear it with their inner ear," he said. It was a solution that even amused him a little.

Karajan wouldn't tangle with the bureaucracy of New York any more than he would deliberately fly his plane into a thunderhead. New York is a rough, abusive city with a tiresome plethora of superstars. Furthermore, Karajan got a shaky start in New York when he first appeared there in 1955.

In 1954, Wilhelm Furtwängler, the revered German musical genius who preceded Karajan as music director of the Berlin Philharmonic, died. Karajan had first conducted the Berlin in 1937 as a guest, and had lusted for that orchestra from that moment. But Furtwängler was insanely jealous of the fast-rising Karajan and had kept him as far away from "his" orchestra as possible. At Furtwängler's death, Karajan was one of three obvious candidates for the Berlin position. The first order of business was to cover the United States tour that had been planned. The American sponsors of the tour intervened on Karajan's behalf. The Senate of Berlin, under whose authority the orchestra functions, asked Karajan to undertake the tour, and he accepted.

Pickets and protesters greeted Karajan in New York in 1955. The *New York Times* announced the Berlin tour on February 8, nearly a month before the first concert in New York. The headline of the *Times* story clearly stated the situation: "Berlin Philharmonic Hopes Art Will Win Over Reaction to Nazi Past on U.S. Tour." Many of the Berlin players had been members of the Nazi party. In return for joining, they received (from Hitler) exemption from military service. But the man singled out for his former Nazi affiliations was Herbert von Karajan.

Unlike many who had joined the Nazi party during the 1930s, Karajan never denied it or pretended it had never happened. From the outset he always maintained he joined strictly for career reasons. Opportunism, and/or survival, were popular reasons for joining the party. The only specific fact that remains in question about Karajan's Nazi affiliation is *when* he joined the party, and there will probably be no end to that debate, as we shall see.

But from the moment the war against Germany was terminated and the Allied Occupation Forces set up a provisional government and began the process of denazification, Karajan's case was in the news. Two years passed before he was cleared and allowed to conduct in public.

He was a leading conductor, of course, ready to contribute to the cultural rejuvenation of Austria and Germany. For reasons both real and political, and perhaps because of the unyielding, unrepentant nature of Karajan's personality—the concept of apology, for instance, is essentially foreign to him—he became a political football between the Russian, the French, the American, and the British military factions that comprised the Quadripartite Alliance governing Germany in 1945. Reading the military documents of those days that pertain to Karajan is a dizzying experience. As soon as he was cleared by one faction, another would block him. If two were for him, two would be against. If three were for him, one would hold out. Within a week, the situation could shift 180 degrees. At best, the concept of denazification was a tenuous one. The theory that all Nazis and all things Nazi (from institutions to art) should be purged, and that all people (and things) that while Nazi in name weren't *really* Nazi should be allowed to function, was divine. Putting it into practice was an extravagant undertaking of dubious merit and marginal success, partly because there was nothing impersonal about the judgments: everyone involved had something to prove. Karajan was subjected to the full brunt of the militaristic, multilingual, bureaucratic process.

The case of Furtwängler, who never joined the Nazi party yet conducted in Germany throughout the war, and that of the then prominent soprano Elisabeth Schwarzkopf, who was a party member, were equally noteworthy and complex. But it was Karajan who first set foot in America to perform, and therefore it was Karajan who was the target of anti-Nazi feelings which ten years had done little to diminish. For those who didn't know Karajan's story, or who had forgotten, organizations like Jewish War Veterans and the Musicians' Union provided information and fanned the flame.

Seven hundred and fifty members of the American Federation of Musicians signed a petition seeking to prevent the Berlin Philharmonic concerts, and protesting "the U.S. Government subsidy" of the tour. The State Department tried to calm the mounting furor by explaining that the Senate of Berlin had subsidized the tour, and that both Karajan and the orchestra's Intendant (manager), Gerhard von Westerman, another target of the protesters, had been officially cleared by denazification tribunals. Nevertheless, at the opening concert of March 1, pickets representing Zionist Youth and various ad hoc groups marched in front of Carnegie Hall. Police detachments were stationed both outside the hall and within. The house lights stayed up throughout the concert for added security. As the concert began, one protester loosed several pigeons into the hall.

The press conference the next day didn't help matters. Karajan, who had registered in his hotel under a false name, said he had been unaware of the demonstrations outside the hall . . . only the applause within. When the questions got sticky, Karajan, who speaks very acceptable English, retired behind the language barrier and let an interpreter carry on. The interpreter, the late André Mertens, who was vice-president of Columbia Artists Management, U.S. organizer of the tour, said "All of Karajan's life has been concentrated on music. . . . He lives in a world of music. . . . Of course he was not sympathetic to the Hitler persecutions. . . . He has never been interested in politics."

Across town, Westerman was telling the *New York Times*, "we must prove that music has nothing to do with politics," while an advertisement in the same paper specified that the Berlin tour was "under the patronage of the Chancellor of the Federal Republic of Germany, Dr. Konrad Adenauer, and under the sponsorship of His Excellency, the German Ambassador." The Orchestra, it was reported, had been sent by Germany "as a tribute to the American people for their many acts of kindness towards the people of Berlin—most notably during the airlift, when Berlin was isolated from the free world."

New York Times critic Howard Taubman was one of several writers who addressed the "art and politics" issue: "The argument that music should be above politics is reasonable. But how often is this ideal practiced? Policy makers, musicians, and indeed many in the audience often act as though they would like to have it both ways. They don't mind if music serves a political purpose, provided it is their purpose. If the political aim conflicts with their conventions or prejudices, then they want music to be above the battle.... The truth is that art cannot be above the battle."

Taubman's conclusion echoed as the Berlin Philharmonic moved from city to city. Karajan recalls that in Baltimore, only twenty-five souls were seated in the audience at the appointed hour. Karajan appeared, regarded the small group, and made rare preconcert remarks. "I am quite aware I am conducting for the smallest audience in my life," he recalls telling them, "but certainly the best. Because against the propaganda, I know you came only to hear the music, and we will make a great performance for you."

Once past the politics, the music was superb, by all accounts, even though the orchestra was in a postwar rebuilding stage and under the baton of a new conductor. Taubman did not write a rave review, but he was certainly enthusiastic: "The Berlin Philharmonic, it may be said in all objectivity, is a fine orchestra, and Herr von Karajan is a conductor of stature.... The visitors gave an impressive account of themselves. The strength of the orchestra is solidarity and tradition. It has a meticulous discipline that is aimed unfailingly at projecting its point of view. It does not go in for brilliance of tone, but it can muster quite a bit of it. Its special gift is for neatness and honesty of phrasing, and it knows how to apply light and shade as if it were one virtuoso instead of a body of more than 100 men."

Karajan was elected music director of the orchestra by the players halfway through that 1955 tour. His position was quickly confirmed by the Berlin Senate, and his work began. Never again would a music writer hold in small regard the Berlin's "brilliance of tone," for the development of an extraordinary "sound" for the orchestra was uppermost among Karajan's musical ambitions.

Listening to the Berlin Philharmonic today, nearly thirty years later, what rivets one's attention is the beauty and perfection of the sound. The softest of pianissimos commands rapt attention. The smooth crescendos peak exactly when they should. The breaks are sliced clean, without the slightest ragged edge. The strings sing with a rich, steely voice whose velvet timbre tightens the throat of the listener. The brass sound so bright and clean one imagines the instruments have been buffed to a silver lustre with a clump of soft fleece. Together the orchestra emits a smooth flow of sound that, like a deep river, swirls and eddies, undulates and bends in its purposeful march to the sea.

Karajan and the Berlin Philharmonic have long been widely acclaimed for their sound, their precision. Andrew Porter, music critic of the *Financial Times* (1952–72) and (since 1972) of the *New Yorker*, recapitulated those qualities during their 1982 visit. "Its tone is broad, deep, full ... it is readier to 'state' than to 'sing.' ... It never sounds febrile or forced but always grandly and profoundly confident, massive in full ensemble, and unhurried even at prestissimo. Those are the generalizations, the constants. Karajan put a high tonal gloss on solid virtues ... the sound became matchless—smoother, more luminous, more beautiful, more exquisite in pianissimos, more rounded at climaxes than anything one had ever heard."

And critic Peter Davis, commenting in *New York* magazine on Karajan's playing of the four Brahms symphonies that were on the 1982 Carnegie Hall program, wrote: "Karajan's success in achieving total euphony is flabbergasting in itself and surely qualifies him as today's supreme orchestral technician."

If critical agreement on Karajan and the Berlin Philharmonic as the ultimate in beauty and perfection of sound is unanimous (and it seems to be), there is a parallel line of musical commentary that is nearly as consistent. It is a thesis that takes Karajan to task for the fact that all that sound and precision, the smooth legato he commands that seems to string entire symphonies—even operas—together into viable units, has submerged the vital essence of the music. As Porter says, "Many will say that Karajan is the greatest living conductor, but no one is willing to say that he took us to the heart of any one piece." It is a theme that has been surfacing in critical writing for at least twenty-five years.

Sunday Times critic David Cairns reviewed a concert given by Karajan and the Berlin Philharmonic in London in 1958. He came away somewhat overwhelmed by the music, but also puzzled, and with reservations. "Yet to say just what was wrong with the perform-ances is not easy. With Karajan, just because there is so much beauty on the surface and so little music below it, it forced one back on vague statements about 'lack of feeling.' "

In an article he wrote about the first Karajan year at the Vienna State Opera (1962), Joseph Wechsberg said this: "Karajan's flair for exactness is evident, but also his love of effect. Everything he does is high voltage, but also missing in depth."

On the event of the Berlin's 1974 American tour, Andrew Porter continued the discussion: "Karajan always gives the audience a smooth ride. In the two Brahms symphonies—the Fourth followed by the Second—that made up his first program, all the bumps were ironed out. The machine started at a touch ... over hill, over dale; now fast now slow; all gradients effortlessly mounted; plenty of power in re-serve; never a jarring gear shift; smooth brakes; perfect road handling. And no direct feeling, you might say, of the road traveled. That's what was wrong."

Porter went on: "When all sense of physical stress has been re-moved from the playing, when nothing sounds difficult, then the tensions of the music disappear. For Toscanini, for Szell, the Fourth Symphony [of Brahms] was a struggle.... When Furtwängler con-ducted, it became a new adventure, for him, for his players, for the audience. Unexpected and wonderful things might happen in the course of it, and they usually did. In Karajan's performance, the music never took one by surprise; astonishments were limited to the none-such instrumental sound.... Between manner and matter there is a Brahmsian paradox which Karajan resolved too comfortably, settling for manner."

Harold Schonberg of the *New York Times* generally found more to like than dislike about Karajan's performances with the Berlin Phil-harmonic. But even when praising Karajan, he acknowledged the prevalent critical theme. After hearing the Brahms Second and Fourth Symphonies in 1974, Schonberg wrote: "From the beginning this conductor has been one of the great baton virtuosos. He can do with the flick of the wrist what others can not do with a bulldozer. But through the years there has been speculation on what exactly he has wanted to do. An articulate school of critics, and musicians too, maintains that his conducting is all technique and no heart, that he is more interested in effect than substance, that music to him is an ego trip.

"There is some truth in these allegations. But certainly, at this opening concert ... Mr. von Karajan was steady, was anything but eccentric, dug into the music and shaped it as he desired. Of course there was an emphasis on pure sound.... It is also true that supreme virtuoso conductors ... sometimes overrefine their performances.

"Perhaps there was this overrefinement to Mr. von Karajan's conducting. But if one listened divorced from the legend, it would have been very hard to take exception to anything that was done."

When the Berlin Philharmonic returned to the U.S. two years later, in 1976, Andrew Porter sounded almost apologetic for harping on the same theme. "I still cannot find words to explain why in concerts—less regularly in the opera house—Karajan's interpretations leave me admiring but unstirred. How can I be so grudging? Why do not I simply cheer executions more polished than I am likely to hear?

"The reason is not any perverse resistance to the 'star' reputation. Toscanini had such a reputation, but at the thought of Toscanini and Beethoven's Ninth, or Toscanini and Verdi's *Requiem*, the Karajan readings dwindle to beautiful but hollow shells, mere sounds. Toscanini took one to the heart of the work. Karajan presents an immaculate surface."

A word must be interjected about the critics, these people who, as David Cairns has observed, offer us "passionate private experience seeking to persuade." The word "passionate" could also be used (as understatement) to describe the negative feelings against critics that have been voiced over the years by those artists, writers, and performers who are the grist for the critics' mill. There is clear-cut, ongoing war here, and with good reason.

There are several types of artistic criticism. The most reasonable is perhaps criticism as consumer service, reviews that help people make selections among established artistic products: films, books, recordings, live theater, paintings, even restaurants. But even in this category the private experience may be jaded, the passion fired by pettiness. And the power, in some instances, is frightful, even obscene. In New York, for instance, a handful of critics are in virtual control of what shows live or die on Broadway. This is an outrageous situation, given human frailties, and it fosters the lingering cliché that criticism is a fallback position for those who are unable to make it on the creative side of the fence. The human frailty applies not only to the critic, but to the greater public, who are all too eager to be told what to think.

Critics who review live music performances are in an unusual position in that they are reviewing unique events. Like sunsets, they never happen quite the same twice. The question arises: For whom are these people reviewing the event? Surely not for those who were there.

They know what they heard (or do they?). Then could it be for those who weren't there? Why, if it can't be repeated? It is reviewed for the record, we suppose, and to give those who didn't hear the performance an idea of what they will hear should they attend a concert by the particular ensemble. And, of course, the reviewers are writing for other critics, contemporaries in this strange brotherhood.

Why, in fact, should we care what the critics say? For most people, music is an emotional experience. The music either catches them or it doesn't. As the well-known flautist James Galway has observed, "music is merely fantasy." What one hears, with the exception of opera, is what one gets, and thus the very abstraction of music all but occasionally defies concurrence. And for the concertgoer there are several variables that further complicate what is already a very subjective experience: the number of alcoholic drinks or the amount of food he consumed before the concert; his general state of mind and body; the acoustic properties of the hall; the weather; and the general mood of the orchestra.

Critical arguments like those above regarding Karajan's musical interpretations—manner over matter—rely on subtle distinctions that require considerable education, or at least musical familiarity. Anyone can hear a wrong note, but to hear minute differences in phrasing and dynamics one must first of all know the music. Then the ears must be good, the music sensibilities keen. And in an age when the quest for perfect sound through high fidelity components has become as common an addiction as sugar, such distinctions tend to get buried even deeper beneath the boosters, equalizers, lasers, and all that wattage.

Perhaps the critics' real service is that they delve into the history and make musical extrapolations that provide us with a measuring stick. So if someone says a performance is good, the critic says, "Compared to what?" This can be annoying, for sure, because when the savage breast has been soothed, it is annoying to have the treatment diluted by a bunch of academic theoreticians strutting their stuff. But that is not to say that the service isn't valid, and even worthwhile.

The best critics are discerning, educated listeners. The best critics have musical educations that rival those of the best musicians and conductors. They are serious intellectuals, music scholars. The best critics can read (hear!) scores, and they have good ears as well. The comparative literature of their profession resides in their musical memories. When Porter compares Toscanini's rendition of Beethoven's Ninth with that of Karajan, he goes to his turntable only to confirm musical impressions that replay readily in his head. The very best critics prove by the absence of malice and sarcasm in their prose, and by the good humor they exhibit, that they truly love music and are not jealous of good players. And they let the reader get to know them, which helps. As one might imagine, the number of such critics is small.

David Cairns once compared a Karajan performance with the Berlin Philharmonic with the driving of a "glittering war chariot." This is among the more complimentary descriptions that have been applied to a conductor at work. Standing with one's back to a vast audience and waving the arms in front of a group of musicians is a tough act to pull off. Often it is most distracting to those trying to hear the music. Conductors are, for this reason, fair game for humorists. One of the stand-by skits of the old *Saturday Night Live* television comedy show was "The Conductor's Club," in which ten or fifteen people would, after some discussion and bickering, stand around waving their arms to records. And actor Danny Kaye's one-man show, in which he satirizes "the conductor" for two hours in front of a symphony orchestra, has played all over the world to enthusiastic audiences. At one point Kaye strides in front of the orchestra with a bundle of batons under his arm. Like a baseball hitter in the on-deck circle, Kaye elaborately tests several for strength, flexibility, and balance before selecting the "right" one.

Karajan says the earliest conductors can be found in Gregorian chant. "The melodic simplicity of Gregorian music allowed many interpretations. And there were no real hints in the music about how to express tempo," Karajan says. "If you listen to different interpretations of the same chant you can hear the differences. The conductors were nameless. Then later on, in the Baroque period, Bach would often roll up a sheet of music and use it as a baton to beat the time. Or the players would watch the bow of the lead violin."

As he chronicles the development of the conductor, the humor of the profession does not elude Karajan: "There was a man named Jean-Baptiste Lully, who developed a different technique. Lully was Louis XIV's music master, composer, and director of the court orchestra (1662). He ruled all music at the Court of Versailles. He had a baton made that was as tall as he, like a majorette's baton. There was a crown on the top, and a silver rod at the base. He would smash it on the floor to beat time. If the rhythm was off, he would help it along this way.

"One day he got angry, and prepared a big smash with the baton. It never reached the floor. Instead, it went into his foot. He got blood poisoning and died. Here was a hitherto unknown event: death of a conductor in the line of duty, a record not equaled since his time. But sometimes I fear that one of Lully's younger followers, in executing his jumps, turns, and otherwise ecstatic expressions which seem to have been born of Indian temple dancers, might end up putting the batón through his own chest."

Karajan is austere on the podium, businesslike from the moment he appears onstage, and restrained in his gestures. He has had his theatrical moments. Those who were in Berlin when he first appeared there in the mid-1930s recall that at one of his first concerts he was led to the podium with his eyes closed. He was young then, trying desperately to make an impression in a city with an embarrassment of outstanding conductors: Wilhelm Furtwängler, Karl Böhm, Bruno Walter, and Erich Kleiber were the resident directors of the major musical ensembles at the time. Karajan is no longer guided to the podium, but he continues to conduct with his eyes closed. He says simply that it improves his concentration, and since he doesn't use a score when he conducts, there is nothing to look at. Seiji Ozawa, music director of the Boston Symphony, doesn't use a score either, but his eyes are open during a performance. Ozawa says that for him, eye contact with the players is critical. Here is one of the fascinating aspects of conducting: there are no rules, only guidelines. The most eccentric approach is tolerated if the results are successful.

The composer Hector Berlioz, in the introduction to his short book *The Conductor: The Theory of His Art*, wrote with passion about those times that were not successful: "The composer . . . depends on a crowd of intermediaries to bring his work before the public—intermediaries who may be intelligent or stupid, devoted or hostile, active or inert, and who yet have it in their power, from the first moment to the last, to contribute to it or to illuminate it on the one hand, or on the other to disfigure, calumniate, or even destroy it altogether. . . . The most formidable of them all, in my opinion, is the conductor. A bad singer only damages his own part; the incapable or malevolent conductor ruins everything. . . . Under such circumstances the most wonderful orchestra is paralyzed; the finest singers are annoyed and benumbed; there is neither spirit nor unity. Under such direction the noblest flights of the author seem but folly, enthusiasm has all the heart knocked out of it, inspiration is thrown violently to the ground, the angel no longer has wings, the man of genius becomes a madman or a fool, the divine statue is hurled from its pedestal and dragged in the mud," etc.

Having divested himself of that stormy prelude, Berlioz acknowledges that the conductor's task is Herculean: "He has not only to direct, in the sense intended by the composer, a work of which a knowledge has already been acquired by the executants, but also to convey such knowledge to them in the case of a work which is new to them. He has to criticize the errors and faults of each of them during the rehearsals, and so to organize the resources at his disposal as to get the best out of them as quickly as possible...."

For those who are mysteriously infected with harmonies and rhythms and great and beautiful sounds coursing about their systems, playing music is a compulsion, and a compulsion is the irresistible impulse to perform an act that may be contrary to the will. The conductor should be an evocative and inspirational focal image—a unifying force—for one hundred or so musicians compulsively and simultaneously performing. It is a big job, a big responsibility. It is a mysterious undertaking as well, because it must be accomplished only with gestures, gestures that can't really be taught beyond a most rudimentary point. Erich Leinsdorf has written that "gesture is of crucial importance in conducting as long as it carries a message."

Walter Legge, who for years was a dominant figure in the recording and performance of classical music (he was head of the classical division at EMI/Angel and founder of the Philharmonia Orchestra of London), has written that "sound comes from gesture, basically. The basic sound a conductor makes comes from the nature of his gesture. What is a conductor's gesture? It's merely the prolongation of his musical will. It's his means of communication.... Because what is conducting? It's the power of communication by the hands of a musical idea, and nothing else."

"Will" is a key word. There is something about the best conductors; they simply exude music. Obviously they know the repertoire in the most complete way, from the notes, from reams of research, from extensive educations that are both musical and humanitarian, and which should include, as Karajan has said, "knowledge of everything that has touched and occupied the spirit." These conductors understand and feel the music in such a compelling way, and their presence is so towering—the mammoth ego harnessed by overpoweringly charismatic quantities of charm, or forcefulness, or vitriol, or pathos, or entreaty—that their will cannot be denied. Karajan says he can tell just by watching a young conductor walk to the podium whether or not the person is going to succeed with the orchestra.

In a brochure "On Conducting," Felix Weingartner talks about Richard Wagner on the podium: "The old flautist Furstenau of Dresden told me that often, when Wagner conducted, the players had no sense of being led. Each believed himself to be following freely his own feeling, yet they all worked together wonderfully. It was Wagner's mighty will that powerfully but unperceived had overborne their single wills so that each thought himself free, while in reality he only followed the leader, whose artistic force lived and worked in him."

Leinsdorf offers a useful delineation between a conducting presence and a technician. For examples he uses Gennaro Papi, a Metropolitan Opera conductor, and Serge Koussevitzky, who directed the Boston Symphony for many years. "Papi," Leinsdorf writes, "never used a score; he cued every instrument and singer accurately; he knew music perhaps better than his antipode.... On the other hand, Koussevitzky was not gifted with an easy conducting arm; he needed help on the musical side to prepare himself; he performed superlatively by the standards of some observers, for others only intermittantly so." But, Leinsdorf points out, Koussevitzky has been welcomed into the halls of fame as a figure of musical importance:

"Koussevitzky, whatever his shortcomings, brought his own personal insights and emotional response to the music. In the bluntest terms, [Papi] handled traffic, [Koussevitzky] made music."

Judith Somogi, music director of the Frankfurt Opera, auditioned for her job with one arm in a cast. The cast may have hindered her, but it obviously couldn't hide the musical will that burned within her.

In *On and Off the Record*, Walter Legge writes of a private session he and his wife, the singer Elisabeth Schwarzkopf, had with Arturo Toscanini at the Maestro's home during his later years. "We went into a smaller sitting room: there were two sofas, one on either side of a low table, and he started, with a glowering brow, complaining, virtually cursing German and Austrian conductors who took Mozart two/fours, particularly the slow two/fours, beating four, instead of beating two, and he said, 'Now I will show you the difference,' and he would hum a Mozart two/four tune. 'Now you sing it and follow my beat,' and with his terribly penetrating eyes and this old slightly bent first finger, he conducted, first in four, than a slow two. And we had to sing. I understood in that moment why he had this power over orchestras. We compared notes afterward, and my wife and I both felt as if we had had steel belts around our waists, slightly elastic steel belts, which were held on to the point of that finger and that finger made it impossible to move more than the tiny liberty that he would allow you."

James Galway played principal flute in the Berlin Philharmonic for several years. In his autobiography, Galway writes that Karajan's main strength is that he conducts in such a way "that he actually moulds the music into phrases, into shapes, so that it comes out sounding the way he has heard it in his head. He is constantly advising and guiding. I remember standing beside him one day while he was playing the harpsichord in the *Brandenburg Concerto* and he turned to me and said, 'Jimmy, would you mind just playing it like this?' The request was couched in such a way that I could not possibly have refused it, even if I had thought he was mad. It has all to do with the expression on his face and the light in his eyes. He achieved most of what he wanted through charm."

Just what a conductor does up there, his effect, was revealed most clearly and unexpectedly in a videotape of Danny Kaye doing his comedy routine with the New York Philharmonic. At the very end, when all the fun and games were over, Kaye spent five or ten minutes conducting a medley of classical passages in a straightforward manner. Even straight, Danny Kaye is a funny, sort of goofy, erratic fellow. As I watched the tape, and listened, I was amazed. Because that is just how the New York Philharmonic Orchestra was sounding: slightly goofy and erratic.

The conclusion is inescapable for the conductor, who takes the stage with only his baton and his persona. His is a form of naked leadership, the results of which are immediately apparent. All else being more or less equal, the conductor plays what he is.

Cairns's image of Karajan driving his glittering war chariot was one that quickly came to mind as the New York concerts of 1982 began. On opening night, the air in Carnegie Hall was suitably charged. The celebrities had turned out in great number. They ranged from Frank Sinatra, whom Karajan was eager to meet, and did, to Henry Kissinger. Black tie prevailed, although the student sitting in front of me was in slacks and a sweater. He split the treasured ticket with a girlfriend, who took his place after the intermission. The water pump had been turned off. Karajan's appearance was accompanied by a sudden burst of applause as he picked his way through the orchestra to the podium, reducing his limp to a barely noticeable stiffness with what must have been a supreme effort. He was dressed in a black suit over a white turtleneck sweater (he hates neckties). His perfectly brushed white hair glowed silver in the lights. Without acknowledging the audience, he stepped onto the podium, planted his black Adidas shoes at shoulder width (they would not move for the duration of the piece), and began at once. It was a Karajan manner that has become classic. His gestures on the podium were restrained, economical.

Most of the time when he was conducting, his eyes were closed.

"On the podium, others conduct. Karajan is being an artist," Ron Wilford says. Wilford is head of Columbia Artists Management, the firm that represents Karajan in America. "He doesn't disturb the orchestra. Phrasing is cued with his fingers. He is like the Spanish dancer who begins a beat with his heels and diminishes it until he is tapping with his fingernails. Karajan too brings total attention to the smallest detail. He is a performer who brings the orchestra and the audience with him. He is the only one I know who can do it; and he didn't have it until he was fifty."

Karajan and the Berlin Philharmonic played Stravinsky's *Apollo*, followed by Richard Strauss's *Alpine Symphony*, a tumultuous, extravagant musical mountain-climbing adventure. The multitudes loved it. The applause was thick and sustained. Karajan obviously savored it. He returned to the podium five times for bows, holding the podium railing, smiling and looking up into the great, sparkling hall, leaning into the applause as if it were a fresh breeze in his face. Then he finally dismissed the orchestra with a floppy wave of his hand and called it a night.

The next evening Karajan and the orchestra played the Fourth and Second Symphonies of Brahms, as they had done in 1974 and 1976. Karajan loves Brahms. This time the excuse was the 150th anniversary of Brahms's birth. Karajan estimates that he has played each of the Brahms symphonies a hundred times, and still he studies all of them, makes changes. During 1982 and '83, Karajan played the music of Brahms continually. After one concert at the Musikfreunde in Vienna, Professor Albert Moser, who is president of that society, told Karajan it was the best Brahms Fourth he had ever heard. "Karajan told me," Moser said, "'I think I know for the first time how I must conduct the last part. Every time before I am too slow. Now I know.'" Moser said he thought Karajan probably conducted the Fourth for the first time in 1929, when he was co-music director at a small theater in Ulm, Germany. After fifty-four years, he begins to understand the last movement. "One of the signs of a great piece of music is that it will never resist further interpretation," Karajan says. "It is like a deep well. You can dip and dip and never come to the end of it."

There was a day off for the orchestra before the last two concerts in New York. When on tour, the orchestra rules call for a lay day after each traveling day, and after every two concerts. But for Karajan this simply means he can pursue other work. Even at seventy-three, Karajan does not take "days off." He has been a dedicated workaholic since youth. Even at play he works hard. He would not know what to do with a day off other than work at something else. And so on the 'day off,'' Karajan spent most of the time in Carnegie Hall auditioning singers.

Every conductor spends more time than he would like auditioning singers. He must, if he wishes to find artists for operas and other vocal works. Today especially, when there is an acknowledged dearth of good, young singers, the search is even more intense. Every conductor is particular about singers. Karajan has a unique set of standards, and they are standards that are not widely shared. No one has been so intimately and famously involved with opera for as long as Herbert von Karajan. Over the last fifty years he has conducted at most of the great opera houses of the world, and has been in charge of many of them: Berlin, London, Vienna, Milan, Salzburg—even New York's Metropolitan, where he once had a contractual agreement. Karajan loves opera. Once he had a grand notion to organize all the great opera houses under one director (himself, of course), package productions, and move them from place to place.

Karajan has a repertoire of fifty operas that, as he says, he could begin conducting at any point upon being awakened from a sound sleep. Mention an opera singer and chances are not only that Karajan has worked with that singer, but that he was instrumental in launching or at least significantly furthering that singer's career. Maria Callas, Birgit Nilsson, Elisabeth Schwarzkopf, and Leontyne Price lead a lengthy list of singers who worked extensively with Karajan.

The heldentenor James McCracken of the Metropolitan tells a story about himself and Karajan that is not atypical. In the 1960s McCracken was trudging along the usual path for aspiring American opera singers. He was in Europe, trying to build a career without much success. Then he got a chance to sing for Karajan. "The audition was in Milan," McCracken says. "My voice coach was my accompanist, and he wasn't so good. Karajan stopped me after a few bars and asked if he might accompany me. I sang with him for about a minute and he stopped. I'll never forget what he said because it was three words that ignited my career: 'that's it, then. . . .' He gave me a role at the Vienna State Opera. It was a big jump. A real plum. I'll tell you about Karajan: he was never afraid to take a chance on a young singer."

Karajan's highly personal notions of casting singers stimulates widespread criticism. "Strange," "against the grain," "improbable," are opinions freely ventured about his choice of voices. It is true he prefers young singers. He likes the freshness, the newness of their voices, and because they are not set in their ways, he can mold them to his liking.

And he will usually choose a lighter, lyric voice over a more powerful, stentorian, typically "operatic" one. He loves a soprano with an articulate, clear pianissimo on the highest notes. The trade-off for this is usually reduced volume in the lower ranges, but Karajan the orchestral accompanist is unmatched for making an orchestra play within a singer's capabilities. And in today's recording studio, of course, such things can be easily adjusted.

That Karajan thrusts lyric voices into roles too heavy and demanding for them is a widespread criticism. Karajan is a forceful fellow who is used to getting what he wants. And until a singer is very well established, it is difficult for him or her to say no when Karajan beckons, because this maestro truly beckons from on high. Karajan doesn't tour the world's opera houses anymore. In the last twenty years he has restricted his operatic work to Salzburg (with occasional appearances in Vienna). But that is like saying one's paintings are hanging only in the Louvre. The Grosse Festspielhaus in Salzburg— the large festival hall—which was built at great expense essentially for Karajan's pleasure, is the most modern, well-equipped opera house in the world.

Until the 1984 Salzburg season, when the same opera was performed at both Karajan's personal festival at Easter and the regular Salzburg Summer Festival, he did two different operas there every year. For the Easter Festival, he recorded the opera the previous year, an extra added attraction for any singer. And with Karajan there is always the possibility of putting the opera on film. When he likes a singer, he asks him to sing again and again, wants him to be "his" singer, part of the Karajan team. So steady work, including records and maybe film, is in the offing. It's irresistible.

In addition, many singers are overwhelmed by the response they feel from him—if he likes them. Nellie Walters, an amazing woman in her eighties who has handled singers for years at Columbia Artists Management, and who has known Karajan since the 1930s in Berlin, watched one of her young artists sing for Karajan while he was in New York. "It was as if he pulled the voice right out of her throat," Miss Walters said. "She fairly squealed with delight. He is like a magician."

Karajan not only knows singers, he understands them. His first wife was a singer. And he cares very much about talent of any kind, especially singing talent. Aside from the power that surrounds Karajan, the possibilities of fame and fortune that are implicit in a successful audition before him, it is the more musical side, the unexpected display of caring, appreciation of the art, that gives singers a shot of adrenalin stronger than any of them have ever experienced. When the "great man" turns out to be a great musician who loves their craft as much as they do, and who takes them by the hand, that is called joy, even rapture.

Such a moment occurred in Carnegie Hall when a young tenor from New York named Vinson Cole began to sing. Cole stood beside the piano which had been rolled center stage and faced the majestic hall, empty except for Karajan, who was slumped in a center orchestra seat sixteen rows back, and perhaps a dozen other people, some from Columbia Artists Management (CAMI), which had organized the auditions, others from record companies waiting to meet with Karajan. Even observing an audition fills one with anxiety. Players at least have an instrument. Singers are naked, empty-handed, alone with their voices.

For an hour Karajan had been listening halfheartedly chatting aside with Ronald Wilford, who had selected the singers, waving and saying thank you. As Cole began to sing, he became attentive. He stopped him, beat out a different tempo for the aria he was singing from the opera *Rosenkavalier*. Karajan asked him to sing it in a flashier style and really make himself heard. "Sing it as if the police are behind you," Karajan said. Cole smiled. "Everyone must think you are singing it for them."

Cole repeated the aria. He finished and stood waiting. Karajan conferred with Wilford. "Very impressive. What is his name?" Wilford told him. Karajan didn't get it. "C, O, L, E." "Ah yes. If he develops, in ten years he could sing *Otello*."

Cole was summoned. He left the stage and approached Karajan via the empty row of seats in front of him. Karajan's handshake was quick, his greeting perfunctory, his praise brief. This was business. "Do you have *La Bohème*?" he asked. "Could you sing it for me?" The question was heartfelt: "For me!" Cole understood. Back on stage he conferred with his pianist. He said later that his regular accompanist was ill. He had never sung *Bohème* with the pianist who was with him. But the man had the music. That Cole would not try was out of the question. He began.

Karajan was now leaning forward, his elbows propped on the seat in front of him, conducting Vinson Cole with the smallest, lazy movements of his hands, speaking to him above the music—"Don't give too much ... hold back ... now!" Karajan was immersed, his expression rapt. Cole finished. "Please could you repeat it once more. You must hold the C longer if you can."

Cole: "I will try."

Karajan: "You must work on it. Why not do it here? You have good lungs."

Cole repeated the aria, held the C.

Karajan (slapping his knee): "There you are!"

Cole was flushed as he returned to the seats. Karajan spoke quickly to him about the future, about coming to the Salzburg Festival, the possibility of *Rosenkavalier*, the special Karajan-sponsored master classes he should attend during the festival, all in Karajan's patented, mumbled way of speaking that is confounding. Heady stuff. As he left the aisle, Cole looked up at the first row of boxes, which were empty, and rolled his eyes like a man whose world had just tilted.

Singers must also look good for Karajan to be interested in them. One might think that the recent emphasis on film and television has something to do with this consideration, but it has always been a prerequisite of Karajan's. Karajan is a consummate aesthete. Ugliness is offensive, distasteful to him no matter where he finds it, in houses, automobiles, music, bassoon players (not so much the player as the instrument), or singers. "The old theory used to be," Karajan says, "that if singers got fat they would have bigger voices. The same idea as sumo wrestlers. So they would eat much. They used to be enormous, tons of flesh. The couples on stage never appeared to care for each other. They just stood there and shouted!"

Singers have changed, and Karajan hopes he will get some of the credit for that. He enjoys telling of one day in Milan when the singers he cast for an opera arrived for orchestra rehearsal at La Scala. "The orchestra wanted to know if the women were the dancers. 'No,' I told them, 'they are the singers!' They couldn't believe it."

The New York concerts continued with more Brahms, the First and Third Symphonies, followed on the last evening by Mahler's Ninth. Andrew Porter, who wrote that the Brahms Second and Fourth had still been "too smooth a ride, without the grit, the almost painful grinding cross-rhythms that is a part of the music," called the First and Third "never-to-be-forgotten events, to be recalled with, if not ranked beside, a Furtwängler Beethoven cycle that in student years changed my life." Porter recalled the baffling mixture of admiration and reservations which Karajan had inspired in 1974 and 1976. "I'm older now, and perhaps mellower, less critical, readier to be grateful for glorious sound and flawless execution."

Perhaps, but the Ninth of Mahler on the final evening seemed to tax Porter's newfound mellowness. "The First Movement was memorable," Porter wrote. "But the brutality, the horror, the madness in the scherzos that follow were minimized—subordinated to a display of carefully equilibrated, highly-wrought orchestral wizardry. And in the finale, expressiveness was pushed, with thick, throbbing string tone, to a climax of brute force rather than full-throated passion."

If Porter was disappointed by sections of Karajan's Mahler, critic Peter Davis was outraged. Deploring what he called Karajan's "detached, Olympian attitude," Davis chastised him for his "coldly calculated precision: Every detail in the gigantic, tremendously complex symphony could be heard as never before, but not for a second did this immaculately conducted autopsy touch the heart." One might be puzzled by what seemed an overly passionate outburst from Davis, but "manner over matter" was again the stimulus, and one man's disappointment was another's outrage. Again, in this subjective, elusive business of music, so much depends on the phase of the moon.

"Karajan has thought about a piece like Mahler's Ninth for so long," Davis said later, "that his vision has become rarified. He has lost touch with what animates. He is a master of the cult of recorded perfection which has purged the spirit from the music."

Davis's position, however legitimate, seemed a lonely one given the acclaim for Karajan and the orchestra within the hall, which seemed to build with each concert. The applause became tumultuous, Karajan's bows more numerous. Whistles and shouts of "bravo" carried above the sustained waves of clapping. As each performance ended, members of the audience jammed the aisles, seeming to be drawn magnetically toward the stage for a closer look at the maestro. Some threw flowers. On the last evening, after the final notes of Mahler's agonized opus to his own approaching death had sounded, the din of appreciation was such that one thought the famous circle of lights high on the ceiling of the hall would surely shatter. Karajan basked in it. Again and again he made the long, difficult walk to the podium to stand motionless, his head thrown back the way one might relish being caught in a sudden downpour in the midst of a heat wave. Again and again he shook hands with his concertmasters, his other principal players. Again and again the orchestra rose as a new burst of applause issued from the appreciative audience. It was a special moment, a wild acclaim, a triumph.

Karajan thoroughly enjoyed New York, maybe for the first time ever. His family was with him, and perhaps that made a difference. Eliette, his wife of twenty-five years, had a good time visiting New York's more fashionable stores. His daughter Isabel, twenty-three, who lives in Paris and is an aspiring actress, sought out theater people. Arabel, nineteen, visited design schools in hopes of being allowed to study photography in New York.

Karajan, an avid movie buff, found time to see *E.T.* and was amused. He even permitted a few interviews, with the stipulation that there be no questions about the Nazi time. Lon Tuck of the *Washington Post* found him "of the grim visage and the Teutonic discipline not only approachable, but even cordial—and, as a conversation develops, jovial." Tuck asked him at what point in sixty-eight years of music making he became famous: "Karajan ... falls silent. He rolls those hypnotic gray-blue eyes, tosses his head back and seems to be searching for an answer. Finally he cracks, 'Am I *famous?*' And then he dissolves into a belly laugh at his joke."

From New York, Karajan and the orchestra traveled to Pasadena, California, for a repeat of the four concerts. Then they flew back to Berlin. Karajan was reported to be as pleased with the orchestra as he had ever been. Indeed, he told the press, "[This orchestra] is one great being. This is a wonderful feeling because you know you are in the innermost sanctum of what music should express. Certainly it is a form of love...." This sentiment would be shortlived, as we shall see. The portent of a stormy future was lurking in Andrew Porter's review of the Berlin tour: "The personnel list in the program was manifestly incomplete. Who was the remarkable first clarinet at the opening concert?" Her name was Sabine Meyer, and soon she would become a cause célèbre.

II
Easter in Salzburg

March 1983

It was Easter time in Salzburg, chilly and dismal, with frequent rain "falling in ropes"—*schnurlregen*—as the locals say. This classically picturesque town, whose rich history recedes into the mists of antiquity when the Celts ventured up what is now called the Salzach River in quest of salt (c. 270 B.C.), is located on a lush, green plain between two steep ridges of mountains with names like Untersberg, Hoher Göll, and Tennengebirge. The Austrian Alps. Inclement weather masses tend to stall out between the ridges and hang over the town. Snowstorms are not unusual in Salzburg at Easter time. Umbrellas sell very well in the early spring.

But Easter in Salzburg is Herbert von Karajan's favorite time, because it is when his festival—the Salzburg Easter Festival—takes place. The event means so much to Karajan that the Easter Festival logo (𝄞) is painted upon the stern of his maxi sailboat.

The festival is an annual event consisting of a new opera production and three different programs of symphonic music, each of which is performed twice. In recent years, a third opera performance has been scheduled for filming. It is truly Karajan's festival. He selects the program and brings in *his* orchestra, the Berlin Philharmonic, for the opera and all concerts. He conducts all nine performances, which are crammed into a ten-day period, in itself a formidable task that would severely test the endurance, not to mention the ability, of a man half his age. He also personally casts the singers for the opera and is stage director of the production. In addition, he is lighting director, supervisor of set design and properties, supervisor of costumes right down to the fabrics and colors, and in charge of special effects. "It is a wonder," Munich critic and long-time Karajan watcher Joachim Kaiser has said, "that he doesn't sell tickets and usher people to their seats." It is indeed a one-man show, and it is such by design.

Karajan created the festival in 1966. It was born partly of his frustration and desperation. For nearly forty years he had been trying, with minimal satisfaction, to produce operas within the confines and restrictions of various opera houses. The Easter Festival occurred to Karajan not long after his bitter departure from the artistic directorship of the Vienna State Opera, where for seven years he had been at the center of a storm that involved management, political infighting on a state level, and a style of administration and a concept of opera production that received mixed—although always passionate—reviews. James McCracken, who often sang at the Vienna State Opera with Karajan, seems amazed anew when he recalls those days. "After many performances," McCracken says, "the place erupted with the kind of noise you hear in football stadiums. Half the audience would be applauding wildly and screaming 'bravo'; the other half would be booing and catcalling. It was incredible."

Being artistic director of the Vienna State Opera is a no-win, impossible job. Many great musicians have tried, including Gustav Mahler, Felix Weingartner, Franz Schalk, Richard Strauss, Clemens Krauss, and Karl Böhm. Most of them departed angrily. "I left twenty days short of Mahler," Karajan says with grim humor. "If I had known that at the time, I would have stayed another twenty-one days." Recently, Lorin Maazel tried, having left the music directorship of the Cleveland Orchestra to take what seems to be an intriguing, irresistible rite of passage for a conductor of the first rank whose ambition is matched by his courage. After one short year, Maazel was already in disfavor. After three years he took his leave. In keeping with the spirit of the task, Maazel held a farewell reception for himself to which he invited "all my friends and enemies."

The problem is caused in part by volume. To this day the Vienna State Opera presents three hundred performances a year of roughly thirty different productions, a schedule which smacks of production-line opera. Guest conductors by the dozen zip in for one-night stands. Rehearsal time is minimal. Attention to the kind of detail Karajan demands is non-existent. At the same time, the State Opera has all the preciousness of a Viennese shrine. London has The Tower, Rome has St. Peter's, Vienna has the State Opera. The music director becomes in effect the curator and is under terrible pressure to uphold tradition, reputation. Since much of any tradition or reputation is comprised of myth, this presents quite a puzzle for the curator. The keeper of a myth is always at the mercy of someone else's fantasy. In this case it is the cumulative fantasy of the Viennese, both citizens and politicians. This provides a serious drawback, because the Viennese by nature are an aloof, calculating people who conceal a basic general anxiety behind a quietly superior attitude, which in turn is couched beneath a facade of elaborate drawing-room manners the likes of which one is not likely to encounter elsewhere. Theirs is a dedication to a kind of macabre introspection. Show them the flower, and even as they enjoy they will wonder about its dark roots. They are convinced that nothing the future holds will quite measure up to the joys of the past, however murky those might be. That makes them benevolently but hopefully negative in most things. No one can bemoan failure with quite the eloquence of a Viennese. This is because no one has prepared quite so well for it. No wonder that a Dr. Freud would emerge from such an environment. And no wonder that Karajan, who is in many respects its prisoner, would come to despise it the way he has.

In terms of time, space, and money, the other opera houses of the world are not run so differently from Vienna's. Most have ensemble companies of singers who do the bulk of the work. Stage time for rehearsals is at a minimum, so small rooms backstage with makeshift props suffice. A pianist fills in for the orchestra. Such methods are dictated by necessity. Even a "successful" opera house depends on the generosity of benefactors for its existence, or in the case of Vienna, a large, annual subsidy from the state. Given the numbers of people, logistics, complexity of set design and construction, and costumes, the task and cost of producing opera is immense.

Necessity be damned, Karajan has always deplored the opera-house way. Whenever he was in charge, he struggled to change it in a single-minded effort that left as much wreckage as music in his wake. When one considers Karajan's rank discomfort in situations over which he does not have total control, one can see why opera production was never very satisfying for him. Vienna was just the last straw, the impetus Karajan needed to invent a solution.

There was an additional motivation in the music of Richard Wagner and the festival he began at Bayreuth, Germany, in 1876, an annual "pilgrimage" that has been run by members of his family since Wagner's death in 1883. No music comes closer to Karajan's heart than the monumental, dramatic compositions of Wagner. Those who stand in judgment of such things agree that Karajan is at his best when Wagner is on the program. Karajan conducted Wagner at Bayreuth twice. In 1951 he did *Die Meistersinger*, and in 1952, *Tristan und Isolde*. He was so appalled by the stage direction, which he considered to be generally overstated, resulting in exaggerated gesticulation on the part of singers and sets that visually collided with the music, that he refused to return. In the back of his mind he always yearned for a Wagner festival of his own, an alternative to Bayreuth.

With the Easter Festival Karajan achieved both his ideal situation for producing opera and his Wagner Festival in a single stroke. Operas by Richard Wagner have highlighted thirteen of the eighteen festival programs. Beethoven's *Fidelio*, Puccini's *La Bohème*, and Verdi's *Il Trovatore* have been the other featured works. After Karajan conceived the festival, it took some time before he settled upon Salzburg. He first spoke to people in Geneva, because he knew their opera house was not fully booked year round. He looked for other houses where he could bring the Berlin Philharmonic and have a free hand. He was still wrestling with the problem during a series of concerts he was conducting in Salzburg. "During one of the performances I thought to myself 'I am such a fool, the place is here.' After the performance I went three hours on a walk in the pouring rain in the woods, and I figured it out. I wanted to prove that we could do what we wanted without a loss. I would not take any pay for it. The next day I asked my people for a meeting and told them. Most of them were shocked. But I worked it out with a man who was at that time music director for all my records. On a flight from Zurich to Stockholm we made the whole budget. In the end our error was only $5,000."

As Walter Legge has written, the festival "was a masterpiece of ruseful planning, a paramilitary operation in organization and coordination."

Salzburg was a good choice. As Karajan knew, people went there for Easter anyway. Why not give them music? Salzburg is a gorgeous town, substantial, unlike so many tourist towns. Its history saves it from blatant cuteness. Salzburg is real, a continuing tradition rather than a theme park contrived by a city planner. When you see "1250" written on a building, that isn't the street address, it is the year it was built. Salzburg has castles looming against the sky, one of which, the Fortress Hohensalzburg (1077), rises impressively on a steep cliff right in the middle of town. And it has churches aplenty, and picturesque squares and fountains, and famous birthplaces, Wolfgang Amadeus Mozart's among them. The deep, cultural roots that provide Salzburg's heritage remain its present-day lifeblood.

It has always been a town of festivals—religious, patriotic, and honorary. The opening of each academic year was cause enough for a substantial festival. Mozart wrote several pieces for such occasions. It continues to be a festival center and a hotbed of schools and organizations that promote dance and other performing arts, and painting and sculpture.

Music is everywhere in Salzburg. To walk through residential sections of town, day or night, is to hear the sound of cellos, violins, and pianos emanating from behind the curtains of apartment windows, or operas or symphonic works booming from stereos and radios. Earnest student quartets play on street corners. Not all of the music is good, of course. In fact, some of the yodeling, oom-paa bands, and polka ensembles one hears on the radio rank with the silliest and most annoying ethnic music east of Scotland. And the fact that the Muzak in the pedestrian tunnel that was my best route from guesthouse to Festspielhaus consisted of a bad studio orchestra playing a lilting version of "On the Street Where You Live" never failed to bring a smile to my lips. I walked the tunnel every day, twice a day, for three weeks, and that tape was never changed. Toward the end of my stay I was laughing outright when I heard it.

Because it is a tourist town, shops, restaurants, and coffeehouses abound. There are lots of wonderful ways to spend money in Salzburg, most of them gilded with old-world charm. Electric-powered buses glide by without leaving a wake of thick exhaust fumes. The police, when one sees them at all, seem more guides than enforcers. The very idea of crime seems foreign to Salzburg. Dozens of immaculate wooden carriages full of tourists ply the streets, drivers dapper in Austian garb, handsomely matched two-horse teams groomed to show-readiness, on pneumatic tires to minimize noise. In Salzburg, one can make a reservation to see a movie.

Everything is immaculate, well maintained, clean beyond what might be reasonable to expect. There is no trash in the streets, no rusty cars in sight. The horse droppings are swept up every few hours by workers in orange coveralls that one sees everywhere in Salzburg doing a variety of menial tasks. Shopkeepers scrub the sidewalks in front of their stores several times a week, and they don't neglect the window ledges, which they attack with suds and stiff brushes. Every morning from 7 A.M. until noon, there is an open market in a small square in the middle of the old part of the town. Farmers come in bringing vegetables, flowers, meats, and fruits, set up their stands, and do a brisk business. Such a market is by nature a messy operation, but the astounding thing is that by 1 P.M. each day, not a trace of the market is left; not so much as a wilting cabbage leaf or a wayward flower bloom. Immaculate. Austrian. The spherical woodpiles standing next to houses in the Salzburg suburbs have the perfect symmetry of dandelions gone to seed.

When chided about their penchant for cleanliness and order, the Austrians are only slightly embarrassed. They suggest if one really wants to see neat, clean towns, one should visit Bavaria. The Bavarians, the Austrians say, are truly compulsive.

On the streets of Salzburg, the remnants of a class society can be seen. The peasants are readily identifiable in boots and babushkas. Otherwise, people are dressed up. Women not wearing heels—with the exception of the jeans-and-sneakers tourist set—can be counted on one hand. Dirndl dresses, with their cantilevered fronts and cinched bodices, are not a rage, but a continuing fashion. They are flattering to the figure, colorful. Women like them; so do men. Men wear Austrian-cut suits with thin woven bow ties, or leather knickers or shorts (lederhosen), and Alpine hats with big, fat brushes pinned to the bands. An overall view of a busy street scene in colder weather reveals a veritable sea of green loden cloth. It's right out of *National Geographic*.

Salzburg is a lively, bustling town, and Karajan is its king. Perhaps he is more revered than a king because he is responsible for bringing in many of the people that buy the plane tickets, fill the hotels, guesthouses, and restaurants, rent the cars, and patronize the shops and coffeehouses. In any case, he is treated like a king. In little Anif, a village five miles from Salzburg where he lives in the shadow of the striking Untersberg, his house is on Herbert von Karajan Strasse. The house is on land that was owned by the church, never to be sold. Karajan got it because the governor of Salzburg intervened with the church on his behalf—the fruits of power. During the festivals the town is painted yellow with Karajan's Deutsche Grammophon record covers, which are crammed into the display windows of virtually every store, sharing space with coats, dresses, ladies' undergarments, sausages, and Mercedes automobiles. At crowded festival time, he is the only person in Austria allowed to drive his car in the special lanes reserved for buses. And he is gossiped about like a king. "Many don't love him," says a lady whose guesthouse was filling up quickly because of Karajan's Easter Festival. "And he loves no one. Do you know that he once told his brother Wolfgang that he had to change his name? He told his brother there could only be one Karajan—him!" And she tells the joke about two other conductors and Karajan discussing who was best. Said one: I have been to heaven and God told me I was best. Then Karajan: Did I say that? She laughs. But the afternoon when dress rehearsal tickets for Richard Wagner's *The Flying Dutchman* were available at the Festspielhaus, the guesthouse lady was observed standing hopefully in the long line.

When the 1975, 350-horsepower Porsche Turbo 911, gray with the wide, wraparound red and blue racing stripes, rear deck spoiler and high-speed driving lights, is parked in the stone archway inside the big iron gate at the back entrance to the Grosse Festspielhaus, it is a sign that the Maestro is there. It needn't be the Porsche. It could be the big light gray, four-door Mercedes 500 sedan with the high-speed driving lights. Or the Volkswagen Scirocco, dark gray with the bright red trim, high-speed driving lights and the word EXPERIMENTAL painted along one side. When someone asked Karajan what was experimental about the car, he told them he wanted to see what color gray paint was fastest.

Karajan's office is on the first floor, a suite of four small rooms laid out end to end, complete with bathroom, daybed, and Steinway grand in immaculate condition. The office is presided over by a comely woman in her forties with the unlikely name of Salzburger, Lore Salzburger. This is a person who redefines executive secretarial qualifications. She is efficient, perceptive, capable, devoted, authoritative, charming, and at the same time, tough and outspoken. She speaks English, French, Italian, and German, as Karajan does, only more fluently than the Maestro. An elegantly stylish dresser, she skis and bicycles for sport. The gleaming 1983 silver Porsche 911 SC in the parking lot with the little oriental rugs on the floor and the Italian flag decal on the rear bumper is hers. Karajan worries about her driving it so fast. The flag, she explains, is so her Austrian-registered car won't be abused on her occasional trips to Italy to see her parents. Lore Salzburger likes to anticipate problems. That she has been with Karajan ten years is a sign that she has succeeded.

If one has come in the front door and has missed the car in the parking lot, it is easy to know right away whether or not the Maestro is in. If so, Salzburger will be practically hidden at her desk behind a bower of cut flowers. If not, the office will be its bare and essential self, with Lore fielding the calls and firing off the letters as the big clock on the wall snaps off the minutes. Whenever Karajan is in the house, Salzburger will be there. Hers is a devotion, not a job.

Salzburger was born in Italy at a time when southern Austria (Tyrol) was northern Italy. She moved to Salzburg when she was still a child, but old enough to remember the dark nights of the mid-1940s when the flares dropped by American planes searching for targets blossomed in the Salzburg sky "like Christmas trees," she recalls. Nearly half of Salzburg was flattened in those raids during the waning days of World War II. After the war, she worked in hotel management and then with the Festspielhaus doing public relations. When

Karajan's previous secretary retired, Salzburger was offered the job. It suits her. She handles the business, the press, the demands of friends, Karajan's ex-wife, wife, children, managers, and agents, all with tactful aplomb. She doesn't hesitate for a moment to replace tact with an icy forthrightness when the job needs to get done.

The Scirocco and the flowers were in place, but Karajan was not in his office this second week of March. It was the first day of scheduled rehearsals for *The Flying Dutchman*, and by 10:30 A.M. he was seated in the darkened performance hall of the Festspielhaus with a crew of approximately fifty technicians and stagehands ready to do his bidding. Karajan was slumped in his seat in the center of the audience, sixteen rows back from the stage. A leather pouch containing two microphones was hanging from the seat back in front of him. His lighting director, Helmut "Richie" Reichmann, sat at a console of dials and switches two rows behind him and two seats to the left. To his right, across the aisle and down a few rows, sat a small man in his late sixties wearing a look of perpetual concern. This was Papier, who has been Karajan's all-purpose valet and errand boy for nearly fifteen years, ever since Karajan rescued him from Vienna, where he had a sporadic career as a policeman and security guard at the State Opera. Karajan puts Papier on his personal payroll for the festivals in Salzburg.

The rehearsal seating plan is important. Karajan seats the off-stage participants with the same care he positions the various sections in the orchestra. He will be directing these people with the same fingertip control he uses for the players, and he expects the same split-second response. The plan also helps him keep track of uninvited people who might try to slide in. I was assigned to the row in front of him, one seat to the right of his.

Spread across the hundred-foot breadth of the stage was the glittering, extravagant set for the second act of *Rosenkavalier*, the opera Karajan would be doing in Salzburg in August. It depicted a most lavish, mid-eighteenth-century drawing room, with French doors that reached to the twenty-five-foot ceiling in which there was an indirectly lit oval containing a delicately painted mural. The floor was shiny black with a white, rococo border. Gilt chandeliers and wall sconces, angelic statuary, and stiff period furniture completed the ostentatious formality of the scene.

There was history here, and Karajan was moved. The late Theo Otto, a well-known designer of stage sets, had drawn this set for the grand opening of the Grosse Festspielhaus in 1960, which Karajan conducted. It had been Otto's last work. Over the years, storage space had been taxed and the Otto sets had been destroyed. Now they had been rebuilt to the most minute detail, and at great expense, and the sight of Act II took Karajan back. "It is as if," he said, "I have been suddenly transported back twenty years in an instant. It is perfect."

He watched while Reichmann spoke quietly into his microphone and the lights played in various ways about the set. The boss of the stage crew came into the audience and sat with Karajan. Soon he, Karajan, and Reichmann were all speaking rapidly in German. Then Karajan picked up one of the microphones. The metallic amplification of his voice echoed in the empty hall. When Karajan speaks English, one must listen with great care to discern what he says. I had assumed this was due partly to his less than complete command of the language. But those he addresses in his native German also struggle to comprehend him. One associate of his says she worked with him five years before she began to understand him without working at it. His voice is low and guttural, like the sound of a large, heavily laden truck struggling up a steep incline, and that doesn't help matters. Among those who have worked more than casually with Karajan, he has become a popular man to mimic. Even a bad Karajan imitation is always worth a few laughs over a beer.

Karajan always seems to speak louder than necessary into the microphone, as if he didn't trust the thing's ability to project his voice. And so his amplified voice is cutting as well. But his message got across, and suddenly figures began to materialize on stage. None of them seemed to know what to do until a man with a clipboard moved among them, placing them here and there on the set. Karajan leaned forward and spoke to me. "These are doubles, stand-ins, just people off the street we hire to test the lighting. The singers cannot be here yet, of course. And these people work well. The stupidest human beings will make the greatest mistakes at any given moment. So I see this with these people and I learn how to prevent the mistakes."

For more than an hour Karajan and Reichmann worked with the lights while the stand-ins remained on their spots, shifting from one leg to the other. Then it was time to go. The set would be struck and replaced within an hour with *The Flying Dutchman* set for the afternoon rehearsal. Karajan put the microphone in its pouch. Papier hurried over with his jacket. "They are marvelous here," Karajan said. "Fantastic. They make all the sets, even the statues. They make the costumes, the shoes. I have worked with them so long now they know just what I will want before I even tell them."

As Karajan left, limping toward the exit with Papier trailing, Festspielhaus administrators who needed to see him rushed to his side to have a few minutes of his attention as he walked to his office. Once there, he would make a phone call or two, sign letters, and quickly be off to Anif for a light lunch, a swim, and a nap before the afternoon rehearsal of *The Flying Dutchman*. Before he reached the exit the French doors on stage were coming down.

Karajan does not exaggerate about the wonders of the Festspielhaus. It is more than just a theater. It is a complex of three performance halls strung together end to end behind a common facade. The long, massive stone building has been built up against (and into) a sheer, narrow ridge of stone two hundred feet high, which forms a natural wall across the old part of Salzburg. If it weren't for this wall, the bulk of which could dwarf all but the mightiest of man's constructions, the Festspielhaus would be a terrible eyesore. But the cliff, which is composed of interglacial gravel geologically compressed into a hard conglomerate—the Mönchsberg as it is called—has provided a natural bulwark and more for Salzburg.

The Mönchsberg was first put to use for performance in the 1600s, when balconies (Italian-style loges) were carved out of the rock for those who came to watch tournaments: bear baiting and other popular sports of the day. In the 1660s, the amphitheater was converted into the Rocky Riding School. Other buildings were added to complete the archbishop's equestrian playground, including an indoor riding school and an enormous room with a graphic mural of luckless Turks being beheaded as part of some grisly sport (bayonet practice?) painted on the high ceiling. "Tilt the Turk," the game was apparently called. The Rocky Riding School became the first of the festival stages. Audience seating was constructed opposite the wall of balconies, which served as a backdrop for the stage. The acoustics were wonderful, but it was open, and rain could quickly terminate a performance.

It was eventually covered with a plastic cloth, which made a racket when it rained. Now it has a double cover, top and sides, and while Karajan likes the charm of it, he avoids it because the dampness bothers his rheumatism.

In 1925, the first enclosed house was added to the riding school complex. The Salzburg Festival, which was begun in 1920 by poet and playwright Hugo von Hofmannsthal, stage director Max Reinhardt, and composer Richard Strauss, moved into the new hall that year. It served well until 1935, when Arturo Toscanini demanded that the house be modified and enlarged. Toscanini was a fanatic anti-Nazi. To him, Salzburg was a bastion from which he could attack the Nazi regime with music. To stem any resistance to his demands,

Toscanini said he would not return to conduct at Salzburg unless the work was done. So the house was enlarged, and the stage moved to the opposite end of the hall for the then idol of the podium.

In 1953 planning began for the Grosse Festspielhaus. Karajan was one of the prime movers, along with architect Clemens Holzmeister. Karajan said he needed a bigger stage than that provided by either the small house or the riding school, which had been refurbished in 1948. A larger audience needed to be accommodated. Politically, it was a bad time to begin such an enormous project. Austria was still under postwar occupation, and other needs were pressing. There were, for instance, many refugees from Yugoslavia, Czechoslovakia, and Germany who were crowded together in barracks. Housing was in great demand. The political left deplored spending money for the luxury of theater for "the elite" instead of houses for the people. But the project was carried out. Josef Klaus, then governor of Salzburg, made the final determination while Karajan publicly flexed his muscles, threatening to leave Austria if the new house was not built.

Klaus's decision cost him his political constituency, but he was compensated with a seat on the powerful, five-man Salzburg Festival board of directors.

The new Festspielhaus was begun in 1956. It took four years to build and came in at nearly double its projected cost of 110 million Austrian schillings, or $5 million (U.S.) in those days. It was no small feat of engineering. In order to unify all the theaters, fifty thousand tons of the Mönchsberg (two million cubic feet) were ground out and carted away. It was tricky, dangerous business. The compressed strata alternated between hard and unyielding, soft and porous. But the work went so well that the project was extended into the Mönchsberg to include a five-story, indoor garage. It holds two thousand cars, and allows festival patrons to arrive in their seats warm and dry, no matter what the weather. Residents of Salzburg are quick to point out that the cavernous excavation, with its imposing, airtight doors, is also an enormous bomb shelter. The fact that rest rooms are minimal and food storage was omitted serves only to amuse them.

The Festspielhaus rivals the garage for sheer enormity. The stage opening spans one hundred feet. Stage and wings together are 300 feet across. It is 180 feet high and 215 feet in depth. Stage portals mounted on tracks allow the proscenium to be reduced to forty feet for small productions and concerts. The stage, all seventeen thousand square feet of it, consists of fifteen independent stage platforms on tracks. There are six bridges for stage lighting equipment, eight towers, and storage space capable of holding four complete sets. At the rear of the hall is an electronics room with computerized lighting control equipment that makes the cockpit of a jumbo jet look simple by comparison.

Inside the hall, nothing was spared in terms of decor. The entrance doors are grand, as are even the most common doors in Germany and Austria, heavy and smooth-opening, with carved wooden pulls. Chandeliers and wall sconces glisten opulently. The arms of every seat are covered in leather, which is promptly replaced when it becomes worn. The hundred-foot, gently curved railing atop the low partition that separates the orchestra pit from the audience is similarly covered in leather. The walls are a teaklike veneer that radiates a warm, restful glow.

Altogether, it is an imposing house in a mighty complex with the finest in wood- and metal-working shops, lofts for painting that are the size of gymnasiums, rooms for sewing the ornate costumes required by the opera—all staffed by the best available craftsmen and women—and it is all Karajan's. Toscanini should have done so well.

As Karajan regarded this great hall in all its splendor, surely the parallel with the god Wotan, from Richard Wagner's opera *Das Rheingold*, must have occurred to him. As Wotan gazes upon his finished castle in the clouds, he thinks briefly of his bargain with the "giants" who built it, then concludes: "It stands now; thank the workers, and forget what it will cost."

Karajan's goal for the Easter Festival was a production of such perfection, a production so completely and totally his, that he would sign his name to it with the same unmistakable authority with which a writer signs a book. During all the years that he had been suffering through producing opera he had been accumulating schemes for the ideal way. All those schemes came together in the plan for the Easter Festival.

A production begins three years in advance, with the selection of the opera and the sketches for sets and costumes. Casting must be done early, because not only are the best singers booked well in advance, the Karajan plan requires more time than a singer would usually devote to a single production. Karajan first records the opera in the fall of the year preceding the Festival. This means pulling the cast together for a week or ten days—twenty recording sessions—usually in Vienna's Musikfreunde Hall, one of Karajan's favorite places to record. Once the recording is edited and packaged, a tape of it is sent to each singer. This allows all members of the cast to listen to the opera they will be singing in the spring, sung by them and the cast they will be singing with, played by the orchestra they will be accompanied by, so that when they arrive in Salzburg for rehearsals the piece will be second-nature. When rehearsals begin, the singers can concentrate on blocking and acting while they lip-synch to the familiar tape being played over loudspeakers in the hall. Day after day they hear their own voices, listen for weak spots, learn ways to improve their performance.

"It is a wonderful system," Karajan says. "It saves the singers' voices, and it eliminates the rehearsal pianist, who typically plays too fast in the mornings when he is fresh, and too slow in the afternoon when he gets tired. It is the best way, of course."

It may be the best way, although some singers say that it can lull one into laziness. Since one isn't singing at rehearsals, one must be disciplined enough to vocalize each day. It is surely the most expensive way. No one but Karajan could induce a record company to front the new recording of an opera every year. Only Karajan, with eight hundred recordings to his credit and cumulative sales in excess of one hundred million records, could command such a process.

Easter Festival rehearsals typically begin with a week of lighting rehearsals. Then the singers arrive for two weeks of staging. Finally, the orchestra arrives for three days of rehearsal, then dress rehearsal and performances. "In two weeks with the singers we have twenty-eight rehearsals," Karajan says, "morning and afternoon, with no delays because of sets from other productions being in the way. Then with the orchestra it comes to thirty-four or thirty-five, and counting lighting rehearsals, nearly fifty for one production. Now in an opera house you can only work five days a week because of the unions, and you can only have one rehearsal each day. So fifty rehearsals would take at least ten weeks. And with the performances spread out, four or five months altogether. We do all this in three to four weeks because we can leave everything in place and work day and night until the thing is done. To me this is the only artistic solution."

Lighting rehearsals are tedious. For six days Karajan sat in his sixteenth-row seat from 10 A.M. until 1 P.M., and from 5 P.M. to 8 P.M., attending to the most minute detail as the sets for all three acts of *The Flying Dutchman* were put up and struck by a stage crew whose efficiency and speed reminded one of race-car pit crews. Two rows in front of him, on the aisle to his right, a tape deck and amplifier had been set up to play the new *Flying Dutchman* performance tape. At the controls was Roberto Paternostro, an aspiring young conductor from Vienna who has been assistant to Karajan since 1977. His job was to unscramble the boss's mumbled instructions and hand signals, find precise entry spots on the tape, run them and stop them at the right moment. Paternostro knew the score. He never missed.

There were bright spots amid the tedium. The most climactic moment of action in the three-and-a-half hour opera comes in Act I, when the ghostly ship of the Dutchman menacingly arrives in harbor seeking refuge from the storm. A typical Wagnerian crescendo of sound is the cue for the ship, a most effective bas relief of foam rubber and cloth sculpted upon a flexible net, to be raised into position (as if quite suddenly rising from the horizon) by a stagehand hauling on a rope high above the stage. As the crescendo peaked, a sixty-foot square of light cloth resembling a sail was to be lifted away as though the sail was being doused. Simultaneously, the music was to be assisted by a box of rocks being suddenly emptied onto a wooden plank backstage to resemble the paying-out of anchor chain. Critical to the visual success of the entire moment was the red glow (danger!) that appeared gradually behind the sail, growing in intensity until the moment the sail was taken down.

Karajan worked on this twenty-second segment for the better part of three days. First the red glow wasn't right. Then there was great trouble with the ship's arrival. Karajan the sailor knew that the sail must be doused before the ship came to a stop, and the anchor chain had to be heard running out *as* the ship stopped and the music peaked. He gave this lecture in seamanship several times, his voice rising and falling in loud, gutteral German, his frustration growing until finally he called for the house lights. Papier came running with his jacket as Karajan made his way unsteadily toward the stage. He disappeared and was gone for about ten minutes, during which time those of us left in the audience saw the ship being raised and lowered several times.

Karajan had taken the lift to the fifth bridge above the stage to talk with the man whose job it was to raise the ship. To him he had privately given the nautical lecture, and, taking the rope from him, had given him a demonstration in smooth hauling technique. To say that the stagehand had been surprised to see the boss arriving at his station would be an understatement. But after Karajan's visit, the ship arrived a lot more smoothly, and with better timing.

There was much attention paid to the blowing "clouds" which were being projected on a diffusion screen, a flat, see-through mesh curtain which was lowered to cover the entire stage opening, top to bottom. The clouds were out of focus for best effect, but there was great discussion about how much out of focus they should be, how fast they should move, and on what musical cues. And the water received a day's worth of attention at least.

The "water" was very realistic. Light blue plastic of very thin gauge had been layered over the stage for Acts I and III, the scenes at the harbor. With small fans placed under it, and the lights glittering off its wrinkled, undulating surface, the effect was striking. Karajan was very pleased. "Most important with this opera is the sea," he said. "Now that I can see the moving sea—all else comes from that. You cannot show the greatness of this opera when not aided by the sea in motion. Over the last fifty years I must have seen forty productions of *The Flying Dutchman*, and all of them were completely silly. When at the beginning of Act I the ship rolled in on the dry stage it made me laugh."

There was a problem with the plastic toward the front of the stage, which was supposed to respond to a wind machine offstage that increased its force when the music swelled to indicate the advancing storm. The plastic billowed nicely, but it wouldn't deflate soon enough. The problem was solved by a stagehand who made more slits in it with a pair of scissors.

So it went for a week. Karajan seemed completely happy with his task. He was occasionally frustrated by the turn of events or by the length of time it took to fix a problem, but he was never angry, never raised his voice, never had a harsh word. He told jokes, hummed along with the music, and was never at a loss for a mumbled, sarcastic aside when he thought he had an appreciative audience.

As the weeks passed, the appreciative audience gathered in greater numbers. As they arrived, they would sit for a while in the row with Karajan, one seat removed from his, and converse about the situation. This was in fact the seat designated for important people who might drop by, but the ritual seemed to be that as the regulars appeared, they would warm it up for a few minutes.

Foremost of those who occupied this seat was Günther Schneider-Siemssen, who designed the sets for *The Flying Dutchman*, and who has been working with Karajan for twenty years. Schneider-Siemssen is a tall man in his fifties with a bountiful, sloping stomach, a pleasant countenance, and a boyish manner. European set designers tend to be scholarly people. Their academic degree requires a rigorous combination of graphic arts, architecture, engineering, lighting, history, costumes, plastic arts, and painting. Perhaps for this reason, Schneider-Siemssen seemed a bit preoccupied.

He squinted at the set and joked lightly and nervously about it being a touch on the dark side. That complaint is not an unusual one, coming from set designers who like everyone to see plainly what is most important about a production, namely their work. But in truth, the lighting was disturbingly low on the stage. Viewers found themselves leaning forward to peer through the diffusion curtain. When asked, Karajan had said that there would be no filming of the performance this year because the film crew had determined that shooting in such low light would be impossible. Karajan was encouraged to know that a new, high-speed film was in the final stages of development and would be ready by the following year. There was no question of increasing the light, film or no film. He wanted it dark, he said, to increase the fantasy of the situation the opera portrays. He obviously had no intention of yielding so much as a watt more light to Schneider-Siemssen. Looking at the dark stage reminded Karajan of a good Max Reinhardt story, about the time during a Reinhardt production when a journalist came into the house, peered at the gloomy scene, and asked if there had been a power failure. Karajan cackled hilariously at the story. Those around him laughed a bit too eagerly. It is difficult to laugh, one of them said later, when you have heard a story many times.

Schneider-Siemssen and Karajan have been struggling over such matters for years. Schneider-Siemssen recalls the production of Wagner's *Rheingold* he did with the Maestro in 1978. There was a dispute over the light in one scene that featured a complex set. After Karajan left the theater one day, Schneider-Siemssen told the technical director he was unhappy with the light and showed him what he wanted. Schneider-Siemssen was taken ill that evening and hospitalized for a few days. The next day at rehearsal the scene was run with the lighting change. Karajan reacted. "What we see here is the fever dream of Schneider-Siemssen from the hospital," Karajan said. "Ten days later," Schneider-Siemssen says, "Karajan was on the podium for one of the final rehearsals. As the music flowed toward the moment we had been working on, Karajan turned around and shouted to the technical director, 'more light!' When I am not happy, he is not happy. But he yields slowly, sometimes not at all."

Schneider-Siemssen met Karajan in 1957 when he was designing sets for the State Opera House in Bremen, Germany. André von Mattoni, who was Karajan's personal secretary and aide at the time, saw sketches Schneider-Siemssen had done for a production of *Fidelio* and showed them to Karajan. Many people had told Schneider-Siemssen he would work well with Karajan because his visual concepts for opera blend well with the music, something Karajan is obsessive about. He heard that Karajan liked his work, but nothing came of it. Two years later he went to Salzburg to see Karajan and show him more work. Again nothing came of the meeting, or so he thought.

A few days later he picked up a newspaper in Hamburg and read about a press conference Karajan had given to announce work on a new ballet. He read that Karajan had named him as the set designer. It was the first he had heard of it.

Schneider-Siemssen wasn't too pleased with the ballet job. Apparently he was filling in for someone who had canceled at the last minute. But Karajan told him he had other plans for him: *La Bohème*, *Carmen*, *Pelléas et Mélisande*. Karajan gave him a contract as his special assistant at the Vienna State Opera. A year later he was head designer. Then Karajan left, and Schneider-Siemssen wondered what he should do. "He told me that I must have a fixed point in this world. He told me to stay and get established both socially and in my career. That I could still work for him out of Vienna."

Karajan's demand that everything in the opera—costumes, choreography, props, colors, action—must have solid roots in the music is nonnegotiable. This straightforward approach, which is tightly focused by Karajan's literal subjectivity, begins with the design of the sets. "This makes it very difficult," Schneider-Siemssen says. "I have to listen to what he is thinking, a collection of details, and come up with the big picture. So I make sketches and we argue back and forth and discuss what is possible from an engineering standpoint. Finally I build a model with light projection built in. Then he can work with the model like a child at the controls of a train, and he is happy. He has talent in so many directions—boats, airplanes, cars, conducting, stage directing—I tell him I am happy he cannot paint." Schneider-Siemssen's laugh is for the understatement. "He has great respect for people who can do things that he cannot."

That seems to be true about Karajan. He speaks with heartfelt admiration of those who can ski, fly, drive, or sail better than he can, those whom he has hired over the years to help him become more proficient in sports. But respect is too strong a word for those who, like Schneider-Siemssen, work closely with him in the theater. Respect can interfere with control, and Karajan would not consciously do anything that would dilute his control. With most coworkers he works at the control factor all the time, sometimes in brutal ways, like the day he took the blind shot at Schneider-Siemssen as rehearsal ended. Schneider-Siemssen had been sitting next to Karajan, who waited until the house lights went up and the attention of people had been shifted from the stage to where he was sitting before he made his move. God knows what Schneider-Siemssen was thinking, not much probably, or perhaps about the difficult set he was designing for Denver, Colorado's opera in the round, but certainly he was not on guard, sitting in the safe, familiar theater (he has an office upstairs) with a man he has known for twenty years. Not that Karajan hasn't attacked him before. Karajan is the Maestro, after all. One shrugs, one forgets, one forgives all too casually, it seems. Or perhaps one continues to hope, so treasured is the work, so otherwise acceptable is the artistic compromise.

Karajan struck like a serpent. He looked at Schneider-Siemssen, who was expecting nothing more than the usual light, postrehearsal banter, looked at him for a moment, then said, "you have brown eyes, the eyes of a traitor." Schneider-Siemssen froze. The color drained from his face. "I never noticed that before," Karajan said, half to himself, half to those within earshot. Then he chuckled, got up and left.

When the singers arrived, all was in readiness to the point that even the places on stage where they would be standing to play their various scenes had been marked and programmed for lighting with the help of the stand-ins. Their first two days were busy with costume fittings when they weren't on stage, because Karajan demands that everyone be in costume from the first day, if possible. "Now, in many opera houses, they dress in casual clothes right up to dress rehearsal," he says. "This is not right. You cannot assume the attitude of an historic person when you walk around in sneakers and jeans. In the costume you will suddenly be uncomfortable, and this will affect your acting and singing."

José Van Dam was to sing the Dutchman, the ghost-man condemned to sail the seas forever unless, on one of his periodic visits to shore (every seven years), he finds a faithful woman to give him true love. Van Dam is a well-known baritone from Belgium with a rich, distinctive voice, an easy manner, and a deadpan expression that conceals a rich sense of humor. Catarina Ligendza, a Swedish soprano, was to sing Senta, the girl who falls for the Dutchman. Kurt Moll, a large man who is a leading bass and a funny, accomplished scene stealer, would sing Daland, Senta's corrupt, opportunistic father. Conflicting engagements kept Moll from all but the last rehearsal; that Karajan permitted such an arrangement was an indication of his high regard for Moll. Victor van Halem, Moll's cover, would sing the rehearsals. Erik, a huntsman who is Senta's local boyfriend, was to be sung by Rainer Goldberg, a promising tenor from Dresden.

Ligendza is a demure creature, girlishly feminine and sparkley-eyed. Shy, yet eager; proper, yet determined. She emits a little sadness. Unlike the other singers, she didn't have a resumé at the ready. She didn't do public relations, she said. She had her career in her head, in her heart. She had begun singing in earnest at age twenty-five mainly because her mother predicted she would never make it as a singer, and she was very happy to be in Salzburg, singing for Karajan. It had been a while since she had sung for him. "That first time, ten years ago, it was terrifying," Ligendza said. "I was new, he was a big giant. I was afraid to see him alive because of the myth of him, all the records, all the time I had watched him on television from Berlin, so far away. Suddenly, when I was in front of him, I realized that I had known about him as long as I had known about music.

"I began singing, and he came to the stage and played the piano, he wanted to make music with me. Once he joined me I lost my fear. At first I sang a small role. The next year he asked me to share a role in *Fidelio*. I was angry that I had to share, jealous. I got sick over it. The next year he asked me to share again, and I said 'Mr. Karajan, I cannot come.' Now, ten years later, he asked me to come back. I was very happy to come back and show him what I could do. I told him about ten years ago, how jealous I was. He laughed. He said he would be honest with me, he didn't think I would be great. He said he missed on me.

"If someone doesn't obey him, he never forgets. But he needed a Senta, I was suggested, and someone talked him into it."

Karajan worked hard with Ligendza on her jump into the sea toward the end of the opera. Again, it was a timing problem that he wanted just right. The Dutchman thinks Senta has been unfaithful to him. He sings a final aria to that effect, then leaves for his ship. Senta is distraught, sings a lament, and rushes to the cliff overlooking the sea. Her family is unable to restrain her. Then as the ship recedes, she jumps. *Then* the ship begins to sink, then explodes. It all happens quickly. It's easy to get it slightly wrong—jump, explode, sink; or sink, jump, explode—difficult to get it just right. But Karajan the sailor knows that just as sails must be struck before anchor chains run out, ships begin to sink and build up pressure before they explode (unless of course they have been hit by a torpedo). And of course it is the suicide of Senta that triggers the sequence, "freeing" the Dutchman. Such details are as important to Karajan as a solo horn entrance.

As the cast swelled in numbers, so did the offstage personnel. Now in the working seats in the audience there was an assistant director, mainly an extension of Karajan, who would spend most of his time on stage with a script, translating Karajan's instructions and wishes when necessary; and his assistant, who sat in the same row with Karajan, six seats to his left, noting all stage directions in a script. Reichmann was still at the lighting console, Paternostro was under the headphones at the tape machine, and Papier was on station with the boss's jacket at the ready. The seats directly behind Karajan were now busy all the time with a variety of people, including the woman who was head of costumes, the properties manager, officials from the Festspielhaus who dropped by to watch for a moment and check a detail with the boss, and Frau Beate Burkhardt, Karajan's Easter Festival manager. This tall, thin, angular woman had worked at the Bayreuth Festival, where she had met Karajan and become a devoted admirer. She had moved to Salzburg, tried to obtain an apartment within sight of his house in Anif (failed), covered the walls of her quarters with his photographs, and made so many overtures about working with him that he finally hired her. In the orchestra pit a prompter now appeared, and a pianist, whose job it was to be in instant readiness in case the tape should fail, or Karajan wanted to work on a certain passage. And there were two young conductors. One, who sat off to the right down front, was a French conductor Karajan had noticed during a competition. His name was Claude Raymond, and he was a devoted student of the Maestro. "He is the greatest conductor in the world," Raymond said of Karajan. "You must write this."

The other was Bruno Weil, music director at the State Theater in Augsburg, Germany, and another conducting competition winner. Karajan had helped him secure the Augsburg job, and had engaged him for Easter Festival as his backup, although Karajan was quick to point out that in seventeen Easter Festivals, he had never needed a backup. "The first year," Karajan said, "there was much at stake, and no money, so I arranged to insure the production with Lloyd's of London. They insisted that from October until the festival was ended, I must not fly my airplane. We never had to collect a cent from them, and I have done every performance since."

Weil sat in the front row, center, concentrating on the score throughout every rehearsal.

There were other Karajan regulars in nonproduction capacities who came and went as they pleased. The weather-beaten fellow with the long gray hair and large girth wearing the bush jacket, looking as though he had just come out of the wild after a few weeks with Ernest Hemingway, was Emil Perauer, one of the few photographers Karajan trusts. Perauer says he has taken fifty thousand slides of Karajan in the last ten years, both at work and at play. The other photographer who would be around as dress rehearsal approached was Siegfried Lauterwasser, an older man. With his shock of gray hair and courtly manner, he could have been a diplomat. Lauterwasser's dramatic images of Karajan conducting are sold in Salzburg bookstores. He has done many of the record cover portraits.

The striking woman in the boots, draped in a soft cloud of flowing, mauve Ultrasuede, was Gela Marina Runne from Berlin, whom Karajan retains to cut the films he makes. Runne first worked with Karajan twenty years ago. She would appear toward the end of each rehearsal in hopes that the Maestro would have allotted time that day to work on the current film project. Karajan had recently formed his own film company (it included Runne) and was in the process of redoing all of the symphonic films (Tchaikovsky, Beethoven, Bruckner, Mahler, Brahms) that he had completed in 1978. He had installed three-head, $40,000 cutting tables in the basements of his houses in St. Moritz and Anif, and he and Runne were in the midst of editing footage of Beethoven's Fifth. Chances were he would not have time (he spent a total of two hours with Runne during the four weeks of Easter Festival), but Karajan's method is to line up the people and projects and have them wait, just in case an hour should pop up in which he has nothing to do. Runne waited with utter composure. It didn't matter to her. She was on salary, all expenses paid. She was sleeping late and taking tennis lessons.

The immaculately dressed and manicured man coming and going throughout rehearsals, looking distracted, clutching an expensive leather envelope, and always sitting beside Karajan for hushed conferences, was Runne's boss, Dr. Uli Märkle. Märkle is a German lawyer who worked eleven years for Deutsche Grammophon promoting classical artists before Karajan hired him to be managing director of his new film company, Telemondial. After law school, the intern sequence in Germany includes terms working as public prosecutor, then defender, followed by a four-month period the younger attorney may fill with work of his choice. Märkle chose theater administration. He had a bent for public relations and was offered a job in that area. He took it, and it wasn't long before he met people from Deutsche Grammophon who brought him to Hamburg. He says it took him five years before Karajan said anything but hello and goodbye to him. Then in 1977 Märkle went on tour with Karajan in Japan, and Karajan became more friendly. Karajan hired Märkle early in 1983.

Märkle is a self-styled deal maker and all-purpose connection who wonders, not very subtly, what poor old Karajan ever did without his services. Märkle takes obvious relish in being "next" to Karajan.

Then there was Peter Busse, a dapper fellow in a state of perpetual anxiety, looking much younger than his fifty years, who charged into the hall the day the singers arrived with the startled, offended look of a man who has discovered a bunch of strangers in his living room. Busse is an actor, so part of everything he does is for effect, and the effect is always aimed at Karajan when he is around. Because Busse is a natural comedian, the effect he usually wants is laughter. This isn't immediately apparent, because as "on" as Busse can be among friends, he is aloof with strangers to the point of being loudly aggressive, almost hostile. The second day he was in Salzburg, Busse approached me and said with obvious annoyance, "Well, the boss said I should take you out to dinner, so I guess I must. What night is good for you?" But one could hardly blame him for feeling ill-used at having to bear the brunt of Karajan's second-hand hospitality.

Busse is Karajan's personal assistant stage director, a complicated arrangement in that Karajan is his own stage director. Karajan says it is not complicated: "I say what I want, and Busse does it. He has no authority." But in the last few years, as Karajan's mobility has become restricted, Busse has functioned more and more as Karajan's arms and legs on stage. He has worked for so long with the Maestro that he can easily predict what Karajan wants in any given situation. So he does a lot of rehearsal planning and blocking out of scenes, and works out a lot of action that is simply presented at rehearsal for Karajan's modification. This seems to be the best way to work with Karajan. The Maestro is a better critic than he is creator or initiator. Give him a starting point, and he is quick to rearrange it. He also seems more willing to accept Busse's ideas than anyone else's. Perhaps that is because Busse has spent nearly twenty years learning from Karajan. He has been a good student and a grateful, not a rebellious one. He aims to please his boss.

"The Maestro is clear in everything he does," Busse says. "The visual side of the performance is totally covered by the music. That's why he has taken everything into his own hands. He can make sure he sees on stage what he sees and feels in the music. The circle is completed. That doesn't happen unless the stage director happens to be right on key with the conductor. Karajan alone has the talent, power, the means to do both. Believe me, I wish I could be the conductor for my own stage productions."

Busse began his artistic career as a dancer, then switched to acting. When he was twenty-five he decided to combine his abilities with his music background and stretch out a bit. So he became assistant to the stage director Margaret Wallmann and traveled with her, learning. During rehearsals for *Turandot* at the Vienna State Opera, Wallmann became ill. Busse was called upon. "I took over rehearsal. It was the big scene in *Turandot* with Leontyne Price and all these extras mourning and carrying on, and I was running around as usual, and I finally saw this man in the wings beckoning to me. I ignored him for a while because I was busy. Then I went over. 'Be careful,' he said to me, 'that when they pick up Leontyne Price they don't lug her around like a sack of potatoes.' I'm sure I gave him a strange look. I didn't know at the time it was Karajan. The next day he offered me a job, and I have been with him ever since.

"I have my other work. They love me in France, which is a great compliment—I am a foreigner, after all. But I keep spring and summer free for the festivals here with Karajan. He is old now. He needs back some of what he gave me, and he has given so much to me when I was young. I was privileged to learn from the best this century has produced. Now I pay him back with loyalty."

There was one gentleman who wasn't at rehearsals, who hasn't been involved with the Karajan organization in several years, but whose presence is still strongly felt, such was his stature within the Karajan clan. This is André von Mattoni, who began as Karajan's secretary and right hand in 1949. The late John Culshaw, a producer for Decca Records in London who often worked with Karajan, described Mattoni when he was in his sixties in his autobiography *Putting the Record Straight*: "The one member of [Karajan's] retinue for whom we had both respect and affection was André von Mattoni, who acted as Karajan's front man ... Mattoni was an exceptionally handsome, perfectly groomed gentleman of aristocratic bearing. In the early days of the talkies he had played some minor roles in Hollywood, but there were dark rumors of some scandal that had driven him away from California. He was multi-lingual without the slightest hesitancy, and without accent. The English thought he was English. The French accepted him as French, and the Italians thought he was Italian by virtue of his name; in fact he was Viennese. With infinite politeness he kept undesirables away from Karajan, but smoothed the path for those who really needed or deserved an audience with 'The Master,' as Mattoni always referred to him. If, as sometimes happened, The Master wished to wipe his feet on someone, Mattoni merely assumed a pained expression and became a doormat."

Mattoni died in 1985 while in his eighties. In the summer of 1983, I visited Mattoni at his house in Salzburg, where he lived during the season with his companion, a young, burly fellow who was involved with church work. He was perfectly groomed and aristocratic in black velvet slacks and Gucci loafers, a silver sliver of a man, an aging trooper; the deep-set eyes still flashing a touch of lust, the voice steady—fragile as antique crystal. He spoke about how he joined The

Master: "I was living in Rome. I was a producer for Viennese and Italian films with my own company. In 1948 the director Marischka said we must do the *St. Matthew Passion*. He had promised this to his only daughter, who had died. He said that von Karajan, the greatest conductor in Central Europe, had promised to do it. I should go and talk with him. So I presented myself to Karajan. He gave me a list of singers to contract. We made dates. He wanted to work with the big chorus in the morning and do the recitatives in the afternoon, when the singers would be in better voice. I asked him how many days he would need in the studio. He said he could do it in twelve days. The day before he came I got on my knees to everyone, pleaded with them to be on time, not to talk, to pay attention. He came, and it was finished in eleven days. He said to me, 'You are my man. You must come to me for good.' It took me a year. I had to close my business."

Culshaw said Mattoni probably knew Karajan better than any man on earth, but that while he would enjoy a gossip about other conductors or singers, where Karajan was concerned his discretion was complete.

It really is a clan that has come together under Karajan, and Easter Festival is its annual reunion. As with any good clan, the common interest is intense. Loyalty—albeit a little one-sided—provides much of the unit strength. Karajan is loyal, too, as long as the voice is holding up and the performance remains at the same high quality, and as long as the willingness to follow orders is still intact. The ground rules are implicit. If those things falter, loyalty (and the contract) is lifted quickly and as a matter of course, with not so much as a glance astern. This is the music business, after all, and it in no way resembles a democracy. Karajan functions ruthlessly behind the scenes as chairman of the board. He would simply say that he works for the good of the music, and he would have a strong argument. Putting Eskimo elders on slabs of ice and floating them off into the sunset is good for the village too, but it sounds a little brutal to outsiders. Musicians speak freely about their shelf life. Brass players know their lips will begin to fail them sometime in their late fifties. Singers begin with the comprehension that they are walking on eggs. So the feeling of clan is strong, with Karajan presiding over the operation from his sixteenth-row seat like a German godfather, joking, cajoling, teasing, laughing, and being as patient as he is demanding with his charges. It is a safe game for him, because it is played from behind the cloak of ultimate power. It is also for the good of the order. The show, after all, does have to go on, and it has to be the best. So the game is moreover a very productive one, a well-conceived, very professional

technique that is designed to relax while obtaining maximum effort
from the players.

Karajan can be generous as well as loyal to those he favors. Seiji
Ozawa continues to call Karajan whenever he tackles an opera that is
new to him. If Karajan has time, Ozawa flies to him for advice and
counsel. If there is no time, they go over the piece by phone, singing
the parts, as Ozawa says, "in our terrible voices." Ozawa says Karajan
is totally open with him. "He knows how many different conductors
have done the piece. He shows me. He tells me everything, how he
once recorded it, how he might change certain things if he did it
again. 'Do it this way and you are safe,' he might tell me. Fifteen
years ago he told me I must taste opera if I am to be really
good."

Ozawa is both grateful for Karajan's indulgence—"He has always
found time for me"—and amazed by his memory. "One time I tele-
phoned him about an opera I know he had not done in many years.
I am sure he had no time to look at the score, and yet he went over
it with me in great detail. I had my score in front of me and was
taking notes very fast. The only problem I have is understanding
him," says Ozawa, whose Japanese-inflected English must be an interesting match for Karajan's Germanic mumblings. It's lucky the
subject they discuss is music.

"I went to him about the Bartók piece for strings and percussion. I
was in Berlin. He had meetings, so I drove around with him in the
car and he reviewed it, front to back, ten minutes here, five minutes
there, in between listening to playbacks of tapes he had recorded,
auditions, meetings. And he hadn't conducted it in six years.

"Once I conducted Brahms's Second in New York, and he came
to hear it. The next day he asked me, 'Why did you do that?' But he
doesn't put me in a corner. It is like when he teaches. He asks, 'What
is wrong?' You have to find it. When I tell him why I do something
he says 'ahhh....'

"My symphonic work he likes, but with opera he thinks I am an
innocent, a baby. What he says about opera is right, but I cannot do
it his way. I must try it my way. I started opera late. I may do it
wrong, but if I don't do it my way, how do I learn? He says that
planning and conditions are important. His mind is great for planning,
mine is not. And I cannot get ideal conditions as he can, keep the cast
from fall to spring. He lectures me. He thinks I understand, but six
months later I make the same mistake again!

"He gets annoyed that I call him Maestro. He says if I keep calling
him that he will call me 'Little Maestro.' I try, but it is hard. I can

call Bernstein 'Lennie,' but 'Herbert'? 'Herbie'? To me he will always be 'Maestro.'"

Most of the stories one hears about Karajan's generosity have to do with material things, and again come under the general heading of professionalism. When James McCracken had trouble accepting a role Karajan wanted him for in Salzburg because of a previous commitment in Vienna, Karajan made it possible by having his plane ferry McCracken between the two houses. And he has been known to arrange for people to look after singers who were particularly nervous or upset. While indeed generous, such matters are indisputably for the good of the order.

The condition that elicits a purer form of generosity from Karajan is medical emergency. He once rushed Ozawa off to the hospital in his plane, and several members of the Berlin Philharmonic have been on the receiving end of his medical intervention. Several times he has arranged for specialists, private rooms, and recuperation in the sun, all at his personal expense.

Karajan is something of a hypochondriac himself, a man who likes his thermostat set firmly at 80 degrees Fahrenheit, and who will not tolerate the slightest draft, even in summer. Unless it is crucial, and a very close friend is involved, he won't dream of making a hospital visitation. His idea of combating sickness is to dive into the best hospital with the best specialists in attendance at the slightest bodily malfunction. He relates sickness to flying: "You wouldn't dream of taking the airplane up unless it was totally checked out. Get everything working perfectly on the ground, and you should have no trouble in flight. It is the same with the body." And yet here he was dragging himself around the Festspielhaus in considerable pain, continually putting off an operation that was not only inevitable, but increasingly critical. It was not so much a contradiction as one might think. He had a schedule, after all. There was no time. There was the festival, recording dates, concerts that should not be canceled. He is a professional: the show had to go on.

"Working with him is not easy," José Van Dam says. "He demands every note. And he knows what he wants. But I can talk with him. He is not closed. If he asks me to do something a different way, and I disagree, I try to understand because he is a bigger musician than I am. And his strength is flexible. Once on stage, he will follow you. And if you make a mistake, he shrugs it off, gives you a sign that it doesn't matter. And you go on. I learn the most when I sing with him."

No one has ever seen Karajan lose his composure on the podium.

He has been known to put on high-voltage scenes over contract negotiations and other business matters, but when it comes to music, Karajan is calm, cool, and collected.

An associate in the U.S. recalls a period in the 1950s when Karajan had a contract for a certain number of productions at the Metropolitan Opera. He said Karajan would call him every evening promptly at 6 P.M. to complain bitterly about the Met orchestra, which was a far cry from today's fine ensemble: "Where did these people come from?" Karajan would lament ... "none of them could pass the first go-'round at the Berlin ... they can't play ... this is terrible." But at rehearsals Karajan's posture was such that one player said he was sure Karajan truly loved them, held the orchestra in the highest esteem. "Now that is being a pro," the associate says. "One has to know, with live art, how to deal with mediocrity and still make a good performance. Karajan knows how to do this. Toscanini would have told the orchestra they were pigs, had a fit, demanded a whole new violin section. Karajan worked it out by being positive. He knew he couldn't change the players. He had to deal with them."

Karajan has set ideas about the function of rehearsal. "Every rehearsal must be an improvement of what went before," he says. "One must learn how to get improvement each time. If you are tired, you cannot gain. Always at the end we are glad if we can say we have achieved something. If we end with dissonance, the dissonance remains with the players. So we say 'we don't know it yet, but it will come.'"

As Van Dam says, Karajan knows what he wants, which is a comfort when the groups to be led are the size of symphony orchestras and opera companies. With the possible exception of the mass gymnastic displays that are held in Chinese stadiums, there is no performing group responding to a single director that is larger than a musical ensemble. Musical leadership is autocratic even in small music groups, and it is essentially so when the numbers reach two, even three hundred, as singers and chorus are added to an orchestra. As has been noted, Karajan's temperament is well suited to the task, and most often his response to his position is self-satisfaction. It is with glee that he tells the story of the time the Salzburg Festival first considered him for artistic director. He was told there were some objections. Some people thought he was a dictator. "I said, 'they are right!'"

On occasion the implications of his singular power give him pause. Once as he sat in his villa in St. Tropez talking about music, he defined what a conductor is: "He is like the hydra of mythology, with nine heads for so much music; twelve arms for so many musicians. He is an ambassador of music, a priest of his profession, a bringer of peace and beauty. He is adored by millions and condemned by the rest as a dictator, shamelessly making business out of art. A charlatan. Has any profession in history suffered such contradictions as that of conductor? It can only be compared with the fanaticism of sectarians.

"This is a unique form of making art: one man is given almost limitless power over players, singers, and budget, the planning, the programs. Where else could this happen? In almost all other professions leaders are controlled by commissions, boards, inspectors, unions, all with the right to change things. In our time this could be the last time someone is so entrusted.

"And there is some taint to the principle of leadership. Hitler called himself 'the leader,' *ja*? So this word has taken on a bitter aspect. It is a suspect word. When people appreciate that someone has to exert his will, they always become suspicious. Leadership—dictatorship. A strong will to express one's self is apt to be criticized today. People seem not to dare to express their opinions openly and with the force to fulfill them. But in the realm of pure art this principle has value. One man must express it, otherwise nothing great will come out."

This philosophy—one man, one expression—is at the core of the Karajan organization as well as the artistic endeavor. The Karajan shop runs from the top down. If Karajan, or Lore Salzburger, or perhaps Märkle, doesn't think of something, it doesn't happen. So there is no public relations, no real organization to keep things smooth. And it is immensely busy, with complex rehearsal and performance schedules, recording dates, program planning, casting of soloists and singers, the logistics of four houses and staff, a twin-engine jet aircraft, ten or a dozen automobiles, a 77-foot, million-dollar racing yacht that demands a full-time captain and four crew; and constant demands from the press, visitors, and people in the business. Then there is a foundation; an institute for the scientific investigation of music; the Easter Festival; the film company; and, of course, last-minute whims and notions of the boss. Salzburger's ability to coordinate the big picture is just short of miraculous. How she keeps the appointments straight, the plane in the air, the boat in the water, her hair in place, and her office immaculate—all at the same time and in four languages—is beyond comprehension. In the ten days preceding Karajan's seventy-fifth birthday (April 5, 1983), she answered 850 pieces of mail in addition to her other duties.

The rest of the organization is a collection of individuals, each of whom has been hired personally by Karajan. Each has been given some, but not all, the information about how the conglomerate works. This, of course, makes them uneasy and insecure, and results in competition among them that can reach nasty, petty levels. And each thinks that he or she is the one closest to the Maestro, that he or she alone has attained the status of "friend." This is just how Karajan wants it. He holds the strings, and doesn't hesitate to jerk them (as with Schneider-Siemssen) when he feels it necessary or when the mood strikes him.

This might seem like a cavalier way to treat loyal workers, and it probably wouldn't be very effective if Karajan were dependent on his people for more than the quick and dutiful execution of his orders. But he is not. Such an organizational method often makes it difficult for those trying to do business with Karajan. In *Putting the Record Straight*, John Culshaw recalled preparations for his first studio encounter with Karajan: "We had decided that Karajan would be treated just like any other artist in the studio, and at first I suspect this bewildered him. Nobody—at any rate, nobody in Austria—ever questioned Karajan's right to do exactly what he wanted. He moved everywhere with a circle of sycophants, who tried to justify their existence by speaking for him whenever possible, and I had to make it clear right away that I could not function as one removed from the conductor. . . . To this day I don't think Karajan ever understood how much of his troubles were due to the people he allowed to surround him."

The best artist, as one music manager points out, is the one who knows what is right for him. The artist who relies on others to make career and artistic decisions for him is in trouble. Karajan doesn't want anyone to tell him what to do about anything. He decides what pieces he will record, what programs he will play, what operas he will do and who will sing the roles, what tires he will buy for his car, and what sailmaker will build the sails for his boat. He makes all business decisions personally with his attorney in Zurich, a Mr. Max Fisher. It is Karajan's success, Karajan's power, and he has chosen to be the one responsible for plotting every detail of its course. If it is bungled, he wants to be the one to bungle it. To date, one can't quarrel with the success of the management. As one long-time business associate says, "Karajan does it all. Man proposes, God disposes. That's how it should be. As for his people, if he had been less successful, perhaps he would have been a better judge of character."

While rehearsals for *The Flying Dutchman* were going on in Salzburg, a Munich production of the same opera was set in a present-day housing development. The Dutchman character was portrayed as an imposter, a man who knew the legend and who was pretending to be the ghost-man for his own gratification. There was no ghostly ship, no sailors in the rigging, no Norwegian coastal town c. 1750. Such a reading of Wagner would revolt Karajan the musician. Karajan staunchly upholds the literal approach against "creative" interpretations, modern sets, and extreme stagings.

"The vision comes from the text," Karajan says. "Here is a man doomed for eternity. Every seven years he may land in hopes of finding a woman true enough to liberate him. In an earlier time he was sailing around the Cape. He should have turned back, given in to the weather, but he did not—he made a deal with the devil. Now he must pay. The man wants to die but he cannot. Nothing ages: the ship, the sails, the man. He can't die."

Karajan says he hates improvisation in art, "anything that happens which is not prepared beforehand. This does not happen with me." And he is disparaging of those directors who have no background in music, who suddenly decide to do an opera. "All they bring to the stage is newness. I have seen outrageous things. Madame Butterfly set in a European brothel! A French production of Wagner's Rheingold in which the Rhinemaidens were dancing beside a canal in French can-can dresses! These directors simply charge around to do something stupid. They love their productions to be booed. All they want to do is create a scandal."

Karajan's dramatic ideal is the Kabuki theater, the highly stylized Japanese tradition in which an actor remains in a particular role, or character, all his life, ideally passing the role on to his offspring when he retires. "Or perhaps the old actor will adopt a young person and make him his heir," Karajan says. So one should not expect to see opera productions from Karajan that are innovative. They will be as literal as his musical understanding and his years of research can make them. If he has done them before, they will be essentially the same, only (he would hope) better, with the roles passed on to new singers whose job is to master every note of the score.

He is not adverse, however, to technological innovations. A production of Fidelio which followed Karajan's enthusiastic viewing of the film Star Wars featured weaponry that looked very similar to the laser guns used in the film. And the gate on the prison that opens in the last act to release the prisoners was electric-powered and push-button operated. Karajan's "gate-o-matic," members of the cast called it.

In animating his singers, Karajan's major emphasis is economy of movement. He urges them to move only when necessary, when the music dictates. "The idea of opera," Karajan says, "is that the actor develops feelings that are so strong he must sing. Like with yodeling. Yodeling is an explosion of pure joy. With opera the idea is to show feelings by singing, to show that one is in a state other than a normal one. The exultation is so big one can only sing about it. Movement, if one is necessary, is only to help fully produce the feeling that comes from the singer's mouth. The change from joy to sadness, for instance. The singer looks at something, feels something. At Bayreuth, when a singer finishes an aria, or even a short piece, he must make this big final gesture, extend his arms, or stamp his foot. This is ridiculous. There must be no 'operatic' gestures."

With *The Flying Dutchman*, this method of operation was carried to the extreme. Together with the low stage lighting, more accurately called "stage darkening," Karajan hoped to emphasize the fantasy of the opera by creating at times a dreamlike effect. With the diffusion curtain forming a flat plane across the entire proscenium, a viewer felt as if he were looking at a mammoth three-dimensional television screen, or perhaps a hologram.

Van Dam, in particular, stood for long periods on stage without moving a muscle. Van Dam is a black-haired, pale-skinned man who has a naturally woeful look to him. The motionless position he assumed was with his feet comfortably spread, his arms rigid by his side, the fists clenched, his broad shoulders squared, and his face tilted slightly toward the heavens, "to invoke the forces," Van Dam explained. When he did move, it was stiffly, and in slow motion, as if his body were partially frozen. It was a difficult assignment. "Acting is not so important as the intensity of personality that one projects," Van Dam said, "and musicality as well. Standing still is also acting. It is easier to move around than to stand still. And the intensity is difficult. It makes singing harder."

Van Dam was not the last to see the potential humor in his rigidly sinister portrayal of the Dutchman. During one rehearsal he broke up the proceedings by pretending to bite Ligendza on the neck. Ligendza said there were times when he really did frighten her. And there were moments in the two-and-a-half hour opera when the spell was broken. At one point the opportunistic Daland, father of Senta, having seen the chest full of jewels the Dutchman has aboard his ship, brings the phantom sailor home to meet his pretty daughter. Daland (Kurt Moll) flings open the door, saunters into the room with obvious pride, and with an expansive gesture shows Senta who (what!) he has brought her. Behind him, the Dutchman had assumed his position. Daland stood gloating, a befitting pose for a man who had just brought home the bacon. And by that point in the opera, with the help of a lighting effect that was making him appear a bit green, Van Dam had indeed projected all the personality of a large, well-traveled side of bacon.

But then, the Wagnerian transitions are time-consuming. If a singer moves too fast, he will arrive at his new stage location with nothing to do but wait. And one must move with the music. It can make for snail's-pace action. Between the dramatic arrival of the ship in Act I and the final scene of the opera when Senta jumps to her death into the sea, *The Flying Dutchman* offers little in the way of real action. But then, that's opera. There is an old, traditional blues song that comments on this aspect of the medium: "Oh a singer comes in from the left / and a singer comes in from the right / by the time they say hello / it's taken up half the night" ("Opera Gives Me Cause to Sing the Blues" by Cletis "Sweet Man" Crowley).

With the singers assembled, Karajan began at the beginning. The curtains were closed, Paternostro started the tape, and the overture played. As the curtains parted, here came Daland's ship, a marvelously realistic construction, drawn by Schneider-Siemssen and built in the Festspielhaus shops, complete with mast, sails, rigging, ratlines, and crow's-nest, gliding in to its berth on tracks. Karajan was pleased, humming along, idly conducting the recording with one hand draped over a chairback. After the Dutchman's ship joins Daland's vessel in the harbor, and the Dutchman is first seen mid-stage, Daland's steersman, who has fallen asleep, awakens and tries to set things right with his master. Spotting the Dutchman, he sings: "I think I see the captain there." Karajan laughed. "One time I saw this production on a very small stage. The steersman used a glass to spot the Dutchman, and my God, the end of the glass nearly hit the man in the face."

Karajan stopped the action to work with those playing the sailors. He gave another nautical lecture about the handling of sails and lines. They ran it through again, and Karajan was shouting into the microphone, "halt, halt, halt!" The house lights came up, and again Karajan made his way to the stage. He got aboard Daland's ship and for ten minutes gave lessons in the proper lowering of sails and coiling of lines. "I should take them aboard my boat and teach them," he said as he returned to his seat.

Karajan the director has always liked the onstage, hands-on approach. Ita Maximova, a set designer who worked frequently with Karajan in the 1950s, recalls him during a production of *Carmen* at La

Scala in 1952. "He showed the singer at rehearsal how to manage with the monkey," Maximova says. "He was the best Carmen I ever saw. He got on stage and did better than she did. Of course, he couldn't sing." Later, in 1967, when he put *Carmen* on film, he donned black wig and moustache and made shifty eyes for the bit part of a swindler.

The stage direction is very important for Karajan because it gives him power to ascertain that the action is the perfect showcase for the music. But being director brings out a whole lot of things about Karajan that are quite charming. He really is something of a ham—a great mugger—and unlike some who put up with the fame that accompanies leadership because they must, Karajan loves being the center of attention. Many were the times during rehearsal when he would keep several hundred people waiting while he entertained those in his immediate vicinity with an anecdote or a joke that came to mind. Like the story about the conductor Otto Klemperer that he told at least twice during the proceedings, about Klemperer walking down the main street in Berlin with a banker named Mendelssohn, of the same family that produced the well-known composer. The two went into a record store so Klemperer could see if they carried any of his records. The clerk checked, and said they did not. Klemperer exploded, told the clerk that he happened to be Klemperer, and he knew better. The clerk: "if you're Klemperer who is this with you, Mozart, I suppose?" Klemperer: "No, Mendelssohn."

Those who have known Karajan a long time say that this story-telling and joking is relatively new. Karajan the younger man did not, or perhaps could not, so indulge himself. One doesn't have time for jokes when one is general music director of Europe; only efficiency and terseness. But it is plain that the "director" job is one that pleases Karajan from every angle. Certainly he is vain enough to appreciate the romantic image that accompanies the power of the job. With his shock of white hair, his black turtlenecks and colorful running shoes, he does look as though he might have come over from central casting.

He spends less time on stage than he used to, because of his reduced mobility. But the times he did go to the stage, once he got there it was evident he was enjoying himself. He physically handles actors—although now one wonders if he isn't partly using them for support—and he gets in close with them, singing the lines with them in his Muppet voice, exaggerating the expressions and postures with his mobile face and body. He gives the women little pats here and there, and the men get their cuffs and shoves of sports-coach appreciation.

When he is finished on stage, there are smiles all around. Karajan the actor is a most entertaining person.

Karajan was most relaxed during the staging rehearsals. This period was when it was easiest to get an audience with him. It seemed that every day a new newspaper reporter or magazine writer or visiting dignitary would join him in the shotgun seat. One day it was Bryan Moynahan of the *Sunday Times*. Moynahan is a sailor, so naturally that subject came up. During the break, Karajan regaled us with stories of the Class A World Sailing Championships the previous summer in Sardinia. He was wearing a black leather jacket with lots of zippered pockets, and as he brightened to the subject, suddenly here was Karajan the sportsman, the big boat sailor, telling stories about Juan Carlos, king of Spain, who regularly sails on one of the maxis. "Gary Jobson was sailing with me, and we were at the yacht club afterwards and Jobson said to this man standing there, 'You guys didn't do too badly today.' I pulled on his jacket and said to him [Karajan acts it out], 'You don't say "you guys" to the king!' And Gary said, 'He's not *my* king.'" Karajan roared.

"Then I had been talking to people, and the buffet was served, so I began to fix myself a plate. Halfway through I realized the king was standing behind me. I'm sure people were wondering what I would do. So I took my time, finished fixing the plate, and handed it to the king: 'Your Majesty....'"

Karajan made sure that Moynahan knew that the ghost sailors on the Dutchman's ship—silhouette figures seen in the rigging—were being played by children. He was proud of this idea. He said the smaller figures made the boat look larger.

Another day the visitor was Klaus Maria Brandauer, Austria's hottest film star, who played the main character (Hendrick Hofgen) in *Mephisto*, and the heavy opposite Sean Connery's James Bond in *Never Say Never Again*. Karajan was at his most expansive for Brandauer. Karajan loves films. Next to being famous as a conductor, he would like to be known as a filmmaker. "I have made thirty-six films," Karajan says. "I am already well known as a filmmaker."

The day after Brandauer visited, an extraordinary thing happened— at least it was extraordinary to a newcomer to the scene. Halfway through rehearsal Karajan wanted to go over a particular entrance several times. It happened that the music he wanted was split between two tapes, so he spoke one word into the microphone—"piano"— raised his arm, and when he brought it down, the pianist in the pit came in at just the right place, at just the right tempo. He played the repeat several times, perhaps it took one minute or so, then Karajan waved him off and nodded to Paternostro, who began the tape once again. It was the first time in nine days that the pianist had been called upon to play, and there he was, totally on guard, totally prepared. I hadn't been quite so prepared when, after five days of saying little more than "*Morgen*" and "*Abend*" (good morning, good evening), Karajan leaned forward at the start of a ten-minute break and said, "Well now, what do you want to know?"

As Busse said, "When you are with Karajan, you have to be prepared for anything at any time." I thought of this one afternoon when I approached the big wooden doors of the hall about twenty feet in front of Karajan, who was having a walking conference with a lieutenant. When I was five feet from the doors, they were magically opened from the inside by Busse. To my questioning look he shrugged: "After twenty years, one knows."

As the third week of rehearsals began, approximately one hundred more performers were added in the form of the Musikfreunde chorus from Vienna. Now the stage was full to brimming morning and night as these seasoned, state-supported, full-time actors, dancers, and singers rehearsed the production numbers. One of these was a dance of drunken sailors featuring the entire company. Bodies littered the stage at the end, much to Karajan's delight. He had designed the choreography, and it was both amusing and effective. "Ah me," he said, watching the scene run through. "The women leave and the sailors get drunk."

The dance scene merges into a confrontation with the Dutchman's crew, coordinated with a sudden stormy, foreboding shift in Wagner's score. It is Daland's crew that has the drunken homecoming celebration. At the outset they hail the Dutchman's ship in hopes its crew will join the revelry. When all is silent on the ghost ship, they celebrate anyway. Then the wind comes up and flickering lights are seen on board the phantom. The music moans and wails as silhouettes of the ghost crew are glimpsed above the bulwarks. Daland's sailors cower in the shadow of the phantom ship and crew. Then rather suddenly, the musical section ends. Karajan the director needed a way to handle it visually, so he told Peter Busse to don the hooded garment of a monk, stride through the mob of sailors, and hold up a jeweled cross towards the Dutchman's crew that would be spotlit as the music climaxed.

Karajan watched it run through a few times and wasn't sure the idea worked. Busse came back from the stage and the two discussed it. Karajan slapped the microphone against the palm of his hand. He wondered aloud what people around him thought. No one spoke. A visitor took a deep breath and said he thought the cross was a bit out of keeping, a little sudden. Karajan emitted one of his patented guttural chuckles as he eyed the visitor. "What would you prefer," he asked, "the swastika?"

Karajan had business to do in Vienna, and he had a doctor's appointment for an examination of the nail he had somehow torn off one big toe that was making it even more difficult for him to get around. He had scheduled these things on the day before the Berlin Philharmonic was due to arrive for orchestra rehearsals, and he had arranged for his private plane to be available. Karajan owns the plane in partnership with another man, and they keep it busy on short charter hops (Salzburg-St. Moritz, for instance) when neither wants it for personal use. Karajan invited me along.

Among those who have not flown with Karajan there is considerable speculation as to his ability, and about who really flies the plane, Karajan or his pilot. The fact that Karajan's wife, Eliette, is loath to fly with him adds fuel to the gossip. Having sailed with Karajan, I assumed he did the flying, and probably did it quite well. He is not a talented racing skipper, but he handles his large sailboat in a comfortable, seamanly way. Since he has many more hours in the airplane (he has been flying jets for ten years), and since methodical fellows like Karajan generally make competent pilots, I did not think twice about going up with him.

He sat in the left-hand seat of the Falcon 10 and went over the preflight list with his copilot. I sat in the jump seat, riding sideways with the second copilot, with a good view into the cockpit and out the windscreen. Karajan taxied the plane to the end of the runway, eased the throttles forward, kept the squirrelly, high-strung jet on track, and lifted off into the rough spring clouds at a wonderfully extreme angle of attack that put away 2,000 vertical feet per minute. He leveled off at 25,200. We all went a bit weightless for a moment at the top, then Karajan slowly settled the plane to 25,000 feet and held it there.

During the preflight and lift-off, I had been conversing quietly with the copilot, asking all the usual airplane questions. Now I asked Karajan if he minded if I took a few photographs of him driving.

"I don't care what you do as long as you don't talk," he said with a grim little smile. I got the message. Even during the taxi run, Karajan's jaw had been working, his eyes narrowed in concentration, much like when he is on the podium. Flying is a great pleasure for him, but one he works at. It is the same with the boat. His aim in both cases is the same kind of perfection he strives to attain on the podium. The concentration and the commitment are as fierce. It is work, not play. It is possible that the concept of play is quite foreign to Karajan.

It was a rough flight. The little plane bucked and tossed as it needled through gray, rolling clouds at 475 knots. Some of the stormier Wagner themes that I had been listening to over the past weeks would have made a good sound track. To one not used to looking out the front window at anything moving that fast, it was breathtaking, especially the descent through the thick, gray weather. The copilot handled radio communications with the tower while Karajan circled. Then he made as pretty a landing in a 30-mph crosswind as one could hope for.

Driving into Vienna, Karajan talked with enthusiasm about flying. "I have been flying in my dreams since I was a boy," Karajan said. He said the Falcon 10 was the sixth aircraft he had owned since he began flying in 1950. Preceding the Falcon, he had a Lear jet for four years. He is pleased to have an older plane. The new ones apparently are built around more efficient use of fuel, and they are not as fast, or rated for as high an altitude as Karajan's five-year-old Falcon.

He is proud of the Falcon's toughness, the fact that Dessault Aviation, the manufacturer, built many military features into the airplane. "This is the only airplane you don't have to throttle back when you hit turbulence like today," Karajan said. "The pilot or the passengers could be knocked out, but the plane will continue flying." That seemed like a dubious advantage, but Karajan was impressed.

Karajan said that the plane could dive from 28,000 feet to sea level in one and a half minutes; that in it, he can travel faster than the orchestra on a large chartered jet; that at full power, he can climb at 4,000 feet per minute up to 35,000 feet. He flies 250 hours a year and wishes it were more. Karajan loves the speed of the plane, the raw, thrilling power of the climb-out, the impressive numbers, and the gadgetry of it all. Improvements in electronics over the last thirty years amaze and delight him. But more than all that, he likes the discipline the airplane demands of him.

He enjoys the mental preparation of flight. "If you fly tomorrow, you must not drink today. You must have a good night's sleep. Flying is not complex, but you must prepare, be organized. Every single thing must be checked out each time. Then if something does go wrong, you have a clear conscience. Then there is the flight itself. There is always the challenge: are you good enough to fly? If everything works as it should, you have great satisfaction. Then I make my work so much better.

"On the commercial planes, there will be a ten-minute delay, and then twenty minutes more, and then ten minutes more, and I wonder, 'Why am I here? I could be outside on the mountain.' Such things give you fatigue, hinder your performance.

"When I bought this plane I was required to take a course at Dessault Aviation. It was very demanding. For the last test they get you up in the middle of the night, put you in the airplane alone, and you must land on the yellow stripe without the field lights on. The course was meant to be sixteen days. I told them I did not have sixteen days, so they let me do it in eleven ten-hour days. On the final examination I scored a 93. My pilot had a 97, but then he is a professional.

"When I got home from the course I had a very short time to prepare a concert. I looked at a score I had not conducted for a long time. I closed it, and the whole piece came back to me because my mind had been sharpened by those eleven intense days.

"When a concert cycle is finished, I get into the plane and by the time I arrive, the concert is finished, history, a thousand miles behind me, and I am rested, ready for the next work."

Traveling with Karajan is to witness an extravagant fantasy being played out. He flies by helicopter from the pasture beside his house in Anif to the airport in Munich, using the trip as an excuse to take a flying lesson (or vice versa?). He sets the chopper down gently beside his pointy-nosed, high-tailed jet, where the crew is waiting, and soars off to wherever he must while the rest of us spend life-sapping hours in ticket-counter lines and slumped wearily in lounges. While we wait endlessly and without hope for baggage, Karajan travels with nary a toothbrush. A complete wardrobe of jogging suits, sporty jackets, running sneakers, sweaters, and performing clothes awaits him at each of his houses. Many of the ways the rich choose to spend their money are laughable, outrageous, unappealing. But who among us much-abused, perpetually disgruntled business travelers wouldn't adopt Karajan's travel scene in a minute if we could?

It is fortunate that flying fits so well into Karajan's hectic life, because he is an airplane nut. Rumor has it that he has held the stick of the Concorde more than once, and he has flown the Boeing 747 flight simulator in both New York and Tokyo ("Please make for me a small hurricane," he told them in Tokyo). One of his favorite books is titled *Handling the Big Jets,* by David P. Davies. An avid plane watcher, he can spot the latest executive jet or a new design wrinkle with the facility that young boys have for new cars. And as he said, the enthusiasm goes way back.

Schuyler Chapin flew with Karajan in 1955. Chapin has been in the music business for forty years. He has been general manager of the Metropolitan Opera; head of a film production company started by Leonard Bernstein; an administrator at Lincoln Center; and head of the Masterworks Division of Columbia Records. He is currently dean of the School of the Arts at Columbia University. In 1955 he was working as an agent for CAMI.

Karajan had asked that an arrangement be made enabling him to fly himself from city to city on that year's Berlin Philharmonic tour. Chapin had flown transports during the war and had retained his commercial license, so the task fell to him. He chartered an Apache twin.

"We met at Teterboro Airport in New Jersey," Chapin recalls. "I had a lot of musical questions, but all Karajan wanted to talk about was airplanes. What immediately impressed me about him was the intensity with which he can listen and absorb information. I think his curiosity and desire for knowledge is one of the things that makes him such an extraordinary performing artist. He picked my brain that day.

"Then we taxied out, Karajan at the controls, and even though he had only fifteen or so hours, he knew what he was doing. He was a natural, smooth. His questions were intelligent. He was also in the midst of learning, and he was very concerned with the instruments. I told him he was in the crowded northeast corridor and he had to watch carefully, although it was a gorgeous day with unlimited ceiling.

"All during takeoff his head was in the cockpit. I tapped him on the shoulder and told him he must constantly be looking around. Ten minutes later I told him again. I was getting annoyed. I had slipped naturally into my old instructor's role, forgetting my student was the Maestro. So I waited until I saw a plane approaching from an angle that should have been noted by the pilot. I waited until it got fairly close, then grabbed the stick and pushed it forward. I chewed him out. 'I survived World War II,' I told him, 'forty trips across the Hump, and I'm damned if I intend to pile up outside Baltimore.'

"Karajan was properly chagrined. He made his approach and a beautiful touchdown, and as we taxied I wondered if maybe I had overstepped my bounds. I said nothing. Karajan seemed remote. At the airport he shook hands, thanked me, and said, 'I am going upstairs and write down "I will look around while flying" one hundred times.' That night before the concert he handed me an envelope. Inside was a sheet of paper with the sentence written out one hundred times."

Two years later, Chapin set up the same flying program when

Karajan returned for another tour. Bad weather forced them to take the train from New York to Washington. "Toscanini had just passed away, and we talked about that," Chapin recalls. "Karajan noted that Toscanini had nothing in his life but music. He was happy that was not the case with him. Then we passed through Philadelphia, and Karajan remembered that it was the home of Eugene Ormandy, who had refused to shake hands with him in 1955 when the Philadelphia Orchestra had given a luncheon for the Berlin Philharmonic. I told him that had been disgraceful. Karajan said it had been stupid. 'Mr. Ormandy would like to conduct in Europe where I have influence that he does not,' Karajan said."

It is like Karajan to have the inopportune eclipse the disgraceful, to regard Ormandy's gesture only as a blunder in career politics. Schulyer Chapin's story came to mind as we sped toward Vienna, to keep Karajan's appointments.

Josef Muller was at the wheel of the rented Mercedes sedan. Josef has been Karajan's driver, gardener, and handyman for seven years. He is a fireplug of a guy in his late thirties. He has the short, stocky build of a boxer, the steady eyes and stoic expression to match. But his smile is easy. Before Karajan hired him, Josef made his living driving a truck between Salzburg and Iraq, a twelve-day round trip over the treacherous mountain passes of Yugoslavia, through Bulgaria, and across Turkey. It's not a route for the faint of heart—good training for his present job.

"I was sitting in a cafe reading a newspaper," Josef said quietly in the passable English he picked up during a two-year stint in the U.S. (he also spent two years in Australia as a construction worker on the opera house). "There was an ad for a private chauffeur, it didn't say for whom. The Festspielhaus number was listed. I had a job. I just went in to see what was up. I met Madame—Eliette. She asked me what I did, was I experienced in gardening and cooking. I said a little. She talked to me for twenty minutes, gave me a glass of orange juice. I left. I didn't hear for six weeks. Then I was getting ready for a trip, in the office picking up road money. I got a call from Salzburger. Would I take the job, yes or no. I said yes, when do I start. Tomorrow, she said. I said OK. I didn't know the wages, I didn't even know why. Maybe I had enough of trucks."

Josef went to St. Moritz the next day and began his job by cleaning the house in preparation for Karajan's arrival. He does everything. He gardens, takes care of the animals, builds things, keeps the cars in order. Even when Karajan wants to drive, Josef will be with him. He accompanies the Maestro nearly everywhere, which makes him more

Karajan's "man" than chauffeur. Some think of him as bodyguard, and he could certainly handle that job as well. If something happened to Karajan, if he really needed help, Josef could sling him over one shoulder, if necessary, and take care of business. Summers, Josef moves to the house in St. Tropez. It's Josef who ferries the Maestro out to his boat in the rubber dinghy and who cranks one of the big winches while Karajan takes the wheel. For a man new to sailing, Josef is an able hand. He is charming, a quick study; he doesn't miss much.

Josef had flown with us to Vienna. In the airport he had rented the car while Karajan waited patiently. He let Karajan struggle in and out of the plane, in and out of the runway vehicle that had taken us to customs, because that is how Karajan wants it. Offer Karajan a hand, offer to take his coat or his package, and he refuses in a way that prohibits a second offer. Some admire this extreme self-reliance as toughness; others would call it macho. Wolfgang Stresemann, who worked closely with Karajan for nineteen years as Intendant (manager) of the Berlin Philharmonic (1959-78), says there is a definite macho side to Karajan's personality. "He works too hard at the sporting life," Stresemann says. "Either you are or you aren't."

Still others see it as part of his need to control situations. That seems to be the perspective offered by John Culshaw in a late 1950s story from his autobiography: "The route from the stage door ... to the conductor's room was a little complicated until one became used to it, and so for the first few Karajan sessions one or another of us waited at the stage door to guide him through. He arrived one day with a raincoat over his arm, which he promptly offered to Gordon Perry, the senior engineer, to carry for him. Gordon simply ignored the gesture, and led him to his room. Of course if Karajan had been laden with a heavy score or parts, Gordon would have been the first to take them from him; but he was not going to be a Karajan lackey and carry his raincoat. Karajan never tried that trick again." So in either case—twenty-five years ago when he didn't need the help, or now when he does—the need is overcome by the posture.

When I see Karajan toughing it out through airports, refusing a hand, I am reminded of a sergeant I ran into in the Army whose job was to teach us how to climb telephone poles. He was a little guy too, and tough. One day during a demonstration he was about five feet up the pole explaining something to us about technique, when he fell. It could have happened to anybody. It was a soft, fuzzy old pole. It wasn't a big drop for him, but he got his feet tangled up and when he landed he drove one of the big, three-sided steel climbing spikes that were hitched to the inside of his ankles smack into the toe of his other boot. He gave a grimace of pain, not much of a one at that; then as the blood flowed freely from the hole in his boot and began making a dark stain on the dry, sandy ground, he spent five minutes or so finishing up what he was saying. Then he walked over to a jeep and somebody drove him to the hospital. I remember as he drove off we all clapped and whistled.

The doctor's office was Karajan's first stop in Vienna. The approach to such an appointment was unusual. Josef eased the big car through a series of narrow alleys, coming to rest finally in a small, diagonal parking area behind what appeared to be a hospital, or clinic of some sort. Apparently we were early, for neither Josef or Karajan made a move to leave the car. I had begun to wonder what we might do for lunch when Josef passed Karajan a brown bag. He opened it and removed a foil packet containing a kaiser roll. It had been split, and one slice of a dry salami had been placed inside the roll. No butter, no mayonnaise, no mustard. That was it. Nothing to drink. Josef and I were evidently on diets. Karajan munched without enthusiasm on his sandwich and spoke with Josef in German. He had eaten only a few bites when a man in a white doctor's coat approached the car. Karajan made a sound of recognition, stuffed the sandwich into the foil, and left with the man.

Josef and I got out with Karajan and now we stood outside, leaning on the car. Josef lit a cigarette.

"He's a tough guy," said Josef responding to my question with obvious reluctance, talking about his boss, dangerous ground. "He is a good manager, that's how I see him. One of the best I've known. He is the best at managing everything that makes up his life. I don't see the music, but I see the cleverness. He's got big knowledge of many things. He knows a lot. He knows what he is doing all the time. What he does he does perfectly. He's always on the correct way.

"He's hard on himself. I never knew anyone so hard on himself. The pain with his feet, his legs. He would never admit it, never let on. He never gives an excuse.

"The music is perfect, the managing is perfect. And he always finds a way to make it better and better. When players get tired he'll keep them interested. He always helps me when he can."

Scarcely ten minutes had gone by and Karajan was returning to the car, having turned his limp into a gait with effort that was etched on his face, the doctor beside him.

Karajan seemed pleased as we drove off. He had received a good report on the toe. "Thank God, I can swim again," he said. "I swim three times a day. I would be in a wheelchair if I did not. The doctor was afraid of infection if I swam with the toe. But he says now I can swim."

Later, driving back to the airport, Karajan talked about Richard Wagner. He said he hadn't heard any Wagner in his head on the flight over that morning. Hadn't even thought about Wagner as we hurtled through the rough sky. Said he had been concentrating on flying the plane. But he said he thought Wagner would like his version of *The Flying Dutchman*. "Of this I am quite certain. You see, Wagner was a visual fanatic. He was furious with his technical director after the first *Ring* cycle. [*The Ring of the Nibelung* includes four operas: *Das Rheingold, Die Walküre, Siegfried,* and *Götterdämmerung.*] He was disappointed in the effects. He didn't think the man had enough talent.

"Wagner influenced art in many ways," Karajan said. "You can be for him or against him, but you must admit that. He was sure of himself. He knew he was great. This made him difficult to handle."

Karajan said that if Wagner were alive today he would be one of the great writers of music for the screen.

The Berlin Philharmonic arrived the next day. Just the sound of this great orchestra warming up—the trills and scales and mournful horn notes, the warmth of cellos and flickering cadenzas of violins, the blats of trombones and throat-clearing of double basses, all in the classic discordant jumble of anticipation—that swelled out of the hall when the heavy wooden door swung open was enough to tingle the spine. The orchestra's arrival was a shot of fuel to the excitement that had been mounting for the last few days. Workers had adorned four hundred feet of street outside the building with long, vertical flags of all nations that were stirring lazily in the spring breeze. And the Festspielhaus was being thoroughly washed (scrubbed!) inside *and out* in true Austrian fashion by teams of sturdy women in long blue work coats whose determination was fierce. The polished wood floors gleamed. The carpets puffed like adders. The full-length mirrors at the ends of the promenades on each level reflected perfect, smudge-free images of life.

There was more than anticipation among the regulars, those of us (actors, singers, stagehands included) who hadn't missed a rehearsal in nearly three long weeks. There was tension. The unpleasantness that had developed between Karajan and the orchestra over the clarinetist Sabine Meyer had been enthusiastically documented in the world press. The unpleasantness was eminating from a contest of wills. Karajan wanted Meyer in the orchestra, and the orchestra did not. Karajan was incensed by the orchestra's rebuff to his artistic judgment. The orchestra was furious that Karajan would interfere with the due process by which players were selected. And there was much more boiling below this surface that had caused the commotion.

When Karajan appeared, the orchestra fell casually, not totally, silent. He made his way to the leather-topped partition on the audience side of the orchestra pit, sat on it, spun around, and lowered himself gingerly onto the podium. Karajan did not greet his orchestra of twenty-eight years that he had not seen in several weeks with so much as a nod or a hello. From the orchestra, there was no customary round of quiet clapping or foot tapping for their esteemed music director. Karajan simply raised his arms and began. In a European setting, where civilized people are expected to exchange a cordial greeting and a firm handshake with coworkers at the beginning of each business day—indeed, often twice a day in some cases—the heavy double slight was not lost on the audience, whose collective release of breath was drowned out by the orchestra's opening notes. Hermann Schreiber, who writes about music for Hamburg-based *Geo* magazine, was sitting next to me. He shook his head. "It's over," he whispered. "It's a broken marriage. They still have breakfast together and talk about what they have to do, but that's all."

We listened to the exquisite sound. It was a rare privilege to sit so close to this ensemble, close enough to lean forward and peer into the pit at individual players, close enough to concentrate on the heady blend of the three flutes in unison, or the soaring horn phrases, matching the persona of players to the music they were making. As one moved from left to right in the hall, it was like having one's own personal electronic equalizer as the volume of sections rose and fell. When I backed off fifteen rows, the mix was perfect.

The house lights were down. Only the low-intensity lights on the players' music stands bathed the orchestra in a soft glow. The neon bulb in Karajan's podium light illuminated the Maestro from below, giving him a harsh, macabre mask made truly frightening by the frowning eyes that glinted in the cold light like steel balls. His mouth was drawn in a tight, thin line, and his jaw worked furiously as he conducted. Given the dramatic tension of the moment, it was the perfect lighting. Hollywood's best technicians couldn't have done better.

Karajan says that from the moment he first conducted the Berlin Philharmonic on April 9, 1938, he wanted the orchestra for his own. As a boy he had grown up listening to the Vienna Philharmonic, which has always been a superb orchestra, and it was that sound quality upon which his initial standards were set. Then when he began working as a young conductor it was with school orchestras, then the small, lesser orchestras of the small-town theaters around Germany, doing the best with what he had. A good way to learn, perhaps the best way to learn, but always the sound in his head soared tauntingly above what he was able to attain on the podium. Then he conducted the Berlin, and for the first time the real sound, nurtured over the years by music directors Hans von Bülow, Arthur Nikisch, and Wilhelm Furtwängler, exceeded his dreams.

It took nearly twenty years before Karajan satisfied his lust for the Berlin Philharmonic. They were uncertain, tumultuous years, during which Furtwängler's monumental anxiety over the fast-rising young Karajan caused the older man to deny Karajan all but occasional access to the orchestra. And there was World War II, during which the Nazis played political havoc with music and the arts in Europe, ultimately bringing them to a grinding halt altogether along with most other aspects of civilized life, if not life itself. Karajan had cast his lot with Hitler's legions, and it very nearly cost him the career he was seeking to enhance. But patience is one of Karajan's strongest suits. When he speaks about the education of a conductor, the talent, the study, and the hard work necessary to succeed at the profession, he concludes, "and then comes life. So many have not the stamina to go through and learn, and then to wait, and wait, and wait . . ."

Karajan's patience was rewarded. The evening of November 30, 1954, Karajan and André von Mattoni checked into Rome's Regency Hotel, changed clothes, and went out for dinner. Mattoni left the restaurant to buy a newspaper. There on the front page was a startling announcement: Furtwängler was dead at age sixty-eight, after a long bout with pneumonia. That evening a telegram arrived, unsigned, from Vienna: "The king is dead. Long live the king." Then the maneuvering began. "The phone began to burn," Karajan recalls.

Karajan says that the Intendant of the Berlin Philharmonic had been in touch with him prior to Furtwängler's death. "He was very loyal to Furtwängler, of course, but he had to make a plan in case Furtwängler was to die. He wouldn't have forgiven himself if he waited until the last minute and I couldn't do it. So he said, 'If somehing happened, would you envision taking the Berlin?' I kept it quiet, but I told him I would do it.

"The evening of Furtwängler's death, at 2 A.M. the next morning, in fact, I was called from the office of Columbia Artists Management in New York by André Mertens, and he said he wanted me to know that Furtwängler had a contract with Columbia to do an American tour with the orchestra. He said he would only honor the contract for the tour if I would take it over. Otherwise he would call it off. I said I would do it only if the Berlin Orchestra appointed me Furtwängler's successor. One thing was clear: I would not go on trial. I would only make the tour as future head of the orchestra.

"They said, 'of course, of course,' so I went and rehearsed the orchestra. After two weeks it appeared the promises were lies. The Senate was not together. Now I was in a trap. My mouth watered to have the job, and they were saying they would see how I managed the tour. If there was heavy political resistance when I came back, I might not get the job. So I called the mayor of Berlin, Mr. Reuter. He could not nominate me. That had to be done by the Senate. But I suggested we hold a press conference about the American tour. During the press conference, he would ask me if, upon my return from America, I would take the orchestra. That is what we did. When he asked me, I said it would give me the greatest pleasure. Sometimes you have to risk the whole thing.

"Then I had to free myself from my appointment at La Scala. I was scheduled to begin a new production of Wagner's *Ring*. I would have to give this up in order to take the Berlin. I went to see the director. I told him if he said no, I would never talk about it again. But I told him, 'if you can let me go, I would appreciate it. If not, it is forgotten and I will honor my contract.' He said it was the chance of a lifetime, and he let me go."

The orchestra elected Karajan their new music director during the U.S. tour. When he returned to Berlin, the appointment was ratified by the Berlin Senate. Then the contract struggle ensued. "I told them I must have the right to pass on the selection of the Intendant," Karajan says. "They told me not even Furtwängler had that right. I knew they were lying because I had obtained a copy of Furtwängler's contract. I also told them the contract must say that I was music director for life. Unless I knew I couldn't be removed, I couldn't give my complete intensity. I told them to make it ninety years if life was a bother to them. It would be the first time they ever gave a life contract. It took twelve years for the contract to be agreed upon. For the first twelve years with the orchestra I had no contract at all. I waited until it was right."

So the love affair was consummated. If the exchange of vows was more an argument than a pledging of troth, more undercut with suspicion and distrust than blessed with honor and respect, well, such is the music business. Most important, the marriage went well. All told, it has been a glorious twenty-eight years that can be measured in the status of "Herbert von Karajan and the Berlin Philharmonic," which is on everyone's top-three-in-the-world list. The two names have in fact become one. In his book *Unfinished Journey*, the great violinist Yehudi Menuhin wrote, "Some conductors are synonymous with their orchestras, at once their creators and creation . . . as Herbert von Karajan with his in Berlin." And when Seiji Ozawa is asked what he thinks Karajan's greatest contribution to music has been, Ozawa says without hesitation, "Karajan and the Berlin; the combination is amazing—it took him twenty-five years."

It is a phenomenon that can also be measured by the income of the Berlin players, who are the best paid orchestral musicians in the world. Their excellent salaries (ten to fifteen percent higher than in other German orchestras)—which are doubled by their share of recording contracts, television programs, films, special events like the Easter Festival (for which they are paid handsomely), teaching, solo appearances, and their participation in various musical suborganizations—give credence to the Jaguar-and-fur-coat image that they have acquired. There are thirteen musical organizations within the Berlin Philharmonic: trios, quartets, chamber groups, brass choirs, the "twelve cellos," and even the double basses. With the phrase "of the Berlin Philharmonic" hitched behind the name of each group, their marketability is great. Many of them make recordings. "The Twelve Cellos of the Berlin Philharmonic" released an album of Beatles songs in October 1983; it was their fifth record. They, like many of the other groups, are in constant demand. It is these subgroups, with their busy schedules, that are a substantial part of the problem that exists between Karajan and the orchestra. This was not always the case. As Menuhin wrote in 1977, "[Karajan] protects his musicians, sees they are well paid, ensures the quality of their instruments, encourages them to divide into smaller groups and play chamber music, and in all manner of ways boosts their morale."

In the summer of 1981, when I first spoke with Karajan in St. Tropez, long before the clarinetist Meyer appeared on the scene, he painted a picture of harmonious family unity between himself and the players, an image of mutual respect and admiration, open communication, and, in general, near bliss. He saw himself as a benign father figure ministering to his charges. He said he knew each player better than they knew themselves, from personal problems to musical habits. He said the players continually came to him to discuss all manner of intimate questions. Eighteen months later, that relationship had seriously deteriorated. The kindest word Karajan had for most of the players after December 1982 was "idiot."

At that time, Werner Thärichen, a timpanist in the orchestra and a composer, was working on an opera called *Expelled from Paradise*, based on an essay of the same title by Leszck Kolakowski, a Polish philosopher. He said the story line paralleled the Berlin situation. "We are a family with Karajan as the big father. The orchestra members are the children. There are problems between the children and the strong father. Some children like a strong father, and some rebel."

The Berlin has its own complex structure. It is two orchestras comprised of the same players. One, the Berlin Philharmonisches Orchester, financed by the City of Berlin, is one of ninety-seven symphony, opera, or radio orchestras in Germany that have a definite function. The Berlin Philharmonisches Orchester is in the "concert only" category. They play a hundred and eight concerts a year in Berlin, plus concerts on tour in and outside of Europe. The other orchestra, from an organizational standpoint at least, is the Berlin Philharmoniker, a cooperative owned by members of the orchestra. All recording, films, television productions, and special events like the Easter Festival are done under contract with this organization. Karajan's life contract is with the Philharmonisches, not the Philharmoniker. By rights, the latter can engage whomever it wants to lead them. But "Karajan and the Berlin" is what sells, first of all, and the crafty Maestro is a fox when it comes to administering such business. He personally holds an exclusive contract with the Philharmoniker for all television and film performances, written with his film company, Telemondial (in Monaco), which opened for business in 1982. It is reported to be a fair contract, which guarantees the orchestra a specific amount of work in those areas per year, and it includes guarantees against Karajan's absence by sickness or death. This contractual agreement would be used against him by the orchestra as the Meyer debate escalated, as we shall see.

Both orchestras must hire guest conductors. Karajan could not do all the work scheduled even if he wanted to. In recent years, in addition to tours, he has conducted only six subscriptions of the hundred and eight concerts a year in Berlin. The Philharmoniker can and does record with other conductors, but Karajan has first choice of repertoire to be recorded, and it is doubtful that the record companies would engage a conductor of whom he didn't approve. An associate points out that in this regard he has been open. Karajan has been both helpful and encouraging to a string of excellent younger conductors, people like Riccardo Muti, Claudio Abbado, Ozawa, and James Levine; he was instrumental in bringing all of them to the Salzburg Festival. He even invited Leonard Bernstein to conduct in

Salzburg. The two are somewhat look-alikes, and too close in age and "superstardom" on their respective sides of the Atlantic to exchange much more than wariness. It has been suggested that Karajan might have invited Bernstein to deny him a martyr's pose. But more likely, the same associate says, it was to show that Karajan wasn't threatened by him.

Within the Berlin Orchestra there are copious and complex ground rules for everything, from how the total complement of one hundred and fifty musicians rotates within sections to how new people are hired. Many of these rules have been around nearly as long as the orchestra, which celebrated its hundredth anniversary in 1982. The players say it is the adherence to these guidelines that has kept the orchestra strong. Chief among the rules of order is how players are hired for the orchestra: the decision is made by vote of the collective orchestra. Karajan has veto power. So both orchestra and conductor must be in agreement about new players.

Players are selected by audition, of course, at which the whole orchestra must be present. The opinion of the section for which the aspirant is playing is given the greatest weight. In the case of Sabine Meyer, the clarinet section invited her to audition in the fall of 1982. In fact, she was invited to play a few concerts with the orchestra in advance of her audition, which is not unusual. When she played her audition, Karajan was not present, although he had heard her play with the orchestra and was favorably impressed. After Meyer's audition, the clarinet section decided that her sound didn't blend with the group. Discussion ensued. The orchestra was divided about Meyer's qualities. Some thought she would adjust, given time. Some thought that hers was a solo approach to the instrument and that she would never blend in. A motion was made to take her on a year's probation. The motion was defeated. The compromise was to try her out during more concerts, and have her play again at the next audition. So she was invited to fill the empty seat in the clarinet section on the American tour. Karajan was asked to keep an eye on her.

On the tour, Karajan liked the way she played. Several people who heard Meyer in New York remarked favorably about her, including critic Andrew Porter. But when the orchestra reconvened in Berlin, the vote was still no. Karajan, who was now championing Meyer as his "discovery," was astounded. He had been very pleased with the orchestra in the U.S. It was the first time since the war that he had felt wholeheartedly accepted in America. Then came the rebuff of Meyer, complete with the political implications that seem ever-present when government funds are part of an orchestra's budget. In this case, it was reported that the cultural affairs minister in the Berlin Senate was behind the orchestra. Karajan felt stabbed in the back. It was a combination of events that suddenly brought a variety of lesser, nagging problems to a boil.

The most disturbing of these, to Karajan, was the behavior of the Berlin Chamber Orchestra, a group of twenty-five players from the orchestra who had been taking ever greater liberties with their orchestral responsibilities. There are two first-chair players at every instrument and other duplication throughout the orchestra. Only 100 or so of the 150 players are needed for most symphonic works. The chamber group was organizing rotation so that on tours, for instance, they could book performances in the same city, and on the same night as the Berlin. Many times Karajan had taken the podium, raised his baton to begin, and noticed the absence of several first-chair players. His resentment over this situation, which had been growing, turned to rage. He declared war.

With the help of the malleable Intendant Peter Girth, Karajan found a loophole in the orchestra's contract—which is a loosely written letter of agreement—and jumped in, declaring that Sabine Meyer had been hired for a one-year probationary period. Aghast at what they considered a double cross, the orchestra immediately filed suit against Peter Girth. Karajan countered with a letter, which was covered by a letter from Girth. Copies of the letters were delivered to each member of the orchestra. Girth's letter was dated December 6, 1982:

> Enclosed is a copy of a letter from Mr. von Karajan, dated December 3, 1982. I received the original on December 6 with a request that I read it aloud at the conclusion of the afternoon full orchestra rehearsal, in order that I might bring it to your individual attention. The head of the orchestra, Mr. Zepperitz, would not allow me to do so, even though I insisted that it was a personal request from Mr. von Karajan himself.
>
> I have no desire to bring a confrontation with Zepperitz before the orchestra. I have therefore arranged with Mr. von Karajan to advise you of the above matter with this letter.

The letter from Karajan read as follows:

> Gentlemen: For over a year we have had a vacancy in the orchestra for first clarinet. Many auditions have been conducted without my knowledge—unfortunately without results. Even the hope to attract the winner of the International Instrumental Competition of ARD [a Vienna television station] fell through because the jury did not feel competent to award first prize.
>
> As a result of an audition at this time, Sabine Meyer, a young clarinetist,

came to my attention and to the attention of the orchestra. In order to more completely ascertain her artistic competence, I allowed her to perform under my direction during rehearsals and concerts in Berlin, Lucerne, Salzburg, and finally America. I am fully convinced that Mrs. Meyer meets all requirements for the position—and have brought my findings to the attention of the head of the orchestra.

One month ago, the orchestra completed a triumphant tour of America under my direction. This tour clearly documents the predominant position of the orchestra in the musical life of the world. It is this very fact that obligates me to utilize all my efforts to promote the orchestra's artistic development.

In a meeting you decided not to secure the talents of Mrs. Meyer for a period of one year. Therefore the unbearable situation of the vacancy persists, and no one in the music world will understand that in the case of Mrs. Meyer, the opposite has taken place [in spite of Karajan's best efforts, the orchestra's artistic development has been curtailed].

It is your right, contractually, to decide upon either a positive or negative recommendation vis-à-vis a candidate. On the other hand, however, I find that my judgment and that of the orchestra are in this instance diametrically opposed.

I will continue to honor my Berlin obligation,

but

—the orchestra tours
—the Salzburg and Lucerne Festivals
—the taping of opera and concerts for television and film
—and all audio productions

are, as a result of the above situation, suspended as of today.

Sincerely yours,
/signed/
Herbert von Karajan

There was much clucking of tongues in the inner circles over Karajan's letter. Such an outburst. Such a hard line. Older and wiser heads were both shocked and dismayed that any conductor would attack his orchestra in such a childish manner. It was, most agreed, an aging dinosaurian response. Werner Thärichen recalled a similar problem from twenty years ago: "There was a horn player he wanted. The orchestra rejected the man. Karajan got angry. He went into a sulk. I went to Vienna to see him, speak with him. I told him it was important to have the opinion of the orchestra, because that opinion had helped sustain the initial sound of the orchestra over the years. We told him we would get him a better horn player, and we did."

Former Berlin Intendant Wolfgang Stresemann has been involved with music all his life. He has written two symphonies, and as conductor, he has been head of the Toledo Symphony in the U.S. and the Berlin Radio Symphony. He has four books to his credit, one of which is about his father, who was chancellor of the Weimar Republic and minister of foreign affairs. Politics was a career Stresemann considered for himself. Stresemann is a tall, erect, dignified man who looks to be in his later sixties. His graying hair is combed straight back from his forehead. His face is long and impassive; his eyes penetrating, intelligent. He listens, and thinks before he speaks. From his own experience—nearly twenty years with the Berlin Philharmonic—he can say, "Karajan constantly threatens you. Conductors are unsure of themselves. If they get to the top, the wind is ice cold. They can't go up, they can only fall. But this letter, you don't write such a letter to your own orchestra. Karajan cannot tolerate contradiction. Instead of talking quietly with his players, listening to why they feel as they do, he explodes. It betrays a lack of security. He is so unstable inside. He doesn't understand people—doesn't trust the people he should trust. He is seventy-five, but he does not have the wisdom of an older man. He is so dynamic, and believe me, he will be dynamic at eighty as well. But he has made no progress towards wisdom. This is strange, because as one grows older a certain amount of wisdom is inevitable. I am seventy-nine.... I know about this.

"As for Meyer, those who have played with her know she is not an ensemble player. She is a soloist who plays for herself. To have her in the orchestra would be like putting Sophie Mutter in the violin section. People have tried to explain this to Karajan. And can he not hear it for himself? When he likes someone it doesn't matter.

"Such a crisis with the orchestra should not have happened. Both sides are guilty. Karajan sees only his own side. On the other hand, the chamber orchestra is at fault too. They have played the same Mozart that he was conducting on the same night in the same city."

Great emphasis is placed on how a new player blends with the rest of the orchestra, as we have seen. This is why musicians under consideration are asked to play rehearsals and concerts before they audition. If their sound is totally incompatible, they are not even asked to audition, regardless of how good they may be. One of the Berlin's two solo oboists, Hensjorg Schellenberger, a young man who is relatively new to the orchestra, talked about this. "The other solo oboe is fifty years old, with twenty-five years in the orchestra. He is double my size, a different kind of person from me. He plays with a fleshy, straightforward, emotional sound. I have a lighter, more intellectual sound to my playing. We are proud of what makes us different, but in the orchestra we must mix, blend in with the sound of the other winds

We are not only *solo* players, but solo *players*. We must both lead the oboe section, and mix with the winds, paying close attention to the entrances of difficult passages, listening, for instance, to the presounds of the flute in soft passages, delaying just a bit in order to blend perfectly. It is not skill that is involved so much as being willing to blend. The most beautiful thing in this orchestra is the clear common interest to create the best sound possible in performance. The feeling of being in one boat together is stronger here than in any other orchestra. We have a name for it: *Philharmonischer Geist*."

The situation with Sabine Meyer was important by itself, but the passions it stirred reflected a malaise that is a common one within many of the best symphony orchestras. Briefly stated, that is the conflict arising from the demands of the organization on the one hand, and the musicians' demands for growth and freedom on the other. This was not the case twenty years ago. Musicians were happier then to have the security of an orchestra job, less inclined to broaden their financial and artistic base by running after every opportunity that appeared. But then, twenty years ago there were not so many opportunities, and the rules under which musicians were governed were more stringent.

Twenty years ago there was not such a plethora of highly proficient musicians, either. Not so long ago the Boston Symphony received over two hundred applications for a second-chair flute position, and that is typical of the competitiveness of the market. Overall excellence in music has taken great leaps, as it has in sports and other endeavors. The best orchestras are now comprised of players of truly exceptional ability. In an orchestra like the Berlin Philharmonic, nearly every player has soloist capabilities, if not soloist potential. Making one of the "name" orchestras is a great coup for any player. But all too quickly, it seems, resentment raises its head over the "meal ticket" that is inhibiting artistic development by curtailing extracurricular activities.

Orchestral musicians pursue a course that is potentially troublesome. On the one hand, they are accomplished, individual artists. Unlike most other artists, however, they work as part of a team. As Manny Borok, assistant concertmaster of the Boston Symphony, once explained, "As you develop and your career takes shape, you are continually playing as a soloist, reaping the applause. Then you make the big orchestra, and at your zenith, you become one of the mass. It is a lot to get used to, the anonymity. You have worked hard for the applause. You miss it." Many orchestral musicians are embarked upon a trade-off that is quite a bit less than satisfactory: they receive union-guaranteed job security and enjoy considerable status in exchange for anonymity and a large chunk of their musical soul. This must be a disturbing compromise for one who is, almost by definition, a blithe spirit, a will-o'-the-wisp. For management, it is like trying to control wild horses after they have submitted to harness.

Musicians are called "players," not "workers," with good reason. On stage, in white tie and tails, an orchestra is a formidable looking group of well-mannered, scholarly, artistic people, committed with steely discipline and concentration to their demanding profession. But in mufti, at rehearsal, they are capricious, mischievous, childlike, like musicians the world over, from rock 'n' roll to country to classical. If they aren't doodling with their instruments, they are talking and giggling, tapping each other with bows, spraying each other with spit key exhaust, or inventing new mischief, always on the left while the conductor is trying to settle a phrasing question on the right, deviously, like school children. Naturally, these tendencies subside somewhat with age and maturation. Some orchestras are worse than others in this regard. It is reported that the New York Philharmonic gives music director Zubin Mehta and others—Danny Kaye excepted—a terrible time. The Vienna Philharmonic is perhaps the most staid group, but then no orchestral tradition is as deep and richly rooted as theirs. Karajan keeps the Berlin Philharmonic in good order, but even this distinguished group perpetrates its share of mischief. Perhaps it is because playing music is a compulsion, and a compulsion is an irrational act. As James Galway wrote in his autobiography, "We [musicians] are not a race apart. Except, that is, when the chips are finally down. In the last analysis we are aware that we are on earth to make and interpret great music and we do find our reward in the expression of our souls' longings." Those who court fantasy have never been known for their regimentation, reliability, or basic stability.

What musicians may have acquired of these characteristics at the outset was usually diluted by the immense amount of time and energy—the intense focus—that was required to master their musical skills. Any serious violinist will have practiced six, eight, even ten hours a day since he or she was a child. Many violinists can't remember life without the instrument. Such concentration, commitment, and determination tend to exclude most of life as the average person has experienced it, from the carefree games of childhood, through the joys and responsibilities of young adulthood. The maturation progression, seduced by the fantasy of music, is thrown out of balance—sometimes blissfully, sometimes disturbingly, always irrefutably. Just as the eighteen-year-old world-class figure skater won't travel without her teddy bear, many musicians tend to behave in surprising ways. The great pianist Vladimir Horowitz seriously threatened not to perform ever again if the Cincinnati Reds lost the 1982 World Series. Horowitz is an old man now, but that has nothing to do with his long-standing demand for fresh beets two meals a day, no matter where he is.

Fantasy is a part of all performers' lives. But of them all, musicians seem the most self-indulgent. For one, fantasy is an elusive siren. Her pursuit is not something readily tolerated or quickly rewarded by a society whose roots are buried in the pragmatic morass of business. Artists, in this world, will always be just a touch suspect. And if conductors are insecure, musicians are paranoid. Like athletes, their playing days are limited. Few of them stay active beyond sixty. The string players can hit seventy, and occasionally a Horowitz or Rubinstein comes along whose agility at eighty is confounding.

Conductors last the longest by far. As one Berlin violin player said, "the conductor and the orchestra are like the hammer and anvil—one hits, the other takes. The critics say that Karajan has never spared the orchestra or himself. But you can hit a lot longer than you can be hit." And so there is a touch of bitterness as well, lurking beneath the surface, contributing to the self-indulgence that seems to pervade the entire profession in epidemic proportions. When the orchestra in question is the Berlin Philharmonic, one must add its celebrity, its world stature, the players' large incomes and individual notoriety, and the fact that West Berlin is their home. West Berlin is a free-world island surrounded by Communism. The Berlin airlift still operates, only now it is commercial and scheduled. West Berlin is a fortress, complete with government tax incentives for living there. There is a fatalistic atmosphere about West Berlin ("eat, drink, and be merry," ... for tomorrow we could be hostages) that attracts artists, free spirits, hustlers, and outlaws. The city is fittingly garish. The facades of old buildings are adorned with corner-to-corner neon advertisements. New buildings are architectural exercises in odd, reflecting glass shapes that glow with eerie colored lights. The restaurants are jammed at 10 P.M. The bars are busy until 4 A.M.

"Karajan clearly needs a hard side to discipline something like the Berlin Phil," Galway writes in his book, "because it is a collection of very highly-strung individuals, each with his own opinion of himself." Karajan has a hard side, and over the years he hasn't hesitated to show it. He, like Furtwängler and Karl Böhm before him, is from the school of iron-fisted tradition when it comes to the care and training and behavior of orchestras. This is part of the issue as well. Karajan is the last of this tradition, and as such he swims against an ever-increasing current. It is not just a gap of several generations that creates the mounting tension, but an anxiety on the orchestra's part based on the inevitability of Karajan's passing. In the summer of 1981, with all the assurance of a man who had seen the schedule, Karajan told me that he had ten years left to accomplish the ambitious projects he had planned. Certainly that is the maximum he will be able to continue working. As is typical in one-man operations when the boss is a senior citizen, all of the employees are beginning to make plans, or at least worry. The father—the idol—will be leaving. When he does, the Berlin Philharmonic will be just another great orchestra. Like all children, the players are already beginning to exhibit resentment.

And so there is tension. The second day the Berlin Philharmonic was in Salzburg, Karajan called for the offstage music to be rehearsed. It sounded thin. Where were the other horns, he wanted to know. It was explained that several members of the orchestra had yet to arrive. Karajan fussed and fumed in his seat, venting anger with a long, abusive monologue about the orchestra. The next day a late-arriving violinist chuckled when he heard about it. "He rehearsed the offstage music? That's like Karajan. He knew several of us were away—with permission. The offstage music wasn't supposed to be rehearsed until today or tomorrow." "That's a bloody lie," Karajan said when he heard this. "They went straight to Innsbruck to play a concert— without permission—and I had to pay for it."

There is a waiting list for Easter Festival sponsorship, and unless one is a sponsor, at a cost of approximately $5,000, tickets for the festival are unobtainable. Even if tickets were available, their price is way beyond the grasp of most mortals. So Karajan opens the opera dress rehearsals to the public—townspeople, friends and relatives of musicians and performers, Festspielhaus personnel—but that doesn't mean they are not working sessions. The first dozen rows are left open so Karajan's lieutenants will have better access (real and visual) to him, and he doesn't hesitate to pick up the microphone during the run-through to make last minute corrections. Karajan sets the tone by appearing the way he does for any rehearsal. Dressed in his baggy jogging suit, he enters the hall from a side door, walks across the front of the audience, sits on the rail, spins around, and lowers himself into the pit. He shakes hands with the two concertmasters and begins.

Bad dress rehearsals are followed by wonderful opening nights, theater people say, and this comforting rationale came to mind as the rehearsal progressed. It wasn't good. For periods as long as a minute, Karajan leaned against the railing, his arms folded, listening instead of conducting. The run-through was nowhere near performance quality, and even as a rehearsal it was ragged, sloppy. There were some strange lapses in Karajan's careful attention to detail. Act II begins with an interior scene of twenty women spinning wool on small, wooden, foot-operated wheels. Several of them squeaked annoyingly. I was sitting with Gustav Kuhn, an energetic young conductor from Salzburg who had studied with Karajan. I asked him about the squeaky wheels. "That's Karajan's idea of realism, I guess," Kuhn said. Kuhn suffered through the rehearsal, not just because it was a nightmare from a conductor's point of view, but because it served to focus with uncomfortable intensity the classic contradictions he had been expressing to me about the Maestro.

That afternoon in a cafe beside the Salzach River, Kuhn had spoken about Karajan, drifting between admiration and disdain like a leaf caught in a confused current. "He is the exception," Kuhn said. "No one can do it like he can. He is so egocentric, so clever; he uses all of his immense power to do the things he wants. I am a strong critic of him, his life, his personality, because I love what he knows about music, conducting. Eighty percent of my profession I learned from him, from talking with him, watching him, listening to him. I admire him totally as the leading figure in his field. Five or six years after I had been with him I went kind of crazy, sweating, red in the face. I began to see him as the Godfather himself. All the defects of his personality roared in upon me. I saw him as a man who cannot separate music from his life. The hero worship I had at the beginning faded, in the same way that at a certain age your parents become human, fallible. It was necessary that I make the separation between the man and his music. I had to decide that he was the greatest, the last great one, the last of the period that started with von Bülow in 1850. His power, his tyrannical attitudes that prohibit discussion make him the last of a type. His career excludes all else. That makes him powerful, but lonely. Look at his face. It is a lonely old face, not a happy old face. If you are not going to love the world, if you are going to live only to gain power, then that is what you will get.

"He was the first one to build a flat opera house," Kuhn said. "The seats don't go up, with overhanging balconies, like at La Scala, the Vienna State Opera, or even Carnegie Hall. They go out, way out. The floor rises, but even so the result is like our society: everyone can see fairly well, but no one can see very well. It is like a big TV screen, which is strange, because the theater is supposed to be for personal contact. Karajan loves television. But on stage, you cannot do close-ups, which is the thing that makes television work. He has built this great house, this enormous stage, huge elaborate sets. What he cannot do is make the actors and singers bigger to fit into this monster.

"Many hate it, but they give Karajan the money. What he does is antisocial. Five hundred dollars a ticket! ..." (Easter Festival membership, for which there is a waiting list, is $200 per couple. Members then have access to tickets, which run $150 each for the best opera seats; $50 each for orchestra concerts.) But if they don't give him the money he doesn't come, and then the hotels are empty. Everybody pays the taxes that support the Grosse Festspielhaus, the festivals, but only the rich can go. God knows what the real cost of the production is ... [Karajan later said it was around $300,000] but there are only three performances, with about 2,000 people at each performance, so it is way up there on the roof. Karajan is the last who can afford to do this. He doesn't know it, doesn't feel it. But the next generation of conductors knows it."

At the dress rehearsal, Kuhn was outraged by the orchestra's performance. "They missed so many entrances," Kuhn said. "There is no excuse. The brass could breathe together and hit it. I could have cried after the first act. How they are behaving is disgusting. Karajan's genius has kept the orchestra on top for twenty-five years. He made them!"

Many young conductors share the dichotomy of feeling that Kuhn suffers over Karajan. Their criticism is harsh, they decry his behavior. But late at night, when the wine is low in the bottle, their voices soften and their eyes acquire a faraway look as they recall some performance by Karajan and the Berlin that awed them, challenged their own capabilities with a standard they can only dream of achieving. Even to come close they know they will have to discover their way, just as Karajan discovered his. What really frustrates them is knowing that they will probably not be willing to make the sacrifices Karajan has, or work at music to the exclusion of all else, or damn whatever consequences may follow in the interest of music, their careers. They worry that if such is the case, greatness—even notoriety—will elude their grasp. They worry with reason. It probably will.

The Grosse Festspielhaus was designed to include long, wide promenades behind the boxes at the rear of both the orchestra and balcony seating. On one side of the promenades are windows overlooking the street. On the other is the gently curving teak-veneered wall behind the boxes, broken only by short stairways that lead to the boxes. The floor is carpeted in gray. In between each set of windows is a bronze head of a musical great (Beethoven, Mozart, Wagner, etc.) on a pedestal. At either end of the promenades is a mirror that measures six by ten feet. Little chandelier sconces between the windows and on the teak wall provide soft, glittery light. Many theaters have "promenades," but they are used mostly as hallways through which one passes on the way to one's seat. The Festspielhaus promenades are used, at least on opening night of Easter Festival, for promenading: "A leisurely walk (or ride), especially in a public place, for pleasure or display."

As couples arrived, he in black tie, she in some spectacular or at least strange and very expensive long creation that included fur trim, or perhaps feathers, or maybe lace, or (depending upon age and quality of body) perhaps a daring design element that revealed a bit of leg or maybe even a subtle glimpse of breast—with the most precious jewels affixed here and there, of course—they would link arms and promenade, slowly, at wedding march pace, from mirror to mirror and back again, all the while looking left and right, nodding with regal, Habsburgian deliberateness when they engaged the eyes of other promenading couples. These were the sponsors of Karajan's Easter Festival, people in their middle to older years, with a median somewhere around sixty-five; people with the sleek, somewhat fierce, self-assured look of conquest; people of substantial means, mostly from Austria or Germany.

The promenades are on the second and third levels of the Festspielhaus. On the street floor is the lobby, with a large room off to one side where coffee, cocktails, snacks, and delicious sweets are served. The large, heavy wooden panel that had been puzzling me from the street as I passed it each day, too large to be a window covering, the wrong shape for a door, had been removed to reveal a plate glass expanse that ran from floor almost to ceiling. Since there was a crowd of people on either side of it, it was hard to say if the plate glass had been installed for looking out or looking in. No doubt there was satisfaction in either direction. Those townspeople standing there across the street in the benign spring snowfall surely had the most interesting view in terms of hairdos, clothes, and cocktail party posturing. Moreover, they had to be reassured by this glimpse of the high life, this bright candle in the palace window. This was Austria, after all, where a few decades of democracy have hardly made a dent in a historical dependency upon royal families and dictators; where castles still rise against the sky, where titles (often in multiples) still define status and identity. This night, this scene, was important to the Austrian psyche. The need and the satisfaction were coming together in blessed harmony.

There was another refreshment room on the second floor, a larger space where an expansive display honoring the Berlin Philharmonic's hundredth anniversary had been set up. Here, the stark white death mask of Hans von Bülow in its blue, velvet-lined glass case competed for attention with the extraordinary show of high society swirling around it. It was here that I encountered one of the young conductors who had been at every rehearsal during the past three weeks. He smiled, asked me what I thought. I told him I was quite amazed by the lavishness of the scene, the costumes, the ambience. He shook his head. "It is the worst," he said. "Worse even than Vienna. These people care nothing about the music. The ticket is a status symbol, something they must do so they can talk about it. Seeing Karajan. It is *the* event."

In the inner sanctum of Karajan's rooms, Eliette von Karajan was hosting a small, private gathering. Eliette had appeared at the last few rehearsals. She had preferred to stay in the St. Moritz winter quarters as long as possible because she loves St. Moritz. There is much more to do in St. Moritz, a better social scene. Salzburg is a provincial little town at best, overrun with tourists at worst, and very dead in the early spring. Bleak. Dreary. Absolutely nothing going on.

Eliette is tall, several inches taller than Karajan. Her mane of long blonde hair is straight as a die and parted in the middle. She is a self-conscious, nervous woman. Her mood seems to shift rather quickly between broody and effusive, the latter complete with hugs, kisses, and the polished repartee of a coquette. She combines heavy makeup with the latest in casual-sport style: expensive sweatshirts and designer jeans. She is a "former French fashion model" at fifty. The key word there is "French." She has a wary, calculating look about her. At rehearsals she came late and twisted in her seat like a teenager at the movies.

Eliette's private gathering wasn't that small. As many people as possible seemed to be jammed into the reception room of Salzburger's office, including Lore Salzburger, who was at her post handling last-minute phone calls and ticket crises, looking very much in charge in a tailored black velvet dress. The guests included old friends of the Karajans' like the Austrian industrialist Dr. Herbert Kloiber and his wife, who had been at the Karajan wedding in 1958. "A local orchestra played for the wedding," Herbert Kloiber said, "forty or so boys from the local town. Austria is full of these small orchestras. The conductor was a local police inspector. He asked Karajan for his autograph. Karajan signed, 'to my dear colleague.'" The Karajans' first child, Isabel, was baptized at their house, Kloiber said. "Five members of the Vienna Philharmonic played. Elisabeth Schwarzkopf sang *Ave Maria.*"

Isabel was at the gathering, having journeyed from Paris, where she was studying acting. She has her mother's large-boned profile and dark brown eyes, and her father's terse manner. Those who know her say she has her father's drive and determination as well. When asked, she said she might have a role in *Look Back in Anger*, a new production scheduled for that fall in Paris.

Others at the reception were administrators from the Berlin Phil-harmonic, including Peter Girth, a tall, delicately handsome man with prematurely gray hair; a few business associates and conductors from here and there; and a long-time professional advisor of Karajan's, who, the story goes, once extracted six valuable Easter Festival tickets from the Maestro, then sold them for big money at the fancy hotel across the street.

Karajan wasn't mingling with Eliette's guests. The door to his private rooms was shut. Inside, he was relaxing, taking a final look at the score—his usual pre-performance habit. "Three minutes before I conduct," Karajan once told me, "what I most want to do is fall asleep. When I come through the tunnel in the car and arrive at the Festspielhaus, I have a deadly desire to sleep."

With five minutes to curtain, all the guests had departed except for Eliette, Isabel, and the three people they had invited to join them for the performance.

In the hall, the audience was hushed. The orchestra was seated and tuned. With about a minute to curtain, Eliette and her small entourage made their appearance, trooping down the aisle to their seats in the fourth row, center, and settling in with a proper amount of fuss. (Once when Eliette and her group reportedly made their entrance quite late, the audience, which was a little impatient over the delay in starting the performance, burst into applause that was not meant to compliment. When she reached her row, Eliette faced the audience and curtsied.)

Then Karajan went to the podium, and the applause was deafening. He acknowledged nothing and went to work. The performance was smooth as silk. The critic from the Italian newspaper *Corriere della Sera* in Milan said it was the best *Flying Dutchman* he had ever seen. The water looked convincing. The Dutchman's ship came out of the red haze, the sail was struck, the anchor let out—all on perfect cue. Moll was just right. Van Dam and Ligendza were touching as the ill-fated couple. The orchestra was in its grandest, Wagnerian voice. The stage crew struck the set for Act I and put up Act II with twenty seconds to spare as the transitional music continued with the curtain closed (their time: 1:56). Ligendza's leap into the sea at the end was properly convincing.

The audience was delighted. There was no whistling or shouts of "bravo" as there had been in New York. This group was more restrained. But then this was Austria, the old country, the source: the home of Mozart, home of Karajan. Brahms had wandered these streets, after all, and Johann Strauss, and a long list of other masters. And this audience was an aloof group, not given to shouting.

Karajan took numerous bows, each one drawing another swell of applause. Never mind that before the first paying customer left the house he would be in his car on the way to Anif for a swim and a little solitary television. He was their idol, their emperor, and he had delivered once again.

There had to be satisfaction for Karajan in all this as well. He has long regarded life's various amenities as his due rather than as his good fortune. He plans projects, he organizes them, he executes them, therefore, naturally, they will be right, they will be good, they will be applauded. The logic of it is irrefutable in his mind. It is not by whim that the Maestro's favorite English phrase is "of course." But the Easter Festival, even after nineteen years, is still special to him. It is the only time he addresses the audience from the podium, as he does annually during an open rehearsal that is not an official part of the festival program. The afternoon following the *Dutchman* opening, with the Berlin Philharmonic in readiness on stage, he sat on a high stool, swiveled around, took microphone in hand and for ten minutes spoke about the festival, did a little promotion for the following year's program, told some stories and a joke or two, all in the best television host manner. The only people who didn't seem to be thrilled and amused by Karajan's monologue were the orchestra players, a few of whom were dozing. But when Karajan got to the music, they played a gorgeous excerpt of Brahms's *Tragic Overture*. Karajan followed up that delicious treat with a surprise visit from the young Yugoslavian pianist Pogorelich, who played Ravel's demanding *Gaspard de la nuit* with artistic mastery that left the audience stunned. Karajan, the former pianist, sat at the bass end of the piano the whole time, leaning in, alternately studying Pogorelich's face and hands, moving slightly with the music—infusing his will—concentrating with rapt admiration. Even here he was in charge, from the best seat in the house, and it is doubtful that anyone enjoyed the performance more than he did.

But there is a deeper satisfaction that Karajan derives from his Salzburg appearances, especially the Easter Festival. Karajan was born in Salzburg on April 5, 1908, an Aries, and he grew up there. He remembers the early Salzburg festivals vividly. He was then in his mid-teens, already an accomplished pianist, and still getting used to the idea that the Austro-Hungarian Empire had ceased to exist. "When World War I ended I was ten years old," Karajan says. "I remember in school one day we had a lesson in geography. In response to a question I said 'The Austria-Hungarian Empire.' And the teacher planted himself before me and said, 'Empire?! What do you say? There is no more empire. It is Kleinstadt!' [small state or province]. I felt as if I had been whipped. One always said the two together as a way of representing more than sixteen states in the empire, all held together smoothly by the wonderful organization plan of the Habsburgs. Now suddenly it was finished. For everyone something enormous had happened, the end of an era, a style that would never exist again. Twenty years ago there were many people called 'monarchists,' because they hoped the monarchy would come back. There are still people today who hope for it. There was a frustration that still exists among my generation, because of course the standard of life was really good.

"At the time of the first Salzburg Festival, the aristocracy still had their big houses and castles, but they couldn't maintain them, they had to be rented out. Into this misery came the festival goers, responding to the chance to enter into the old grandeur of the Habsburgs. The festival was well publicized, and quite different from what it is today. People came for a whole month because they wanted the social contact. Max Reinhardt was a great influence. He was one of the greatest stage directors who has ever been. And his brother was a great promoter who knew how to sell what they had for the most money. Reinhardt had a wonderful castle in Salzburg that was the center of the social scene. To be admitted to his circle was critical. He sold to the Americans invitations to a dinner party because he told them they would meet a real princess. And for the real princess, my word, people went for it. All the highest clergy would turn up at these events. I know this because with my piano playing I was nearly always invited. Reinhardt always had a singer, a dancer, a musician who entertained at the end of dinner for ten minutes or so. So I met all these people.

"And when they arrived, it was not with one automobile, but two. One came in front with the luggage, and the people came in the second car driven by two chauffeurs. It was a fairy tale for the local people, just to see the visitors arriving. The road would be lined with two thousand people, including young people like my friends and me. It was incredible. Many of my friends dreamed of going to America to make a fortune so they could do the same thing."

Now, sixty years later, Karajan finds himself at the core of the fairy tale, the center from which the drama unfolds. Given the circuitous, uncertain path Karajan traveled to this position, he must register at least a shred of amazement as he bobs in his heated, indoor pool, alone, after another Easter Festival opening night, in his house in the shadow of the Untersberg. Because Salzburg has not always been the place where he wanted to be. Like any self-respecting, monumentally ambitious, world-beating prodigy, he wanted to leave his provincial little hometown.

III
A Picaresque Beginning

Karajan was the youngest of two sons born to Dr. Ernst von Karajan and his wife, Martha Kosmac von Karajan, a woman of Slavic descent. Christened "Heribert," he later dropped the *i*. His paternal ancestry can be traced to a Greek-Macedonian named Georg Johann Karajannis, who founded the textile industry at Sachsen, a province of Germany. It was he who shortened the family name. His son Theodore, Karajan's grandfather, was a professor of Old German philology at the University of Vienna. He was also librarian, and later became dean. Theodore had two sons, Max and Ernst. Max was professor of classical philology at the University of Graz. Ernst became a physician and eventually head of surgery at the Landeskrankenhaus, Salzburg's only hospital. But before that, the family lived in Vienna.

Ernst Karajan was very musical, and an actor as well. "People made much of themselves in that time," Karajan says. "Viennese society was deeply committed to music, literature, and art. My father played piano, and clarinet too. Social evenings revolved around small groups that would get together and play music. There were two pianos in our house. At least twice a week there would be music. Of course there were no recordings, no television in those days. Live music was the only music.

"My father was a handsome man with a straight nose and a beautiful Greek face. Women were drawn to him. He was a very human man. He loved his patients. If he made a mistake, he wouldn't talk for days. He was soft in some ways. He would be terribly hurt by the bad judgment of his colleagues. He always walked to the hospital, which took twenty-five minutes. One time I asked him why, and he said that while he walked he would review every aspect of the operation he was going to perform. When he arrived, he would be completely ready. Much later I found that this idea influenced me a great deal. I take much more time for planning and preparation, organization, than most people. Sometimes I sit over the schedule for months. If I do this, I will never be overwhelmed. If not, I will not be ready, and I cannot stand not being ready.

"It was difficult for my father to make up his mind in everything but his work. Always he would say, 'ask your mother,' when we came to him with a question. Then he wouldn't be happy with her decisions. I think this made a big impression on me also. Because from childhood, it has always been me who commanded."

Karajan calls his mother the most unselfish person he ever met. "She was always in the background. She had no need to prove herself. My father once told her, 'you would be happy as the head sister in a covent that serviced the whole world.' I remember when I was twelve years old I fell while climbing. I fell seventy-five feet, broke my ankle, and hurt my spine. I got away with it then, but now I pay for it. I'm sure all my back trouble stems from this fall. But when I was brought in I remember my mother said 'thank God!'—not because I wasn't dead, but because she had me, in bed, dependent on her love and care. When she came in to check on me she would move the door handle a millimeter at a time so as not to disturb me.

"She lived in fear of everything. For me to be a conductor was as if I were mounting an expedition to the moon. She would say, 'if only you went into something safe, like the civil service.' Then when I made my career she said: 'but what if he becomes deaf!' She always worried about the worst thing that could happen. As a boy, I didn't appreciate it.

"I didn't have much family life. My father couldn't communicate with young people. He didn't participate in our interests. My friend's parents were different. They had a car. My father didn't have one. So we would go with my friend's father, and my father was left alone. This made me want to be as near to my own children as possible. We built the St. Moritz house with one large section for them. There is a big playroom, and it is acoustically shielded. As a kid I always had to go to my friend's house. My parents didn't want noise. And we weren't supposed to bring girls. The subject of sex was taboo in my family's home. They said it had to do with health. What does health have to do with love?"

Karajan's brother Wolfgang is sixteen months older than the Maestro. "I was always smaller than him, younger. I didn't belong to his gang. This had its effect in school. Since I was born in the middle of the year, I couldn't go to school when he went. I should have gone—

I was ready. But I had to wait. Then there were music lessons. My parents wanted Wolfgang to learn piano. I said, 'me too!' But they told me I had to wait a year. So I used to hide behind the curtains while Wolfgang took his lesson. Then when I was alone I would try to do it. After three weeks I was discovered, and they allowed me to continue with lessons. I quickly caught up with Wolfgang and went beyond."

The need to best the older, bigger, more socially active brother must have been chronic. It is difficult to assess the brothers' relationship at present. Indications are that the two are distant. Referring back to the story about asking his brother to change his name Karajan says: "What happened was that Wolfgang went to tour America with the Bach organ quartet he had formed. On the poster they were printing for the trip they planned to make the 'Karajan' huge and put the name 'Wolfgang' in very small type and thus make people think it was me. I got very angry about this and made them change it." (Wolfgang refused to be interviewed when I called him, saying that in the past whatever he had said had either angered the Maestro, or had been taken as jealousy, so he had decided that saying nothing was the best course.)

Karajan speaks well of Wolfgang for the record. "We raised hell all the time," he recalls. "We were taking chemistry in school, and of course our goal was to find the powder that would explode with the most noise and smoke. Then we would choose for who had to light it. Once it went off with an enormous bang. The fire department had to come. We frightened pedestrians with our bicycles, and we had a secret language that our parents couldn't understand."

Wolfgang had a penchant for engineering and electronics. As a teenager he built a radio receiver and set it up in the middle of the footbridge that connects the two banks of Salzburg across the Salzach River. Two hundred people gathered at the bridge, with the police finally having to intervene. Karajan says that Peter Siemens, head of one of Germany's largest electronics manufacturing firms, once told him that if Wolfgang had possessed a more stable disposition he could have made a fortune. But as Karajan says, "you couldn't make an appointment with him, because when you arrived he might have taken his dogs for a walk in the mountains."

Wolfgang had a small electronics lab in Vienna which he moved near the Swiss border during the war. The Silberman organ factory was nearby, and Wolfgang and his concert pianist wife became interested in the instrument. He and his wife collaborated on a Bach program called "Art of the Fugue" which they (and two others) played on four organs. They toured with success all over the world in the 1960s.

Karajan took lessons for two years, progressing rapidly enough so that by age five he played at a public benefit concert. He remembers it well. "I couldn't reach the pedals, but I wasn't all that nervous. They promised me a cake if I would play." When World War I began, the elder Karajans sent their sons to live with their aunt in the Steiermark, a mountainous region southeast of Salzburg. When it became clear that the war would not affect Salzburg, they returned home to their studies. Wolfgang temporarily left the keyboard to study violin, while Herbert was taken on by the well-known teacher Franz Ledwinka at the newly erected Mozarteum in Salzburg. This was considered quite an honor. "We lived right next to where the Hotel Österichischerhof is now," Karajan says. "I watched them build the Mozarteum. On the cornerstone they carved a theme of Mozart, and do you know, it includes a wrong note." He laughs.

Karajan was known as a promising young pianist. "I was playing six hours a day," he recalls. "I don't know why I did this, but I always had a strong tendency to learn things and acquire skills. If it weren't for music, I would have sat down and learned Russian, or something else. People say you are a prodigy. Perhaps, but you don't realize it. You are so involved in what you are doing that you forget. I have the ability to concentrate on what I want to do, and shut out all else." A story Karajan tells of when he was six or seven reveals that even as a child he was thinking about more than technique:

"My mother had gone to Bad Gastein to take the waters and had taken me with her. She was a good-looking woman who enjoyed the attention of men, and at Bad Gastein, a man was attracted to her. They were formal with each other, but children are more aware than one thinks. Now my brother and I had seen an electric car that was in a big toy shop in Vienna. We were dying for this car—it would be like having a jet interceptor to fly today. That car was it. So one morning my mother and this man were sitting near each other, and my mother asked me to play a certain piece on the piano. I didn't want to for some reason. So she said if you play the piece, I will buy you the electric car. And I said no thank you. Later I realized that I wanted to play for the music, not the money. The money would have to come by itself." Like many of youth's ideological stances, this one would be modified along the way.

"I had a nice childhood," Karajan says, "but I took it as it came."

Summers, the Karajan family moved into the spectacular mountain lake region east of Salzburg. Within an hour-and-a-half's drive of

Salzburg there are a string of slender lakes from two to six miles long. Each is fresh and clear with its own delicate blue-green hue, and each is concealed like a glittering treasure within a dazzling border of mountains that rise from the water's edge.

The lakes are deep. It is said that the Nazis used some of them as vaults for their more valuable possessions, sealing them into deep, underwater crannies with large, metal plates. If so, those caches have never been discovered.

The Karajans had a house at Grundlsee, the lake farthest from Salzburg, a small, precious gem of a lake. The neighboring mountains are in the six-thousand-foot range. Some wear snowcaps all summer. It has been sixty-odd years since the Karajans summered at Grundlsee, and even with the few guesthouses and souvenir shops that have been added, the town is fortunately quiet, blissfully unadorned; the lake, the mountains, the overpowering natural beauty of the place are quite enough for anyone's sensibilities.

One's early environment establishes certain criteria. For one who was raised in Salzburg and Grundlsee, it would be difficult to find much that equaled his initial aesthetic vision. The mountain lakes of Austria have Colorado's grandeur without its roughness. They are green, lush settings that feel hospitable, not hostile or threatening. The air is very crisp, even in summer. The edges of scenic objects are sharp. One can look across panoramic vistas with good distinction of both color and mass: the near meadow, the far edge, the middle-distance green line of hill, the far purplish backdrop of trees, the craggy mountains beyond—and in the V where the two peaks dip their profile against the sky, the breathtaking snowfields of the really high, far-distant mountain ranges emerge with a clarity that astonishes, as if they might be the spume-drenched faces of monstrous, gathering waves.

Confronted with such a vista, one reconsiders Karajan's music, his emphasis on gorgeous sound, his insistence that every shading, every nuance be heard, his demand that there be precise separation as well as the dark blend, the legato of the whole. He is the mountain man indeed, the child of idyllically beautiful Grundlsee, magically mysterious Grundlsee, where the rest of the world doesn't exist when you are just a boy growing up.

Perfect Grundlsee. A stocky young fellow in white shorts pauses in his reverie with the radio and a beer to rent an electric boat (no dirty, noisy outboards are allowed on the lake). Top speed is three knots. One cruises silently around the placid lake speaking in low voices when at all. It feels safe, like having a toy boat on an amusement park lake. There are no life jackets in the boat. Sailboards glide about in the light breeze. A few high-performance *Flying Dutchman* sailboats bring a smile.

At the west end of the lake on a high knoll, against a backdrop of dark, distant mountains, one can see the old Karajan house. It has not been in the family for years. A sign outside indicates rooms for rent. It is a large house with a commanding view of the lake from the screened porch. There isn't a cranny on the lake where Frau von Karajan couldn't have kept track of her boys, with a little help from binoculars.

"The house was in three parts," Karajan recalls. "My father, his brother, and his sister owned it together. There were three cooks and one wood-fired cookstove. Everyone quarreled all the time. But this is where I began sailing at age six or seven. The wind came straight down off the mountains, like in the fjords. The beauty of it was something. Salzburg and Vienna were crowded, a mass of stone buildings. I didn't like the cities."

Electric car or no, Karajan continued to play the piano in public while he was still very young. His notices were good. Like most boys, he took to sports at an early age. From his father he inherited an intense love of nature. He began skiing when he was five, and to this day he prefers to be surrounded by mountains. He played team sports too. There are old pictures of soccer teams with goalie Karajan seated cross-legged in the front row holding the ball. But it was the more solitary, nature-oriented pursuits—skiing, climbing—that received his fuller attention. The study, the devotion to music, didn't leave much time for other organized endeavors.

The Karajan parents kept a sharp eye on the way of the world, and made demands upon their sons. When Herbert was fourteen, he and Wolfgang were sent to London for a few months to polish their English. They stayed first at a pension, then as paying guests of a London family. Back in Salzburg, they became friendly with Bernard Paumgartner, head of the Mozarteum. He became teacher and advisor to the brothers. He played chamber music with them and taught them how to ride motorcycles. It was Paumgartner who first observed that Herbert would never be satisfied with the amount of music he could produce with his ten fingers, and suggested that he consider conducting. "He wasn't a good conductor," Karajan says today of Paumgartner.

When Karajan was growing up, anyone interested in music had to study piano. "You mustn't forget that in my time, in a town like Salzburg—besides the festival—there was a very decent orchestra, maybe sixty members, but they only played six concerts a year. You couldn't learn much from that. There were no records until that great, great achievement began between the two wars. We had to learn opera and orchestral music from piano scores. An orchestra reduced to piano. Of course, it never gave the real sound. If you played a certain chord you had to imagine the full complement of horns or whatever. We always had to transpose our experience of the music into the real sound. Today a pupil learning will have five, ten different tapes of a Brahms symphony. In our time it took us longer to learn, but I think we got it more solidly into our systems than students do today. I am convinced that I am right."

As a boy, Karajan's thirst for sound was satisfied in part by frequent trips to nearby Vienna, where he came in contact with the work of artists like Leopold Godowsky, the great pianist who was trained by Camille Saint-Saëns, and where he heard symphonic music and opera. Upon graduation from Humanistischen Gymnasium (Humanistic Grammar School—the equivalent of American high school), he went off to study in Vienna, where he would be more totally exposed to music. That was not the original intention, however. Karajan says his father wasn't keen on a music career for him. He suggested something more practical. No doubt Frau von Karajan was similarly concerned. So Karajan enrolled in a technical college in Vienna, with the provision that he study piano on the side. He did so with Professor Josef Hofmann, one of the great pianists of the day.

"I wanted to make a career as a pianist," Karajan says. "There was one trouble: the tendons in my fingers were not anatomically normal, and they would become inflamed. So I had to stop from time to time. I was in the school, in humanistic studies—psychology, philosophy, general educational courses.

"I was also taking lessons with Professor Hofmann. After three months Hofmann (like Paumgartner) told me, look here, you have a feeling and imagination for sound which will not be fulfilled unless you have eight hands. In the same way that there are people who will not go to string concerts because the size of the sound is not sufficient, for you it will be the same if you play only one instrument. If you can, try to become a conductor, because this is the only thing that will satisfy you."

Karajan convinced his parents that he must proceed along the path he proposed. He entered the Academy for Music and the Performing Arts in Vienna in order to study conducting with Clemens Krauss and Professor Alex Wunderer. Kurt Stern, a classmate of Karajan's from those days at the Academy, remembers him well. (Mr. Stern can be found most evenings playing popular classics on the piano in the Palm Court lounge of the Plaza Hotel in Manhattan.) "He was a serious fellow," Stern says. "He didn't bother with the girls. The rest of us were struggling to conduct, while Karajan was already doing Brahms from memory. There were no jokes. It was all hard work. You had to be above average to be accepted at the Academy. Of two hundred and twenty that tried to get in, maybe eighteen would be accepted, and of that number, three would graduate. So if there was someone more talented than you, it was all right. Karajan was like that. He wasn't offensive, but no one could get close to him. There was a buffet downstairs where we all ate. Karajan would arrive, eat his sandwich quickly, and disappear. At that time he had only one desire: to make a good career. Every student had to write a composition that would be played by a string quartet. I played viola in the quartet that played Karajan's piece. When he came to hear it nothing special happened. It was a very traditional composition. He was determined to do everything just right.

"Vienna in those days was the world's music capital. We were exposed to the likes of Furtwängler, Kleiber, Krauss, Richard Strauss, and the voices of immortal singers. We were only one generation away from Bruckner, Brahms, and Strauss [Johann Jr.]. We were surrounded by music and the tradition of music. A successful musician in Vienna had status like in no other town in the world."

Even in his student days, Karajan had easy access to the Vienna State Opera, which was often the hottest ticket in Vienna. His uncle was in charge of security and safety at that theater, and could usually find a ticket or two for his nephew. So Karajan got to hear more than his share of the day's great singers doing a broad selection of the opera repertoire.

The academy's reputation aside, Karajan says the conducting classes were low level. "Clemens Krauss, who was leading the class, was conducting at the State Opera. Then he left to become the conductor at Frankfurt. The class was entrusted to a member of the Vienna Philharmonic who wanted to conduct. But he could not teach us because he didn't know how himself."

Eight of the students got together and formed their own study group. They would learn the score of a production that was coming up in Vienna. Then they would meet at someone's house, preferably where there were two pianos. People in the group would take various roles—orchestra (on piano), singers, chorus, and of course, conductor. They would switch roles and keep going. Then they would attend the performance. Afterwards they would gather to assess what they had seen. "Naturally, we never thought the conductor did it right," Karajan says. "It was a system that worked very well. Probably better than if we had had a good teacher. We probably worked harder."

There were the inevitable recitals to show the work of Professor Wunderer's conducting class. By all accounts, Karajan starred.

"After I had conducted three of four concerts, I knew I could do it," Karajan says. "But the student orchestra wasn't the right thing for me. I wanted to see how I would do with a professional orchestra in a public concert. So I raised all the money I could and financed my own concert. It took me a year to get it together. It was in Salzburg, where I was well known as a pianist, with the Salzburg orchestra. My father played clarinet in the orchestra that night. The Intendant of the opera house in Ulm, Germany, was at this concert. He was impressed, and asked me if I would do a production of *Figaro* at his theater."

"Karajan presents Karajan" (January 23, 1929) was important not only because it landed him a job at Ulm, which began his career, but because it revealed a classic Karajan approach. When he wants something, he quickly makes an assessment, designs a plan, and plunges in without hesitation—his way. In this case he knew he was outstanding among his peers. He knew he could conduct. Rather than wait for an opportunity to show what he could do, he created one. True, he had the means. His parents undoubtedly contributed heavily to the effort. But he also had the courage, the bravado, the determination—and the organizational ability—to make it happen. And of course the Intendant at Ulm was not in attendance by sheer coincidence. It is typical of Karajan to imply that he was. Considerable scheming and effort went in to making certain that the man from Ulm was at the concert. In fact, everyone else could have stayed home. Karajan surely knew that the music director's job at Ulm was about to be vacant. The concert was designed as Karajan's audition—and it worked.

Ulm had one of the eighty small opera houses within Germany at the time (many still exist today). Towns in Germany that are too small to support sports stadiums have an opera house, and often it is a surprisingly grand structure. The houses are usually called the "Staatsoper," because their operation leans heavily upon the federal budget. Both East and West Germany support opera and classical music the way America subsidizes farming. And so it was that the young conductor Herbert von Karajan ventured one hundred and fifty miles to the northwest of Salzburg to begin work in Ulm, population (then) sixty thousand.

"During the two years in Vienna," Karajan says, "I did all the things I did because I knew I had to learn. All I wanted to do was work, work, work. What I really wanted was to have something in hand that was mine. I was mad for it. I was really glad for the first time I had this theater that was really small, true enough, and I had to rely on singers who had lost their voices, and on youngsters—but it was mine.

"There were two of us who shared the conducting responsibilities. We each had one month's time to prepare and present an opera. We did it all. We helped build sets, we organized the costumes. I would often get on my bicycle in the winter and ride around all morning reminding people about the rehearsal that afternoon, or rounding up extra players I needed for certain productions. We had no coaches. The first time I did *Rosenkavalier* I had to study the bass part, which is very long, in order to coach the singer. Then the man came in and confessed he could not read music. I said all right, you will learn it as you hear it. I worked so hard with this man that when it was finished I had this opera in my head for all time. You can wake me up at 3 A.M. any morning and say, 'now you must whistle what is on page 14 of the score,' and I will do it straightaway. This was my great advantage over today's generation, who learn pieces by tape recorder. We had to put these things together ourselves, and we knew every part of them. My salary was 80 marks ($40) a month. It is ridiculous to compare it with today's inflation, but it was very low. Below minimum wage.

"And of course I arrived in Ulm with the acoustical feeling of the opera house in Vienna in my head. You can imagine what a shock it was to hear the twenty-two-piece orchestra at Ulm. I had an image of the sound I wanted to hear, and I tried to put that in synchronization with the music that I conducted. I tried to force my concentration on the side of what I wanted to hear—not what I was hearing—which, of course, I could not do at the time.

"But all of the small theaters in Germany operated with great care for the material, not like other countries, where singers were thrown together and performances were tossed out. We took time, time to prepare and think the thing out. And I had an opportunity for the first time to conduct all the operas I knew from my years in Vienna. Each was prepared, rehearsed, then performed eight or nine times.

"The audience was different from what we have today, certainly. Every German wants to be educated in art, science, music. He may not really be interested in music, but he will have a great wish to perfect himself in the knowledge of music. Theaters in those days were institutes for education. It has changed, of course. Today everyone wants perfection, the best. Yesterday the civil servant would go to a small spa in Germany for a fortnight for his holiday. Today he goes to the Caribbean. Today people know from TV what can be had. So they are more reluctant to go to the small theater when they can see the best on TV.

"But at Ulm I could express myself, get to know my faults by what I did. By repeating pieces you have done, you get to see the mistakes you have made. We two conductors got to know each other's productions. We had a mutual understanding, and we substituted for each other, which expanded our repertoires. Then, as today, it was a must to have conducted forty operas."

Karajan considers the Ulm years of great importance to his development. Such a slow, sure learning process has lost its popularity in a time when jet travel, television, and instant gratification—as much as possible as soon as possible—have drastically rearranged both the pace and values of life. But there are those who continue to see merit in such tenure. One is Bruno Weil, the young conductor who was Karajan's backup at the Easter Festival, and whom Karajan helped get his post at the theater in Augsburg, Germany. Augsburg is bigger than Ulm, yet it is still a small town.

"A conductor gets better with age," says Weil, who is not yet thirty-five. "Karajan didn't become famous until he was fifty. Karl Böhm was sixty before he was famous. A conductor can have a fast career now, and many go for it. But I feel I must resist it. The more experience you have, the better. A pianist can practice at home. But it takes many years to gain sufficient experience with opera, even with the symphonic repertoire. You must conduct an opera once just to know what is going on. I feel it is foolish to stick my neck out in Vienna or Berlin before I have done the opera in a smaller theater.

"Karajan told me," says Weil, "after the Brahms he did at Easter Festival, that it took him twenty years to be able to do it that way.

"Singers," Weil continues, "used to polish their roles in provincial theaters. Now they just begin in Bayreuth, and after five years they are gone, finished. Opera has become too much like the movies. They want an eighteen-year-old to play Siegfried. You must be forty-five to have the experience to sing Siegfried. Caruso would come to sing at the Met in the old days, and he would come by ship. It would be like a vacation for him between roles. Today a singer will perform in Vienna on Monday, London on Wednesday, New York on Friday."

Karajan's season at Ulm began in September and ran until April. The *stagione* system was used: one, possibly two, operas would be prepared, performed eight or nine times over a two-week period, and would be finished. Houses like the Vienna Staatsoper, on the other hand, have a repertoire of thirty-five to forty operas scheduled throughout the season. Karajan says he prefers the *stagione* system, in that the opera is always fresh, rehearsed and ready. In April, Karajan would have free time, which he used, as one might expect, to full advantage.

"Guest conducting on my level was not done. We were not asked. We were unknowns. So in the off-season I would go to several places where I could learn new things. I went to Milan, because it was a great time (1930s) of Toscanini and others, and the way of Italian singing fascinated me. It was not known in Germany. Operas in Germany were sung exclusively in German at this time. In Italy, opera was sung in Italian. So I was soaking up this sort of knowledge. I heard two or three operas in French also."

Since he was already a prominent young musician in Salzburg when the festival began in 1924, Karajan's connection with it was automatic. In the 1930s the Salzburg Festival enjoyed great popularity and attracted the best singers, musicians, and conductors. It took place only in August in those days, which suited Karajan's schedule perfectly. He had both the connections and the ability to become involved with the production, and soon was chorus master, in charge of conducting offstage music. In this way he attended every rehearsal, and got to assist the rehearsals of Toscanini (whom he admired greatly), Richard Strauss, and all the others who conducted there. "I got a close look at what was done and how it was done by the great masters," Karajan says.

"I know from colleagues who started in big theaters and were engaged all year round that they missed the sort of thing I was getting in my off-season. They heard only what was done in their own theaters. As a result they acquired a narrow artistic view. This was in 1930. Recordings were primitive, not yet a source of what was going on. So I jumped at any way of getting new knowledge, of hearing what I needed to hear." He did indeed. He once got on his bicycle and rode two hundred miles to hear Toscanini conduct.

In 1933, Ulm Intendant Erwin Dietrich suggested to Karajan that it was time for him to move on. Karajan persuaded him that he should stay one more season. But as the 1934 season drew to a close, Dietrich was adamant. "He came to me," Karajan recalls, "and it was one of the most impressive moments of my life. He said, 'I have followed your work five years. You are better, more experienced. We are a small town, and people who work here don't become well known. Guest conductors here are rare. You are in danger of getting stuck here. I think you are born for greater things, and we will not take you back next year. You must swim or drown.'

"When I first conducted the opera in Berlin six, seven years later, Dietrich came to me and said, 'You see, I was right.' He was very generous."

Karajan's retrospective reassessments are always brief, and they usually rely on highlights that have been modified for the sake of experience. One can extend David Cairns's criticism of Karajan's music to his recollections: "... a symphony is a drama, and truth arrived at by argument. Karajan, the Superman of the musical establishment, does not like argument, and sees to it that awkward facts ... are safely smoothed over."

Leaving Ulm had to have been traumatic for Karajan. For all his confidence about making music, he has never been a secure man. His obsessive need for control, his insistence upon loyalty, his machismo approach to the sporting life, his grim drive for perfection in all things, and his insistence upon a life contract with the Berlin Philharmonic all attest to this. Fifty years later, when he speaks further about making the transition from Ulm, one can still sense traces of anxiety, desperation.

"At the end of the 1934 season I left Ulm. The only place to go was Berlin, where singers, conductors, agents ... the business was there, the contacts. I joined others who were accompanying the singers and making deals—the scramble to meet directors who might engage us."

Karajan bumped around Berlin for three months without much success. That's not such a long dry spell, unless one is Herbert von Karajan. "Everyone said, 'you have been five years at Ulm, we haven't heard you.' Most of the others moved around in two-to-three-year hitches. I wasn't sorry that I had stayed in Ulm so long, because I had built up my repertoire. In the shorter stints you were forced to do the same things over and over. But I wasn't getting any work. Then at the end of June I met the Intendant of Aachen. I can frankly say that I hypnotized him to give me a chance. I was so determined becase it was more or less the last chance. His season had finished in June, so one could not guest conduct, but he invited me to conduct a rehearsal."

Musically, Aachen was much more important than Ulm. There was an orchestra of eighty, a chorus of sixty, better singers, and a more enthusiastic, sophisticated audience. Aachen at the midpoint of Germany's western border, only a few miles from Belgium and Holland, enjoyed a great flux of people from all three countries. It was a cultural center. The post Karajan wanted was a desirable one.

"I told the man," Karajan says, "'don't give me a contract until after you have watched me conduct a rehearsal. If you like that, give me the first production in your season. If I do it well, then you take me.' He agreed; I prepared Beethoven's *Fidelio*. The performance was in September, after which I was appointed music director at Aachen. Suddenly people got interested in me. They saw it was a big jump."

In fact, it was just a few months after his initial connection with Aachen in August of 1934 that Karajan was asked to guest conduct the Vienna Philharmonic for the first time. He did Debussy's *Fantasy for Piano and Orchestra* and *Prelude to "The Afternoon of a Faun,"* and Ravel's *La Valse*.

At Aachen he followed *Fidelio* with Wagner's *Walküre* and Strauss's *Rosenkavalier*. Then, in the absence of the Aachen general music director, Peter Raabe, who was guest conducting in Berlin, Karajan conducted a few symphonic concerts. The reviews were excellent. The aging Raabe quickly saw Karajan as a rival. Karajan was becoming known. He was asked to conduct in Frankfurt and Karlsruhe, theaters of the next rank. He was not yet thirty, and moving fast. "When people began to compete for me," Karajan says, "the mayor of Aachen, who was broad-minded, said 'whatever they want to pay you, you will get here.' So I made a contract for six years."

The contract was for more than music director of the Aachen Staatsoper. In six months Karajan had already advanced. By early 1935, he had replaced Raabe as general music director, much to Raabe's annoyance. "I had complete control over musical life in Aachen," Karajan says. "I was the youngest director (twenty-seven) when I got the contract. I was known as one of the ascending people in the business."

Raabe was compensated politically: he became head of the Reichsmusikkammer—the chamber, or bureau of music for the Third Reich—a division of the Reichskulturkammer, which was presided over by Josef Goebbels, who had been Adolf Hitler's minister for public enlightenment and propaganda from the Nazi seizure of power in 1933. While others might debate the separation of art and politics, Goebbels was clear about such matters. "Culture," he had said at the outset, "is a poster for the Third Reich."

According to Karajan, it was at this time (1935) when the pressure was put on him to join the Nazi party—when his perilous and misguided affair with the Nazis began. "I was not a member when the party came in," he says. "And, as music director of the Aachen Opera, I was not so exposed politically. But when it came time to sign my contract as general music director, my secretary came in and said that the man who was head of the party in Aachen had mentioned that my appointment was difficult to pass. I was about to be named general music director and I was not a member of the party.

"Now I will tell you what I compared this problem with. I used to ski a lot. My companion was an Austrian guide, whom I took everywhere with me. Once we went to a certain mountain in Switzerland, where they told me that I could not ski with my guide unless I joined the local Swiss Alpine Club and also hired a Swiss guide. I wanted to ski the mountain, so I said to hell with it, and I took a membership and hired the guide. For me the Nazi party thing was just the same.

"Before me was this paper, which stood between me and almost limitless power and a budget to provide for an orchestra with which I could do however many concerts I liked, including tours. I had a secretary, an office, I was in heaven. And they were saying that I must be a member, that maybe I would have to do a concert for them once in a while, that's all. So I said what the hell, and signed. But afterwards people said, 'of course you are a Nazi.'"

In 1947, after the war, Karajan ran into a man named Edge Leslie at the Salzburg Festival. At the time, Leslie was a British diplomat stationed in Zurich. He was a government official, but he lived for music. He harbored notions of conducting, and he occasionally wrote pieces for classical music journals. He and Karajan hit it off immediately, and are friends to this day. In 1947, Karajan was living in St. Anton while waiting to be cleared (denazified) by the Quadripartite Commission. Leslie had a place in St. Anton as well. The two met often over dinner. "Karajan told me," Leslie says today, "that he would have done anything to get the job at Aachen.

"But you have to understand about his mission. Once I arrived at his flat to pick him up. He was out walking and left me a note to wait in his room. There were religious books of all sorts scattered around. Passages in the books had been underlined, and notes made in the margins in his seismographic hand. When he returned, I asked him about it. He said that you don't need any faith to believe in God, because there are plenty of signs available of His existence. Mozart wrote a symphony as a child. Heredity can't account for this, Karajan said. There is only one explanation: the Creator chooses people as His instruments to produce some beauty in a world that is all too ugly. 'I was given special tools,' Karajan told me, 'special talents. I never had any doubt that my talents came from the Creator. My duty is to exploit them to the fullest. My ambition is to make music as perfectly as possible and reach as many people as possible. I also must make music on film.'

"The critics call Karajan an arrogant god," Leslie says. "Karajan would say he is an instrument of God. And he is ruthless in his mission. He told me, 'I have done terrible things,' but explains them as part of the fulfillment of his mission."

The story of how he came to join the Nazi party has often been told by Karajan. It is the best known of his retrospective reassessments. The fact that documents are available that lead to a different conclusion fails to move him.

These documents were revealed as far back as 1957 in an article by Paul Moor about Karajan—"The Operator"—published in *High Fidelity* magazine. "Once and for all," Moor wrote, "to set the record straight: Herbert von Karajan joined the Nazi Party not in Aachen but in Salzburg, and not in 1934 under pressure but on April 8, 1933, only two months and eight days after Hitler came to power. He was assigned membership card #1 607 525. He paid his dues for that month, but before the end of April, he left to return to Germany, which caused a small administrative snarl, since he did not actually pick up his membership card. However, back in Ulm, he got this straightened out on May 1, 1933, and received another card, #3 430 914. These facts are on record in the master file of the Nazi Party in the Document Center of the United States Mission in Berlin, and would seem rather more reliable than Herbert von Karajan's memory."

Twenty-five years later, these documents were rediscovered, this time by German musicologist Fred Prieberg. In his book *Musik im N.S.-Staat*, Prieberg documented Karajan's "double" membership in the NSDAP (Nationalsozialistische Deutsche Arbeitspartei—Nazi party for short). The dates and the numbers matched those Moor had found in 1957.

Karajan's immediate response to the publication of the documents Prieberg had obtained from the files of the Berlin Documentation Center was outrage. "It is such a fabrication," Karajan told me, spitting out his words with contempt, waving his hand in the manner he would use to still an orchestra that had gotten completely lost, "that I refuse to even talk about it. It is ridiculous. Prieberg said those things just to make money."

A few months later I had obtained my own documents from the Documentation Center in Berlin, including copies of the membership cards mentioned above. I showed them to the Maestro at his house in Anif. He first wanted to know where I had obtained them, and registered annoyance that such things would be made available. Then he took the papers, regarding them with wary curiosity. He held them under a lamp to see them better, and examined them for several seconds. "Where is my signature?" he asked. "They are not signed, you see?" I asked him what he made of them. He shrugged, looked at me: "They are false." (NSDAP membership cards were not signed. They were filled out by party officials.)

Oddly enough, it is within the records of the NSDAP itself that disagreement with Karajan's assertions is found. On file at Berlin's Documentation Center is an interesting series of letters that were sent between various central and divisional NSDAP party headquarters for the specific purpose of trying to make a determination on the very issue under discussion: when Karajan joined the party. It is impossible to ascertain who initiated the correspondence, who made the request or who asked the question that got the bureaucratic machinery rolling. But the rest of it pieces together handily:

—Letter dated January 5, 1939, from Nazi Party Headquarters in Munich to the Nazi Party Financial Administration in Austria pertaining to Karajan's eligibility for an NSDAP membership book. The letter states that Karajan apparently joined the party twice: April 8, 1933, in Salzburg (#1 607 525), and again (without reporting a change of address) on May 1, 1933, in Ulm. The letter asks if the "provisional" membership of April 8 is in effect.

—Letter dated February 4, 1939, from the Nazi Party representative in Austria (Vienna) to the treasurer, NSDAP Munich, stating that it is up to the Salzburg headquarters to determine the validity of Karajan's April 8 application.

—Letter dated February 4, 1939, from (apparently) NSDAP Vienna to the NSDAP treasurer in Salzburg requesting a determination on the above question.

—Letter dated May 15, 1939, from the Salzburg city group "Neustadt" to NSDAP treasurer in Salzburg. The group leader relates a conversation with party member Herbert Klein, who signed Karajan as an NSDAP member in Salzburg for five schillings. He said he gave Karajan a receipt and filed the application at the recruiting office in Salzburg. After the party was forbidden, Karajan left for Germany. After his departure, Klein said he didn't hear from him again and believed that Karajan never paid any party dues in Austria. Klein intended to check this out to verify his statements. (Copy sent to Munich.)

—Letter dated July 7, 1939, from Party Headquarters Munich to the treasurer of the party in Cologne-Aachen, which declares the Karajan application of April 8, 1933, to be invalid because Karajan did not remit his dues; declares the date of May 1, 1933, to be valid;

and transmits Karajan's party book with the request that it be given to him.

—Letter dated December 12, 1942, from [Oberberreichsleiter Schneider] to the Reich's Chancellory in Berlin stating that the official date of Karajan's entry into the party is May 1, 1933; that his party number is 3 430 914; and that his book was made available on July 13, 1939.

And so we have the documents on the one hand, culled, collated and filed from the tangled, incomplete and frightful mess of paperwork hastily left behind by the Nazis, who were in full flight—and Karajan's steadfast denials and assertions on the other. Given that he had never tried to hide his membership in the Nazi party, why does Karajan stick with such tenacity to guns that seem to have lost their pins? One must suppose that Karajan still insists upon the 1935 date to temper the deed of joining, perhaps to provide a rationale—the preservation of one's career—that people could comprehend, even safely accept. To have joined in April or May, one or two months after Hitler had taken power, would have been to appear a touch enthusiastic in his support of Hitler, his politics, and his plans. This would not be so easily understood.

"It is the most difficult thing in life to understand for those who did not live in Germany or Austria at that time," Karajan says. "I have tried to explain this to my wife, and she still has no idea of what happened there. Even with the enormous interest in that period, the saturation by films from all sides—German, French, U.S., Jewish— outsiders have no idea what was happening there. Discontent was widespread because of the aftermath of World War I. Debts of war are always paid in some difficult way. The Communist thing had started. Germany and Austria were really battlefields for different parties trying to get power. And at this time Hitler was becoming stronger. If you look back with objectivity and perspective, you see things that were happening economically that were basically good ideas. This is what will always be in the mind of the whole world: how could such horrible things go on for so long? On the other hand, if you say Hitler was only a murderer, he wouldn't have been followed by seventy million people. Impossible."

When trying to comprehend the Austrian response to Hitler, it is vital to remember that until 1918, the feudal system prevailed in Austria. Until then the Habsburg dynasty took care of business and provided a regal point of focus that was without parallel for grandeur and elegance. Most of the people did their work and had few worries. The Habsburg Empire was reasonably efficient. One Austrian socialist described the Habsburgian attitude as despotism diluted by sloppiness. Their multiracial empire was enormous, and its presence fostered contentment and pride among most Austrians. Most amazing of all, perhaps the most difficult for non-Europeans to comprehend, the Habsburgs were in power for more than six centuries.

A wave of republican feeling swept across all of Europe during the period of American and French revolution, but there was little continuing democratic sentiment in nineteenth-century Austria. Workers' education clubs, which were formed in the 1880s in Austria for the purpose of politicizing the people, didn't catch on. One such club closed quickly when no one came to meetings. Why? The beer at the inn where the club met was inferior.

In 1919, when democracy was suddenly foisted upon an Austrian nation already reeling from drastic, geographical reduction by the Treaty of Versailles, the results were catastrophic. How does a nation resolve the sudden termination of a way of life that is sixty-five generations old? Very slowly, for certain. In 1985, monarchistic shadows are still cast upon Austria. In 1919, most Austrians basically thought democratic principles and a republican form of government were ridiculous. The number of parties was confusing. Few people participated in elections. Social tensions grew amid hatred for the Treaty of Versailles. Schemes abounded for bringing back the emperor. The prevailing attitude ranged from dissatisfaction to outrage.

There was, as Karajan has indicated, great economic misery. Starvation was a nationwide threat. The scramble for jobs was ruthless. Imperial civil servants became firemen, barons became bar-pianists, and colonels became innkeepers. By 1921, inflation was out of hand. Hand-to-mouth charity was keeping Austria going (the Hoover Relief Organization, the Quakers, etc.). In a few short years, Austria had fallen from being a world power and multilingual empire to a state in shambles.

There was a moment of hope in 1930, when internal order was stabilized and Austria's credit with the League of Nations was high. But when Hitler won six million votes in the German elections that year, Nazi disturbances broke out all over Austria, and the clamor for Anschluss began against a backdrop of fierce internal bickering among political factions and prohibitive tariffs established by neighboring states. By 1933, Austrians had very few choices for the future: Communism, Catholic authoritarianism, or union with a strong Germany. In the absence of any national political unity, most Austrians thought the best way toward economic (and political) survival would be to join Germany. That Hitler had exhibited dictatorial tendencies wasn't alarming to Austrians used to a powerful monarchy. As for Hitler's anti-Semitism, which had been clearly stated (along with his desire to absorb Austria) in his book *Mein Kampf* (1924), that was not something to be taken very seriously. Anti-Semites in Europe, like racists in today's world, were a dime a dozen. Mainly, to the struggling Austrians, the situation across the border looked very tantalizing. They wanted to join a greater Germany.

"We could see the improvements Hitler was making from Salzburg, which is only seven kilometers from the German border," Karajan says. "At this time there were six million Germans unemployed, so Hitler said a network of highways would be constructed, unheard of at this time, and he said people would be employed, and they would be able to buy things. Of course he was counting on the possibility of war. He knew from World War I the value of mobility. He promoted the Volkswagen factory and brought out the VW beetle. You could take away the body and make a military car in no time. It was useful, cheap, reliable, and could move until the road was nearly nonexistent. Dr. Porsche was a genius, of course. Hitler said every workman would have a car. We laughed. It couldn't be possible. Tractors were unknown, and we always yearned for cars. A car, and I have felt this myself, changed you. When I was in Ulm I was too poor to have a car, but after three months in Aachen I had one, and when I first drove to conduct in my own car, my work was more valuable because it had brought me a car.

"People said, I have more respect for work which brings me this, and a house, of course. The poor Austrian people, in the backwoods, saw that the Germans on the other side had a better life. The train going across the border every day was full with people who brought things into Austria. What they wanted was to be taken by Germany."

In his fascinating study *The Meaning of Hitler*, Sebastian Haffner comments on Hitler's successes and achievements (between 1930 and 1941), citing this "economic miracle" that Karajan mentions, above all others. "By 1936," Haffner says, "there was full employment. Crying need and mass hardship had turned into modest but comfortable prosperity ... helplessness and hopelessness had given way to confidence and self-assurance ... the transition from depression to economic boom had been accomplished without inflation, at totally stable wages and prices. Not even Ludwig Erhard succeeded in doing that later in post-war Western Germany.

"It is difficult to picture the grateful amazement with which the Germans reacted to that miracle, which, more particularly made vast

numbers of German workers switch from the Social Democrats and
the Communists to Hitler after 1933 ... anyone who still rejected
Hitler seemed a querulous fault-finder."

Even as meticulous a historian as Joachim Fest seriously addresses
this issue in his biography of Hitler: "If Hitler had succumbed to an
assassination or an accident at the end of 1938," Fest writes, "few
would hesitate to call him the greatest of German statesmen, the
consummator of Germany's history. The aggressive speeches and
Mein Kampf, the anti-Semitism and the design for world dominion,
would presumably have fallen into oblivion, dismissed as the man's
youthful fantasies ..."

Haffner points out that Hitler accompanied his various accomplishments with carefully measured injections of fear: "On the whole, the
management and dosage of terror during the first years must be
described as a masterly psychological achievement by Hitler." A case
in point was the screw he turned upon Austria in the form of the
thousand-mark tariff he initiated, to be paid by every German who
crossed the border into Austria.

"This tariff had a great effect," Karajan says. "One thousand marks
was twenty-five percent of what a car cost. It ruined the tourist
industry in no time. All the middle-class hotels were empty. The
other hotels were reserved for people who had more money, mostly
foreigners."

When the Germans "invaded" Austria in 1938, the Austrians were
more than ready. "It started in Tyrol," Karajan says. "There they
opened the frontiers and the Germans came in and they were greeted
like liberators. The Austrians were much more 'Nazis' than the Nazis
themselves. Converts. The fanaticism of converts. Then came the war,
and people knew the truth: the machine of informing people was
built on lies."

It is easy to see how the fervent and very focused young Herbert
von Karajan, assertive and sure, willful and commanding, loaded with
talent, could have admired Hitler in 1933. Certain similarities between
himself and this fast-rising statesman could not have been lost on such
an ambitious, perceptive fellow as Karajan, who was himself preparing to take his own world (music) by storm. They were born within
fifteen days of each other in the month of April, nineteen years apart.
They both had artistic temperaments, and strong-willed, egocentric,
driven personalities. The list of comparisons is long, from their love
of fast cars and the operas of Wagner to their elitist attitudes. Hitler
knew what he wanted; so does Karajan. Both operated one-man
shows, and both demanded total control.

Those who know Karajan best, and those who have worked closely with him, protest that he was not even a moderately enthusiastic supporter of Nazism. Karajan is certainly not a follower, as all proper Nazis had to be. He once mentioned a slang expression for Nazi that translates literally as "bicyclist: he bows for the people who are higher," Karajan explained, "and beats the people who are lower with his feet." Bowing down isn't Karajan's style.

And yet, as the German magazine *Der Spiegel* noted (June 18, 1984): "During the regional party-day celebrations held in Aachen in 1935, Karajan directed 750 singers and 100 instrumentalists in the production of a cycle entitled 'Celebration of the New Front.' Created for Hitler, among others, the text was written by Baldur von Schirach." (Schirach later became head of the Hitler Youth Movement.) "Individual titles included, 'Hitler'; 'The Guardians of the Future'; 'O Land'; and 'Horst Wessel.' When it became necessary to celebrate Hitler's entry into Austria, their [Hitler's and Karajan's] shared homeland, Karajan quickly added Beethoven's freedom-drama *Fidelio* to Aachen's program."

Politics, beyond those relating to music, do not seem to interest Karajan. He is the complete political pragmatist, interested only in fortifying his position in the world of music. It behooves any leading musical figure in Europe to be on the friendliest possible terms with mayors, governors, presidents, or chancellors, especially in Austria and Germany, where a man in Karajan's position has nearly cabinet-member status. Then he can engage these officials on equal footing to secure the all-important budgets upon which the various musical organizations and festivals depend.

Perhaps it was Hitler who soured Karajan on political participation, because that early foray certainly got him into trouble. Trouble with the Nazi high command when he married a woman who was one-quarter Jewish (his second wife, Anita Gütermann, whom he married in 1942); trouble with the Allies after the war during the denazification process; trouble that continues to plague him to this day. Reaction to the Prieberg book was widespread—his findings were published in newspapers throughout the world—and Karajan and the Berlin Philharmonic are still not welcome in Israel. But more important, there are a few indications that his Nazi affiliation troubled him personally. He will not admit such a thing (no apologies!) or even discuss it. When the subject arises, his pat assertion is definite, strong: "I would not change anything I have done." And he quickly relegates the whole matter to his career: "What would have happened if I had not stayed in Germany, if I had gone to the U.S.? I don't know. I had one chance, to take over the Radio Symphony Orchestra of Stockholm. It was a pretty good orchestra. They liked me. But their schedule was very busy. I would have had to give up La Scala, and not been able to conduct in London. I declined. I do not think I would have accomplished as much if I had left. Probably I would have a job with a U.S. orchestra, but I would not have this all-around music activity. In the U.S., the music director is bound by too many duties. He does not have enough time."

But on another day, when Karajan was speaking about musical expression beginning with an emotional trigger in the composer's mind, one of his frequent digressions led him to psychoanalysis, and Carl Jung, whom he admired, and the notion that unconscious events must be relived emotionally to understand the basic reason for whatever complex was causing a problem. "This is difficult," Karajan said. "Man guards against the intrusion, but if he can, he beats it.

"I underwent psychoanalysis once," Karajan continued, "mainly for my own interest, of course; I wanted to know myself better. It lasted two years. It was after the war. Because after the war there was a time when I would walk down the street and all I would see were people with one leg, or one arm, or no eyes. I concentrated on only the worst things—the wounded, the mutilated. Time heals too, of course, but after analysis I knew that I had acquired another sense which helped me so much, and the music, of course. After analysis I never had another pessimistic phase. I concentrated on creation, not destruction."

Aachen is the base from which Karajan's career began to flourish. His first season there was 1935-36, and right away he was able to attract name soloists for guest appearances. The fact that his demand for high quality was published in the local newspaper helped attract the talent he sought. Also that season, he conducted the first of those occasional concerts for the Nazi command. It was on April 26, in Brussels, only a few days after the German army had taken the demilitarized Rhineland.

He began guest conducting in Stockholm and Amsterdam, and in June 1937, conducted for the first time at the Vienna State Opera (*Tristan und Isolde*). Following the performance, Karajan was offered the post of orchestra master. It was a plum for a young conductor, but Karajan refused the offer. Although not yet thirty, Karajan felt it would be against his nature to be on the third, or even the second rung of the ladder.

Karajan was operating from strength. As he said, he had control of

Aachen's musical life, he was bringing in desirable outside talent, and Vienna wasn't his only offer. There were two calls from Berlin. One was from the Berlin Philharmonic to guest conduct a concert. Karajan refused the tempting invitation because they would not guarantee him enough rehearsal time. The other call was from the Berlin State Opera with an invitation to do an opera in Berlin.

"Furtwängler had left the year before," Karajan says without further explanation. (Furtwängler had resigned from the State Opera in one of his early, frequent skirmishes with the Nazis. The premiere of Paul Hindemith's opera *Mathis der Maler* had been canceled by Hitler himself, who didn't like Hindemith's music. Furtwängler tried to reverse the decision by writing an open letter in defense of Hindemith's music. Unsuccessful, he resigned his posts at the State Opera, the Berlin Philharmonic, and as vice president of the Reichsmusikkammer. He subsequently returned to the Philharmonic, but not the State Opera.) "They were looking for someone to replace him. I was the last of six or eight people to be auditioned, and I was offered the post. I would not leave Aachen because I was happy there. I could not let them down. So I asked if I might have a guest contract for thirty performances, and I would share my time. I spent three days in Berlin, four days in Aachen. Two nights a week I spent on the train. People today tell me how tiring it is to commute, and I can only think back to those days. Never a holiday. Working seven days a week."

Karajan's season at Aachen lasted until June. He continued working with the Salzburg Festival, and with their summer academy in July and August. "The big names were there, of course, but they came, gave advice, and went away. The real work of training the youngsters fell to me. But it helped my English and made my contact with the music stronger. I expanded my repertoire and could compare pieces others did with how I did them.

"My guest conducting schedule was busy, and there was some broadcast work, and then in Berlin I did a new production of Mozart's *Magic Flute*. It was received as a sensation. It was a dangerous time in my life. Things were going so fast, I was having so much success that I was always apprehensive. Because wherever I went it was a sensation, people said it has never been like this. First, this put other conductors in opposition to me. Second, the expectations were at a level that one could not hope to fulfill. I would do one concert, and the next time I didn't know, the hall must come down around me because it is so wonderful; but it was just a concert, maybe a good concert. And people began to say that I was a fast-burning candle, that I would soon burn out."

The various pressures had their effect on Karajan. "In Aachen I began having problems with concentration. Perhaps I was over-worked. I couldn't express myself as I wanted. Maybe I felt I couldn't master the music. I felt enclosed in a case of glass, restricted. It was one of those changes men go through.

"I spent much time wondering how I could overcome this weakness of concentration," he recalls. "Then one day I was in a bookstore, and this book nearly jumped off the shelf and said 'read me.' It was an English book called *Yoga Explained*. So I bought it, and read it. I began exercises in the morning and more or less never stopped. I collected all the books on the subject I could find. I located teachers. There were periods when I did yoga for two hours every day, and it helped my concentration enormously."

Even a hobby is not treated casually by Karajan. When he is interested in something, he must pursue it, study it until he is an expert. So it was with yoga, which he began as an antidote for lapsing concentration, and continued lifelong because of its compatibility with his inner feelings about music. His knowledge of music, even in his twenties, was immense, his repertoire enormous for his age. He was an outstanding pianist, who had more understanding of the technical aspects of playing the various instruments than many of the players. For Karajan, the thorough student, that was the easy part. So, at thirty, he was already fully immersed in the confusing, complex, abstract elements of his profession: the transmission of his will; the attainment of sound quality; projecting the inner fabric of the music. The more he progressed with yoga, and later Zen, the more he realized that these meditational, intuitional philosophies contained important keys to the riddles he was confronting.

Today, Karajan states simply that for him, standing on the podium, moving in his understated manner, with his eyes closed, "conducting is a mystical experience. In a good moment, I forget completely the knowledge of what I do. I have trained my hands for thirty years. They are independent from what I feel. They will move of their own accord, and the music will run. To be able to take part in the real meaning of the music is something. It has to be done, and done again, until you forget your hands do the thing. In the meantime, if there is a singer who makes a mistake you can correct that, but it goes by so fast nobody knows. A musician who plays a long phrase and is suddenly going faster—that was me speeding him up because I felt the man was getting short of breath. So I let him play a little bit faster. The next day he comes and says to me 'I can't believe what happened.' I say, 'I was in you, and I felt you were short of breath, and you would have broken up the phrase, so I speeded up.' That is the kind of contact you have with the players, which is difficult to explain."

From the stories he tells, one learns that along the way, Karajan's eyes were very much open to a wide range of clues for achieving this oneness with music and orchestra. "I had the good luck," Karajan says, "that from my youth in my father's house I was always in contact with people who represented something. I admired them for their knowledge. They were best at what they did. So I saw what could be accomplished. I still have that feeling today. I don't spend time reading romances, novels. Instead I study because I know there is more to learn. In what we do there is always more to learn. This is what makes me seek the company of people who can teach me something—doctors, scientists, friends, whoever is better at something than I am. You know I can command. But if I see someone is much better than me I will be a slave."

He tells of the doctor who made his patients get undressed for their examination in front of him, rather than in a private cubicle. "By the time they had their clothes off," Karajan says, "the doctor knew what was wrong with them just by how they had moved during the process." And there is his oft-told story about the first time he took a horse over a jump: "The night before I could not sleep. I wondered what I would do to lift this massive thing over the fence. 'Don't disturb it,' my teacher told me. 'Set up at the right angle, and it will lift itself and you over the fence.'" There were more clues from skiing, from aviation, and from mountain climbing ("Every mountain has its own pace"). And from driving: "To be one with a road, you must know how fast to go over it. Lift your speed by 10 mph, and it will be a constantly nervous trip."

As Karajan has said, how to transmit one's convictions in front of an orchestra is something that must be inherent. But it can be polished, refined. His early insistence on conducting without a score in front of him was such a refinement. From the outset, Karajan has said that the score came between him and the music; it affected his attitude toward the music. "When I have learned scores," he says, "I try to forget at the end what I have seen, because seeing and hearing are two different things.

"We say we must know a piece *auswendig*—inside out, or by heart. Because then you have the ability to produce inside yourself a sound which does not exist. I can, if I want, while alone in a room without orchestra or tape player, hear the whole opera of *Tristan*."

When yoga jumped out at him, Karajan the scholar was committed to further research. When a particular book appealed to him, he would seek out its author for conversation—the way he has sought out the best drivers, skiers, and sailors to help him become proficient in those sports. In such a way he established a relationship with Pater LaSalle, a Zen master who is head of a monastery in Tokyo. "His book is called *Zen Buddhism*, and is signed with his religious name, Enomiya. It was so important to me, it gave me so much that I nearly have all of it in my head," Karajan says. "When finally I met him I felt as if I had known him twenty years." With the old Zen master, Karajan explored refined states of consciousness. "They give you a 'koan,' a short text where something is put that may seem ridiculous, like the idea of a ring that is in a pond, and how one retrieves it without getting the hands wet. For this they give you six hours of concentration. Because when you really can do it without stopping you get to another world of experience—a place where the intellect ceases to function. Then you feel that things are different, and they are.

"There is a nice story about the boy who comes to the guru and says he wants to study with him. The guru tells him to go into a small hut and concentrate on his parents. He tries, but cannot. So the guru asks him what is most dear to him. The boy says his buffalo. So he enters the hut and for three days concentrates on his buffalo. The guru goes to the hut and tells him to come out. The boy says he cannot. He cannot get his horns through the door. And the guru says, now you have taken the first step.

"The Zen master I know conducts communal meditations in the mountains with twenty-five people. He can feel if someone is sleepy, or on the verge of *sartori* (the state of illumination), and he assists them with this bamboo flyswatter on the back of the neck. He hits them, provides an adrenalin rush, as if you are driving around a curve and there is a car in the center of the road coming at you, and they reach another state of mind, a spiritual equilibrium.

"People who were tortured have achieved another state of mind, of that I am sure. When the first terrible pains were over and it went on, they didn't feel it anymore. I have had many illnesses, great pain—too much—and suddenly I went beyond it.

"In a way the orchestra and I do the same thing. We concentrate on a riddle which is the content of the music we do. In every rehearsal we concentrate on the riddle. We accept it the way the Catholics accept the miracle: 'I believe because it is absurd.' And then if we have the common focus of concentration, something else comes to life. And this we feel, not twenty-five of us, but a hundred of us. It is like taking off in the airplane. It lifts us up.

"The language of Buddhism says not 'I shoot,' or 'I operate,' it says 'it shoots—it operates.' The 'it' indicates that something behind you is governing everything. You are only giving it the first control, then you must let it go where it goes. When I forget I make music, I know that it is right.

"During any concert that is done with great preparation, I don't hear the music anymore—I just live it. It absorbs me. Every concert is a mystical experience, an ecstacy. You step out of yourself, or what you think is yourself. You can no longer command it. It is a form of grace."

If the musical pressures of his career were enervating during the Aachen years, the Nazi politics swirling around Karajan were equally complex, disturbing, and also very dangerous—guided, as they were, by whim and considerations of personal advantage. With the aim of removing Jews and their music from the German concert halls, Josef Goebbels had, by the mid-1930s, systematically "nationalized" all music, art, and literature under his Reichskulturkammer, where it could be meticulously fashioned and directed (propagandized and corrupted) for the maximum benefit of Hitler's Third Reich ideology. Membership in the Reichskulturkammer was mandatory. Those who dissented from "Nazi aesthetics"—a contradiction of terms, given the intellectual dead ends encountered by the maniacal need to redefine the racial foundation of the German musical classics—were threatened with concentration camps.

"They started by saying they didn't want the *St. Matthew Passion* to be sung," Karajan recalls. "Word was passed around. People lower in the Nazi management tried to enforce it. I said to them, 'Give me the document which forbids it and I won't play it.' Otherwise I would not stop playing one of the greatest musical pieces. They tried always to beat you down. People who wanted something and who were not strong enough did what they said and were given new posts because they were friendly with the party. I got myself in great trouble."

The strong-willed Karajan was fortunate in several regards. The Berlin State Opera, where he had a contract, was part of the Prussian State Theater system, and was under the control of Prussian Ministry President Hermann Goering. Berlin State Opera Intendant Heinz Tietjen, who had hired Karajan, had a good line to Goering. The procuring of the talented Karajan was a feather in Tietjen's cap. Karajan became an important man to Goering, who was determined to keep his parcel of music and theater out of Goebbels' hands.

Karajan had accepted the second invitation from the Berlin Phil-harmonic (1938) to guest conduct, and that turned out to be politically advantageous for him as well. This time he had been afforded suffi-cient rehearsal time, and on April 9, 1938, he had conducted the *Haffner* Symphony, *Daphnis and Chloë* by Ravel, and the Fourth Sym-phony of Brahms. The reviews had been most favorable; enough so to provoke the anxiety of Wilhelm Furtwängler, the Berlin Philhar-monic's music director, and a most powerful figure in the musical life of Germany. Karajan conducted the Berlin Philharmonic one more time—April 14, 1939. After that, he was pointedly kept away from the orchestra by Furtwängler, whose jealousy was obsessive. Karajan did, however, reconstitute a Sunday concert series by the Berlin State Orchestra (made up of members of the Berlin State Opera orchestra) that had fallen into limbo after the emigration of conductor Erich Kleiber. His foothold in Berlin was strengthened in spite of Furt-wängler's efforts to prevent it. "I announced a series of six concerts, which were sold out in one day," Karajan recalls. "This made the others furious, but I was untouchable. It was done and there was nothing to stop it."

Furtwängler, who had never joined the NSDAP, had tangled with the Nazi regime on many occasions, and had worked hard on behalf of many Jewish musicians in the Berlin Philharmonic. He was a thorn in the side of the regime for these reasons, but too august a musician (and too valuable politically) to be treated with anything but defer-ence. With virtually all of the Jewish conductors driven out of Ger-many (Bruno Walter, Fritz Busch, Erich Kleiber, Otto Klemperer), Furtwängler had become even more powerful. The Nazis needed to find some kind of leverage to keep Furtwängler at least a bit off balance, and it seems evident that in Karajan the Nazis found an ideal stimulus for Furtwängler's well-known paranoia.

Dr. Oliver Rathkolb of the Institute for Contemporary History (University of Vienna) summarized this situation in his doctoral dis-sertation: "In 1938, Heinz Tietjen, Intendant of the Prussian State Theater, brought [Karajan] to Berlin, and only two months later, after the second performance given by Karajan in the capital [*Tristan und Isolde*], the Berlin critic van der Nuell wrote about 'Das Wunder Karajan' [the Karajan wonder, the Karajan miracle]. This re-view was in part an attack against the aging Wilhelm Furtwängler. The question of how much Karajan was used to eliminate, or at least to neutralize, the artistic base of Furtwängler, who had become a political liability, has not been clarified to this date. However, there is proof that Karajan should function as a counterweight to

Karajan conducting
in 1957

Karajan and his wife, Eliette,
walking in Mayfair in 1965

Michael Glotz, Karajan's artistic collaborator for recordings

Gela Marina Runne, Karajan's film editor

Karajan and Peter Busse, his personal stage director, with the silver rose from *Der Rosenkavalier*

Helmut 'Richie' Reichmann, lighting director at the Festspielhaus

Dr Uli Märkle, managing director of
Karajan's film company, Telemondial

Lore Salzburger, Karajan's secretary

Günther Schneider-Siemssen, set designer

During the Salzburg Festival music dominates everything and display material appears in the most unlikely shop windows

One of Salzburg's horse-drawn carriages passes the front entrance of the Grosse Festspielhaus. The Hohensalzburg fortress rises in the background

Karajan rehearsing *Der Rosenkavalier* for the 1983 Salzburg Summer Festival: (*above*) coaching Vinson Cole and (*below*) playing Baron von Ochs in a scene with Agnes Baltsa

Karajan at the controls of his
Falcon 10 jet and (*right*) being
seen off by Francesco, his
major domo, and Josef, his
chauffeur, in the chartered
helicopter that he flew from
his house in Anif to Munich;
there he boarded his jet which
he flew on to Hannover
where he was to have a back
operation (June 1983)

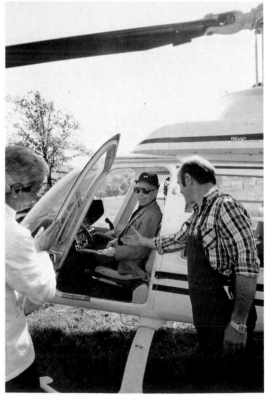

A water view of Karajan's childhood summer home at Grundlsee; located on the right of the picture with two chimneys

Karajan's home at Anif

Karajan holding a falcon during rehearsals of *Tannhauser* in Vienna in 1963

Karajan during orchestral rehearsals two years before his death on 16 July 1989, aged 81

Furtwängler. Karajan is reported to have been politically indifferent, but nevertheless had become a member of NSDAP in 1933.

"His agent, Rudolf Vedder, Obersturmfuehrer of the SS with excellent connection to H. Himmler, was therefore able to influence the events around the competition between Furtwängler and Karajan in Berlin."

Karajan has often said that Furtwängler (and Toscanini) had the strongest influence on him as a young conductor. While a student in Vienna, he would attend Furtwängler's concerts whenever he could. "He was an uncommonly fascinating personality," Karajan says of Furtwängler. "I went to his rehearsals as often as possible. Each was a reciprocal searching with the orchestra—quite different from those of Toscanini." But he says he never actually met Furtwängler until he (Karajan) invited him to Salzburg after the war to conduct at the festival. "We talked on the train," Karajan says without further exposition of this presumably momentous meeting with Furtwängler. "If he was jealous of me, I never sensed it from him."

On July 26, 1938, in the midst of the confusing times at Aachen, with Karajan commuting to Berlin every week, he married Elmy Holgerloef, the first operetta singer in the Aachen chorus. Not much is known about her, although people who have met her say she was a charming, delightful person. Soprano Elisabeth Grummer, who was married to the concertmaster in the Aachen orchestra during the time Karajan was music director there, and who frequently sang in Karajan's opera productions, told Lanfranco Rasponi (in *The Last Prima Donnas*), "I have only the finest memories of Elmy Holgerloef. What a superb artist she was in her repertoire, which was operetta. Very few have ever equalled her, for she had grace, style, and musicality." Love of nature is what brought her and Karajan together, though their marriage lasted only two years. She died in 1983.

Also in 1938, two young Austrians that Karajan had never heard of—and who were only vaguely aware of him—were making careful plans to leave Germany. Their names were Henry Alter and Ernst Haeusserman. Both of them would later be important to Karajan. But in 1938, they were simply two men taking the prudent course of emigration. Alter was one-half Jewish; Haeusserman, one-quarter. Such things were measured precisely in those days. Alter was a student at the State Academy of Music and Drama, and an assistant director when he could find work; Haeusserman an aspiring actor. They wore the letter *J* on their shirts and stood in line for days to get their quota number for the U.S. They got visitor's visas—the only visa available after March 1938—and arranged deferments from the army for the

alleged purpose of visiting the U.S. World's Fair. They were supposed
to take a German ship. Instead, they booked passage on the *U.S.S.
Aquitania*. They arrived in New York on August 1, 1939, and were
processed at Ellis Island. Alter was granted a six-week visit; Haeusserman, who had better connections in the U.S., was granted six months.
Four weeks after they arrived in the U.S., the war began. Neither
man would return to Austria until 1945, when they would be wearing
the uniform of the U.S Army.

They are very murky, those strife-torn days in Berlin that were
leading inexorably to a war that would be accompanied by racial
persecution and atrocities of the vilest order. The style of those in
power in any country is quickly reflected in the streets, where it is
emulated by the population, which never fails to learn the rules of
the game and then play to best advantage—especially when the power
is vested in a popular dictatorship. The atmosphere of fear created by
the Nazis fostered deceit, back-stabbing, double-crossing, blackmail,
and physical abuse. Even those closest to Hitler bobbed and weaved
to further ingratiate themselves with that unpredictable and dangerous
psychopath—or to save their own skins. So it went through the ranks,
with the paranoia and hysteria swelling to the approaching beat of
boot-heels echoing on night pavement.

Even in a benign society the art and culture business has more than
its share of rough, nasty edges. In Nazi Germany, sequestered as they
were for the good of the order, and as important as they were to the
very fiber of life at all levels, art and culture carried on in a particularly vicious jungle. Music, particularly, had long been hailed by
German intellectuals as the most spiritually ennobling of all the arts,
a reflection of the loftiest of human aspirations. When it came to
music, everyone, Hitler included, wanted to exert influence.

There is no easy window into what went on. Even Prieberg's
monumental book—the product of twenty years of source gathering,
329 interviews, and letters and research from 192 archives—was criticized for shifting blame from the totalitarian state to the musicians
("Do musicians learn anything but music?" Prieberg laments toward
the end of the book). As Dana Mack wrote of the book in *The New
Criterion*, "[Prieberg] refuses to acknowledge that even for famous
musicians, like Furtwängler, who had the choice of emigration, love
of homeland and family may have been the regime's allies in enforcing
obedience."

Many who were there, and remember, seem to fall quickly into
the old survival mode, as if even now there could be recriminations

if the wrong things were said. Others are reluctant to speak at all about those days. From Karajan we have some glimpses that enlarge the picture somewhat. He says of his agent Vedder, for instance, that he first encountered him in Aachen at the Karlsruhe State Theater. "There were two Vedders, father and son. They were sometimes rough people, but good businessmen. One was in sales for the Steinway Piano Company. The other got me invited to conduct the Berlin Philharmonic, but there would be no rehearsal. I said I preferred not to do it, and I would want four rehearsals. I told them I was not yet the person they needed. So I waited, and it worked.

"Vedder was a personal friend. I knew suddenly toward the end of the war that he was in SS. I understood why. His artists were like his children. It was his duty to protect them. He used to say, 'You don't need me when all is well, only when things are difficult.' But the Reichsmusikkammer sent spies into the various orchestras. They would listen to what the musicians talked about, observe what they bought, and write nasty reports about them that got them in trouble. Within SS, Vedder could stop these things and protect his clients."

But Karajan says it was Tietjen, not Vedder, who manipulated the competition between him and Furtwängler. Why or how Tietjen became interested in Karajan is not clear. Perhaps in his capacity as Intendant of the Berlin State Opera, he simply had the eyes and ears for recognizing talent that were the requirements of his job. With Furtwängler gone, and with Furtwängler's replacement, Clemens Krauss, having gone to Munich, Tietjen was left without a "name" opera director. So he went after Karajan, and from the beginning found he had his hands full. Karajan was not the typical young conductor, grateful for handouts.

Tietjen began a correspondence with Karajan, offering him the opera *Der Bürger von Calais*. In his reply, Karajan said that would be fine, but first he would like to conduct *Fidelio*, *Tristan und Isolde*, and *Die Meistersinger*. Tietjen made it clear that Wagner operas were out of the question, since they were under his direction. He offered *Carmen*. Karajan suggested they forget the whole thing. Tietjen suggested a meeting, saying that he was charmed by Karajan, and offering him *Tannhäuser*. Karajan thanked him, saying that he wanted to do *Fidelio*, *Tristan*, and *Die Meistersinger*. Karajan said it was not a condition, just a request. Tietjen replied, "you are right; I was in error."

After Karajan's first rehearsal at the opera, Tietjen called him over. As Karajan recalls it, "he said, 'You are a great meteor.' I started to say something, but he interrupted me. 'Say nothing. Keep conducting as you have. I have heard your rehearsal and we don't need to discuss these things any more.'"

And so Karajan conducted *Fidelio* on September 30, 1938, and *Tristan* ("the Karajan wonder") on October 21. On December 18, he did *The Magic Flute.*

The relationship between Tietjen and Karajan was one of convenience. They were not a good mix, since both men were too used to having things their own way. "He was selfish," Karajan says. "He couldn't stand other opinions. And I knew that I had not been born to obey others. We had terrible fights. But Tietjen was at odds with Furtwängler, who had left him because of the Hindemith controversy. I was the tool of Tietjen to be used against Furtwängler.

"It got to be like a cockfight, with people betting on Furtwängler or me. There were personal notices in the newspaper: 'Seek Karajan concert—will trade two Furtwängler tickets,' or 'I seek Karajan subscription, will give five onions.' Goebbels didn't care what Furtwängler said about the Nazis. It was serious for Furtwängler, but not enough for Goering and Goebbels to get into an argument about it. But Tietjen used it, even when he saw that Goebbels would never replace Furtwängler."

The Goebbels diaries are specific about his continuing support of Furtwängler. In December 1940 he writes, "Furtwängler is complaining about Karajan, who is getting too much fawning coverage in the press. I put a stop to this. Furtwängler is behaving very decently. And when all is said, he is our greatest conductor." And a few days later, "Row between Furtwängler and Karajan. Karajan is getting himself feted in the press. Furtwängler is right. He is, after all, a world figure. I put a stop to it."

Against this background of political intrigue which he is recalling some forty-five years later, Karajan interjects a curious remark: "I had not the slightest idea of what was going on. I only wanted to conduct in peace." It would hardly seem possible that he could not have known what was going on. The peace he sought, in any event, was still a long way off, because Tietjen suddenly betrayed Karajan. Exactly why he turned against the man who had served his purposes so well is still not clear. Perhaps Tietjen acted on direct orders from Goebbels; one doesn't know. In any case, Tietjen pulled the rug from beneath Karajan. Karajan read about it in the newspaper.

"I picked up the paper and was astounded to read that Tietjen had given Furtwängler an opera that he had promised to me. I was so outraged I nearly lost control. I was in Tietjen's office in three seconds. He said to me, 'When Furtwängler comes back into this house, you will leave by the back entrance. Do not try to understand. This is high politics.' I told him I only knew what he had promised to me. He changed the subject: 'You have done such a good *Magic Flute*. Why not do it again?' *The Magic Flute* was no substitute for *Meistersinger*.

"Then I changed my tack. I wouldn't argue with Tietjen. I am a good actor—I have even rehearsed the girl opposite Hans Sachs—so I decided to copy him. 'Ah yes,' I said, 'I must think, yes, that might be a great idea, to do *Magic Flute* again, a little breather after Wagner. Well, we have to talk further, perhaps after a few days.'

I went to see my dentist. His daughter was the private secretary to Mrs. Goebbels. I told him to look at my teeth because I was going to enlist. I had met a general in the Luftwaffe some months before. I had told him I wanted to fly. He said I was over age. I couldn't be a fighter pilot, but he said he could make me a courier. He told me if I ever got drafted to let him know and he would put in a request for me. So my dentist looked at my teeth, and he called his daughter, who contacted Goebbels through his wife.

"I went to see Goebbels. He had this intense concentration on your person. Only you existed for him when he was speaking with you. I felt this immediately. He said, 'so you want to leave us.' I said yes, to defend my country. He said 'why not defend it with your baton? We will send you to Rumania, Bulgaria.' I said, the baton is nice, but the stick of an airplane is better. He said, 'When the war is finished, you can fly. For now, please conduct. You know how to handle people.'"

Edge Leslie says it was Goebbels who tried to have Karajan drafted. As a result, there is an apocryphal story that Karajan joined the SD (Sicherheitsdienst—the Security Service) to become immune from the draft. The Nazis suspected a dodge, so the story goes. So to prove himself, Karajan had to fire two musicians from the Aachen Orchestra for listening to an Allied radio broadcast. "Legge chuckled about this," Leslie says. "His remark was, 'Probably they were bad players.'"

The Sicherheitsdienst was the intelligence branch of the SS. Its purpose was to discover the enemies of the National Socialist concept and initiate countermeasures through official police authorities. The Gestapo and the SD were closely related groups. At the Nuremberg Trials, it was found to be a crime to have been a member of the SD, but members were tried individually. Karajan's alleged SD membership was not proved by the Allied Denazification Commission. And Karajan won't talk about it. "These are not important things," he says, when asked. History has absolved him. So be it.

In amongst this tangle, there is a rumor that Goebbels, the wom-

anizer, wanted to draft Karajan so he would have free access to Karajan's second wife, Anita. Karajan says he never heard of such a thing.
In any case, despite his self-proclaimed willingness, Karajan did not
serve in the military during the war.

Karajan's lot in Berlin was not improving. Tietjen had turned on
him, Goebbels had administered what sounds like a brush-off, and the
Führer himself was less than enthusiastic about Karajan's approach.
Karajan says he met Hitler only once, for a handshake, when he
conducted a *Meistersinger* production. According to Karajan, Hitler
stormed out of the theater during the performance, angered by one
of the male singers, who was obviously inebriated and causing havoc
with the proceedings. (Hitler knew the part word for word.)

"Naturally, Hitler demanded to know what caused the problem,"
Karajan says, "and someone suggested I never used a score. Furtwängler was asked if it was possible to do the opera without a score,
and he said no, it wasn't. So Tietjen said that I must have the score
on the podium. So I did, but turned it backwards. I wouldn't have
liked to deal with me at that time. I was terrible."

There is one note in Goebbels's diaries (November 1940) that refers
to Hitler and Karajan: "Midday with the Führer ... I tell him about
Vienna. About the city's love of music, about Furtwängler and Professor Sauer. . . . He praises the old school's capacity for hard work, its
nimbleness, systematic approach, and good, basic technique. The
Führer has a very low opinion of Karajan and his conducting ... "

In October 1942 Karajan got into further trouble with the authorities by marrying Anita Gütermann, who was (according to the Nuremberg racial statute book) one-quarter Jewish. (Karajan's previous
marriage to Elmy Holgerloef had been officially terminated, one sup-
poses—perhaps as casually as it began.) Gütermann was from a pros-
perous industrial family. Her relationship with Karajan would last
well beyond their divorce in 1958, as we shall see.

Next, Karajan lost his job in Aachen. He was still commuting
frequently to Berlin. Even after the blowup at the State Opera, he
continued with the Sunday concert series, and he was guest conducting wherever he could. In the spring of 1941 he was in Italy on tour
with the Berlin State Opera (apparently he and Tietjen had made a
temporary truce). On one hand, the tour was viewed as an enormous
success. Others called it a Nazi propaganda effort. But as Edge Leslie
says, "Anyone working in Berlin in those days would have given
anything to get work outside Germany. The tour of Italy saved
Karajan. It was an enormous success." But it cost him his job.

Karajan picked up a newspaper in Rome and read that he had been dismissed as general music director in Aachen because he was absent too frequently. So now he was truly afloat in Berlin, with his Jewish wife and his uncompromising musical working prerequisites, at the geographical center of impending peril. He says that during this time he often took refuge at the country estate of the Swiss ambassador, whom he had met at some musical affair, where he would ride horseback and relax, and no doubt imagine what it would be like to conduct in peace.

He kept working, however and wherever he could. Some of the jobs were very strange. One in particular casts revealing light upon the absurd extremes that existed in Germany in 1942. "There was a man named Glasmeier," as Karajan tells it, "who was general director of German Radio. He had been a cavalry officer in World War I. He was a typical Prussian aristocrat who loved horses, high society functions, and women. When the war ended, he had a good knowledge of the social order, so he would approach wealthy families and offer to trace their lineage for them, construct their family tree. So he mingled with the rich, and kept next to the good life.

"After he became head of German Radio, he made a plan. He said to himself, Bayreuth is for the Wagner Festival, but Bruckner has nothing. We should make something for Bruckner. He knew Hitler loved Bruckner. He knew of a convent twenty kilometers from Linz. It included a church and a great library. When the Nazis came it was secularized. So Glasmeier commandeered this convent, then he went to see Hitler. He extolled the virtues of the convent, the beauty of the courtyard, the perfect setup for the concerts that Furtwängler would conduct there, the pleasures of the Spanish Riding School in the moonlight. He was a salesman. He told Hitler the convent must be restored and made into a shrine for Bruckner.

"Hitler went for it. He provided unlimited money. Furnishings were bought in Paris. A coach and six matched horses were obtained—the coach was light blue damask inside. Glasmeier took a corner room for his office. From the windows he could look down the left cloister 120 meters; down the right cloister, 80 meters. There was an endless number of rooms, incredible space, all beautifully restored. He assembled a personal orchestra of twenty-five pieces.

"He lived there, and how! He wore a monk's coat lined with sable and a mortarboard. He carried a silver cane. Each evening he dined with the old master of the convent.

"He decided he needed a bigger orchestra, and that was easy. He was head of German Radio, and there were many radio orchestras to choose from. So he auditioned all the orchestras with the radio system and took players he wanted. They would have one rehearsal a day, with the conductor always being a guest. Every Sunday there was a concert before the altar. The main piece was always Bruckner.

"I met Glasmeier in Berlin. He asked me, will you come? And I said, of course. I was so impressed by the place. The orchestra was wonderful.

"After rehearsal a man came to my room. 'Are you happy?' he asked. I told him yes, I was happy. 'Do you have the right spirit?' I said yes. To make sure of this, he said he would take me to the crypt under the convent. It was dark and damp. There were niches in the walls full of skulls and bones. In the center of the room were Bruckner's bones. 'You are beneath where the orchestra will play,' this man said. 'Bruckner has never heard his Eighth Symphony. You have the opportunity to play it for him. Now you will have ten minutes alone with him.' And he shut the door and left me there in the dark."

It is difficult to learn much of what Karajan did between 1940 and 1945, when the war ended. He continued his six concerts a year with the Berlin State Orchestra, moving from hall to hall as Allied bombing took its toll. And there are brief notices in old newspapers about him conducting here and there. There were many concerts in those days (one in Paris in particular) where he conducted the Nazi "Horst Wessel" song prior to the program. And there was some job hunting. Karajan tells of his efforts to secure the music director's job in Dresden. "Karl Böhm had left Dresden and gone to Vienna." he says. "So I inquired about the position. I needed to have an opera house to myself. But the party said 'no, we don't want him.' So I never did really apply. I left for Italy two or three months before the war was over."

Perhaps the way Karajan feels about these years is best revealed by the otherwise very complete, four-page, single-spaced, official biographical summary of his career that Lore Salzburger hands out to inquiring reporters. It notes family history, the first piano lesson, important concerts, various job appointments, marriages, festival appointments, his major awards—even his daughters' birthdates. Hardly a year in the chronology is without a highlight, with one exception: 1940 to 1945. The listing for 1940 is his marriage with Gütermann (a misprint—the marriage took place in 1942). The listing for 1945 is "passes the war's end in Italy." In between is blank space. Amid such Austrian attention to detail, the omission is a glaring one. The fact that even now, toward the end of his life, Karajan refuses to be forthcoming about those years, indicates that he prefers blank space to what might be "awkward facts."

★   ★   ★

Karajan left Germany in late 1944, about six months before the war ended. "The bombardment was becoming more severe every day," he says. "If they saw you in the street they would hand you a gun. I had a friend in Milano who was director of a radio station. From him I got an invitation to do a radio concert. It was just a pretense. Then after I got permission to go I had to find a plane. This was almost impossible, because the flights were saved for generals. For ten days I ran around Berlin airport looking for a way. Finally I found a man, an official at the airport, who was a music lover. He said he would do what he could. He took my number and said when he called I would have to be there in thirty minutes. I remember when he called I ran out into the street and there was a bombardment. I ran through the debris and got there at the last moment."

Karajan checked into a cheap hotel in Milan and waited. Anita was apparently with him. For going underground, the Germans would have punished Karajan by death. If recognized as a Nazi German, the Partisans in Milan would have shot him on the street. The Karajans met an architect named Aldo Pozzi. Pozzi was a music lover who immediately invited the Karajans to move in with him. Gun battles between the Germans, the Americans, and the Partisans broke out continuously on the streets. Two weeks after he had taken the Karajans in, Karajan says Pozzi was grabbed on the street and shot for harboring Germans. (This contradicts what Karajan has said previously. In Ernst Haeusserman's book, *Herbert von Karajan*, it was reported that Pozzi was not shot for harboring the Karajans.)

According to Karajan, he then took to the hills outside Milan, near Lake Como, where for six months he and Anita lived a hand-to-mouth existence. "I was warned that I should report in every day to be transported back to Germany. I knew it could be my death. I said constantly to myself, what will happen now? I decided if I could come through with my health intact I would not mind anything I did until things were normal. With persecution, there is always lots to go through that is unpleasant, but all of it just passed over me. I said to myself, if I let this unpleasantness influence me, if I acquire hatred in myself, I will not be able to make music. The policeman must hate or he can't kill the man who is harming other people. But the musician must not. If he gets involved in emotions like that, he loses his personality. This is quite clear. So all the unpleasantness ran off me as rain runs off the roof.

"At the end of the war, I made the most of my time in Italy. I studied Italian. I made a very strict schedule for myself, and studied as hard as I could. I got into discussions with people as much as possible to improve my speech, and this is where I really learned to use the language as I do.

"I remember one thing very clearly, how in three afternoons I saw all the beauty of the upcoming spring in Italy, and I thought that in two weeks I might be here no more. And I said if that happens, I will take nothing bad back with me.

"We were not living with friends. We were black sheep. It would have been damaging for the friends to be with us because I was not cleared at the time. I could not be invited to La Scala because the Allied Forces said we have to clear all the artists, see what they have done politically, and determine if they have been repatriated."

Letter from Rome Area Allied Command, APO 794, U.S. Army, Office of the AC of SM G-2; TO: Counter Intelligence Corps, Rome; December, 1945; Subject: Herbert von Karajan—1. According to SHAEF records, the above person described as General Musik Direktor, born Salzburg on 5th April 1908 was an agent of the Sicherheitsdienst (S.D.), Aachen.* 2. It is known that subject was recently in Rome and his wife is said to reside at the Albergo San Giorgio, Rome. 3. Will you please conduct an investigation and submit a report to this office.†

"I went to Trieste in mid-September, because it was closest to Austria, and I had heard they were sending some transports into Austria. I ran into an old friend, a colonel in the British Army [Trieste was occupied by the British]. He said, 'what the hell are you doing here?' 'Looking for a way to get back,' I told him. He said, 'why don't you conduct?' I said, 'you know exactly.' He said, 'conduct for us. We do what we want. You will conduct. Are you ready to conduct three concerts with us?' Because the British were reorganizing art and culture, as it was with all the occupation forces. I said I could think of nothing better. They had quite a decent orchestra. You see, I was so full of music after six months that I just took them and it went. He wanted to do more concerts, and he said if I did them, he would see I got British transport back to Austria.

"We were transported in lorries like the beasts. Everything was in shambles, as you can imagine. We learned what had to be done and how you must be cleared for permission. Salzburg was under American occupation. People were standing in the road to see a man who

*Karajan's alleged membership of the SD was not proved by members of the Allied Denazification Commission.

†The National Archives; Record Group 260, ACA Austria; ISB; Theater and Music Section Reports. All subsequent military documents excerpted in this section are from this source.

had the power to tell them that they were not Nazis. I was so fed up I would not do it. Later on, when they got interested, they said, 'why didn't you come?' and I said, 'mein Herr, I am young, I can wait. I will wait until I have the right to conduct.'" In Salzburg, Karajan stayed with his parents.

Letter (excerpt) from Counter Intelligence Corps, Rome, to Rome Area Allied Command; 4 January 1946: 2. Subject is believed to be in Salzburg, Austria. Mrs. von Karajan ... was interviewed 21 December 1945 ... and divulged the following information: subject is presently in Salzburg to clarify his personal affairs with Allied Authorities before continuing with his career as an orchestra conductor. In a recent letter, subject informed his wife that his affairs in Salzburg were being cleared up favorably and that he hoped to join her soon. Mrs. von Karajan has not seen the subject for two months. During the war the subject had appeared professionally in various European cities, including Berlin and Aachen. Subject had been permitted very few appearances in Germany, however, because of his disfavor with the Nazis which grew out of Mrs. von Karajan's Jewish ancestry. Before going to Salzburg, subject had been in Trieste in his professional capacity.

While in Salzburg, Karajan was contacted by the head of the Vienna Philharmonic, who invited him to conduct the orchestra. "They had no conductors," Karajan says. "So I went to Vienna and did a concert. That was the beginning of 1946. Of course it was a roaring success. Then they wanted more concerts, but there was opposition from the Russians. A four-party commission was governing Austria and Germany, and of course there were always quarrels. Everything had to be approved by all four parties. There were always arguments about petrol. The Russians wanted all the petrol. They were rebuked, so they said they had to personally clear me. I went before the commissar on the day of the second concert. He held me from 9 A.M. until 2 P.M. At this point the first violin, who was president of the orchestra, came and told the man he had to make up his mind because the people were already standing in line for the 3 P.M. concert. I quickly changed and made the concert. After that the Russians said, 'No more.'"

Henry Alter was present at the first concert Karajan did with the Vienna Philharmonic. Alter had arrived in Berlin on July 6, 1945, with the first American occupation units. He was with an Army information control team as film, theater, and music officer. In November he left for Vienna. On January 18, 1946, he heard Karajan and the Vienna Philharmonic play Richard Strauss's *Don Juan*, a Haydn symphony, and Brahms's First.

Sitting in his office at Manhattan's Cooper Union College, where he was dean of continuing education until his retirement in 1984, Alter vividly recalls that concert. "It was a seminal experience for me," he says quietly. Alter is a slight man. His skin is very white, his eyes pale behind rimless glasses. On his desk is a framed photograph of Karajan, personally inscribed. In 1983, Alter helped Karajan's youngest daughter, Arabel, with her successful application to the Parsons School of Design in New York. He also helped find her an apartment.

Alter's lifelong association with Karajan is tied immutably to that postwar concert, that "seminal experience." Not for a moment does one suspect overstatement. Strauss's *Don Juan* is melodic, uplifting, evocative, emotionally stirring even in recording. And the Brahms First is a treasured possession that becomes further enriched with each hearing. Both are memorable, with themes that haunt. One can barely imagine the mighty impact of that concert on the war-ravaged, music-starved audience of Viennese.

"Like any well brought-up Viennese," Alter said, "I had been going to concerts since I was a child. But I had never had an emotional experience before. The hall was cold. People were wearing overcoats. The *Don Juan* was incredible, the Brahms unforgettable. After the concert I hung around. I went backstage and Karajan was sitting by himself in the green room. I asked him if anyone was with him. He said no. I asked if he needed a ride home. He said that he did. I had been at the concert with my mother and a young lady. We drove him home in a rickety old army vehicle.

"He was supposed to do more concerts," Alter says. "I was captivated by him as a musician, but it was clear we would have to blacklist him for a long time. It would be penalizing the public more than him. He understood. He knew me as one who had to enforce the edict that he could not work in public, but he respected me for that. Our conversations were cold and matter of fact. With one exception. He said, 'If you want me to stay for interrogation, you must do something to prevent me from starving.' So I got him supplied with food and necessities from army stores.

"There was one Russian officer in particular, a Colonel Epstein, who was opposed to all Nazis. He knew we wanted a smooth resurgence of cultural life, but he could not forget a particular scene he had come across at a concentration camp as part of a liberation unit: he had seen the earth moving from the people beneath it who had been hastily buried alive."

When the Russians blocked Karajan's concerts in Vienna, an emissary from the Army Information Services Branch, Otto de Pasetti, theater and music officer, was sent to interview Col. Epstein, the Russian censorship officer. "Karajan is known as a strong Nazi," Epstein opened. "He got many honors in Berlin. He was a very successful conductor under the Nazi regime, joining the Nazi party in 1935, and hence he is an 'old Nazi.'"

De Pasetti reported: "I gave a short story of Karajan's family, education, and professional background. [I] described him as an arrogant and ambitious and not very sympathetic character with a strong personality and a great power of will, whose mentality makes it very unbelievable that he was a Nazi supporter or even only a sympathizer.... The reasons Karajan joined the party were purely professional. He encountered difficulties in Ulm and also in Aachen. Those difficulties were encountered through his character. In order to strengthen his position he became a party member. In 1942 he married a partly Jewish woman. At this point [I] was interrupted by one of the woman officers (Russian) who mentioned the fact that he could not marry a Jewish woman under the Nazi regime. [I] replied that the woman was half or quarter Jewish and Karajan had to meet hard consequences. He was put before a party court and there he declared to quit the party. In the future his concerts were considerably reduced and in order to make a living he had to conduct in Italy and Hungary." De Pasetti softened Epstein up somewhat, but he didn't get him to change his mind about Karajan's concerts with the Vienna Philharmonic. Nor did the controversial press release published in the Vienna *Kurier* on December 21, 1945: "The Theater and Music Section of the American Information Control Service is of the opinion that Herbert von Karajan had paid sufficiently for his membership in the Nazi party through the stand which he took for his non-Aryan wife and the consequences of this step." While this struggle was going on over Karajan's person, a man arrived in Vienna who would have a strong and lasting positive effect on Karajan's fortunes. This was Walter Legge, the highly regarded producer of classical records for the British firm of EMI. With the hostilities over, Legge was on a scouting trip. He had arrived in time to slip into one of Karajan's rehearsals with the Vienna Philharmonic, and he had been impressed. In *On and Off the Record*, Legge recalls his first encounter with a man he would work closely with for the rest of his life.

"I was absolutely astonished at what the fellow could do. The enormous energy and vitality he had were hair-raising. It's a great experience to watch him rehearse, to see him take a piece for the first time with an orchestra.... He just reads it straight through, then corrects. And I have never heard him raise his voice at a rehearsal. Hardly a word is spoken. The whole thing done visually. He knows exactly what he wants, and has this strange, quiet authority. As he has said to me many times, 'If I don't raise my voice, they'll listen to what I say, and the less I speak, the more important each word is.'

"[Then] the Vienna Philharmonic phoned to tell me that the Russians had forbidden Karajan to appear and the concert was canceled. So I rang him up and said that I was awfully sorry to hear about th's, and would he like to have lunch with me and talk things over? He said that he was sorry, he was going to sleep but he could see me at 4 o'clock. So at 4 o'clock I went to the appointed address. I knew how difficult it was to get anything in Vienna at that time, so I took him a bottle of whisky, a bottle of gin, and a bottle of sherry. Years after he told me that after I left that evening he divided each of those bottles into thirty portions so that he had one drink for each of the next ninety days, but he did not touch them that day.... He has that sort of iron will.

"He was living in the most uncomfortable conditions on the eighth floor of a block of flats, sharing a room with people he didn't know. And we started to talk. I tried to make it a business conversation but he was obviously out for a real chat. He probably had not talked to anybody for a long time....We met almost daily, and the negotiations for the contract went on for six months.... He was in no hurry to sign, even though he had no money and no work—and no possibility of work—yet he had an inner sense of repose that I have never met in any man in similar circumstances ...

"Our collaboration became the foundation upon which Karajan's great fame and fortune were built.... He more than any other conductor, except perhaps Stokowski, was really made by gramophone recordings...."

Karajan remembers the meeting with Legge:

"He came after the second concert was forbidden. He was in Vienna. I was a little bit confused, and suddenly a man is there saying he would like to make a contract with me. I said how can you say that—you have seen what has happened here. And he said I have the power to make you a contract. He had cleverly done one thing: he had formed a Swiss company. That gave him the right to talk with 'the enemy,' because an English firm could not make a contract with an Austrian at this time.

"His people came in with new equipment, but it was still 78 rpm with a three-and-a-half-minute playing time. We recorded at the

Musikfreunde, Goldene Hall. I could do it because I had no job. The Vienna Philharmonic must first of all do their service at the opera. After that they can do other things if there is time. So I waited, and if they suddenly said next week we can do three recordings, then we would do it. We began with the Eighth of Beethoven.

"The equipment was enormous. The cutting was done on wax. It looked like a big cake."

Karajan says he didn't stay in Vienna for long that year. Short of patience with the bureaucratic red tape that engulfed him, he went to St. Anton. "I said, 'I am so fed up I will come back only when the Allies are gone from Vienna.' I was in the mountains that I love, and I said, 'I will wait here.' I spent a year there and in ski huts further into the mountains with an instructor and a guide." (How Karajan financed this venture is not apparent.) "I had time to think about my repertoire and consider new aspects of it. For a year I had a self-imposed retreat. No playing of music, just thinking about it."

Karajan left the mountains that winter long enough to take part in preparations for the Salzburg Festival and become a cause célèbre. The Allies were doing all they could to put the festival back on its feet that year. It would be the first festival since the war concluded. Karajan and Furtwängler were the two best conductors available. But Furtwängler was far from being cleared—although not an NSDAP member, his musical eminence during the war (he was officially a "Prussian State Councillor" in addition to the other high posts he had held) would hold him up longer than Karajan—and while some of the Allies (and the Austrians) wanted Karajan at Salzburg, there was no way to rationalize his participation.

"Music wasn't the big question," Karajan says. "The problem was finding rooms and places to eat. The city was full of occupation forces. There was no place to sleep.

"Between February and August I had traveled from Vienna to Salzburg eighteen times," Karajan says. "Each trip took twenty-four hours. I would wait on the Russian-manned frontier to be treated like a beast in order to consult about how to make Salzburg work. It was agreed that if clearance came by August, I would conduct. There were two operas to be given that year, *Figaro* and *Rosenkavalier*." The problem was, there was no way to enlist Karajan's musical talents without confronting his political past.

In 1945, when Henry Alter arrived in Vienna and took stock of the cultural situation and how it was being affected by the denazification proceedings, he wrote a memorandum containing some provocative observations. "[Over the past nine months] we have not succeeded in cleaning out Nazi influence but have very severely impaired cultural activities through indiscriminate denazification measures.... European artists have always considered it their privilege to be honored and flattered by the existing governments without giving them any true allegiance and without, in fact, ever acquiring a political conscience.... The fact that they continued to work [under Nazism] is partly due to the professional vanity without which they would not be artists.... If it is assumed that the artists should have refused to be active under the Nazis, then there are no differences and everyone belonging to that profession who received a salary while the Nazis were in power should be banned.... As a possible solution to the problem it is suggested that only crimes against an orderly society be charged against artists."

As plans for the 1946 festival took shape, the following letter was received in the Theater and Music Section, Information Services Bureau (U.S. Army). It was from the acting municipal music director in Aachen, Professor Th. B. Rehmann, who went slightly overboard in his steadfast support of Karajan:

I was in the closest collaboration with Mr. von Karajan in the years of his work in Aachen ... both privately and in his official actions, he openly disclosed his rejection of National Socialism. His policies as Generalmusikdirektor were, pervasively and consistently, no less than a provocation to the NSDAP [Nazi Party] leadership of Aachen. Warnings and well meant advice were ignored by him. [He] ... publicly scorned demands by the local party leadership that instead of the customary great religious choral works he perform others, recommended by that leadership ... the suggestion that he advanced his career by pro-Nazi acts is simply absurd. To the contrary: I have personal, positive knowledge that Aachen's party officials left no stone unturned to derail Mr. von Karajan's career....

I was present during a telephone conversation between Mr. von Karajan and the then Kreisleiter [top regional party boss], in which Mr. von Karajan refused, with firmness bordering on rudeness, to remove from the schedule such works as the G-minor Mass and St. Matthew Passion of Bach and the Missa Solemnis of Beethoven, until and unless the Kreisleiter were able to suggest to him works of comparable greatness. Verbatim, he said then, "The time when budding composers of the Hitler Youth reach the point where they can create works of this rank is still far in the future."

Shortly before he left Aachen, Mr. von Karajan was planning a great Bruckner concert featuring the Fifth Symphony.... He wished [also] to have the Cathedral choir sing the *a capella* motets, on the grounds that they particularly suit the Fifth Symphony (subtitled the "Sacrale"). [But these pieces] had been officially rejected by the Reich Propaganda Ministry. To this, and in the presence of numerous singers nearby (who had to overhear parts of the conversation), Mr. von Karajan's very audible response was, "Really ... then we'll do it for sure!"

Many other incidents of this type could be reported.

The integrity of Mr. von Karajan's attitude is further attested by his consistent refusal to conduct at official party-sponsored concerts, trouping of the Colors and similar occasions. This caused strong resentment in party circles, but which left him quite unimpressed. When he spoke of his own membership in the party—even in the presence of strangers—he was in the habit of joking about it. Another favorite way in which to underscore his dislike of Naziism was to stress his favorite conductors: Toscanini and Bruno Walter, which he did publicly....

The situation with Karajan and the Salzburg Festival of 1946, however, suggests that denazification had become thoroughly ensconced as an untamed, bureaucratic animal. The care and feeding of this beast fell to a large chain of occupational, multilingual military personnel representing four nations. Each of them, it seemed, had a personal (if not highly emotional) stake in the beast. The breadth of the conundrum is evidenced by the following excerpts from U.S. Army documents of the time:

—Report #33 from Hq US Forces in Austria, Information Services Branch, Otto de Pasetti, Theater and Music Officer, dated May 31, 1946: 4. A list of all members of the Salzburg Festival was submitted to this office by the Festival Committee. Herbert von Karajan was listed as the main conductor, although he is not yet allowed to perform.... Request is hereby made to get a quick decision on Karajan. Karajan is scheduled to conduct 10 opera performances and two concerts.... It is obvious that they will try to put pressure on the Allies and especially on the American element, that the Salzburg Festival cannot take place because Karajan cannot be replaced at the last minute.

—Semi monthly report from Hq US Forces in Austria, ISB, Dr. Ernst Lothar, Theater and Music, dated June 15, 1946:* ... the findings of the Hurdes Commission which cleared Karajan last March, mostly on the grounds that he is indispensible, will be discussed on Monday, June 17, by the Interallied Denazification Board.... According to [Capt. Allen], the Board will find Karajan unacceptable because he was a party member since 1935 and is considered an "illegal Nazi under Austrian law." ...

The undersigned had Mr. Karajan come to see him at this section's office.... Mr. K. impressed the writer as a man who thinks of music first.

*Lothar, an Austrian writer of note in the 1930s and '40s, was part Jewish. He sought to leave Austria quietly after Anschluss. He put his wife, child, and personal belongings in his car and drove to Austria's western border. There he was stopped by the Nazis, who took his car and its contents. He and his family were allowed to walk into Switzerland with the clothes on their backs.

As it is the case with many other creative and recreative artists, Mr. K.'s love of music comes close to some sort of obsession. The intensity of his speech, his gestures, his emotional attitude add to the impression of a 100% musician. It appears from the files that K. is overbearing. With this writer he was not ... asked how he felt and what he did when Hitler marched into Austria in 1938, he replied that he not only did not come to Austria from Germany where he then stayed, but went to Switzerland. With this he wanted to imply that he disapproved of the Anschluss.

... it would appear that Mr. K.'s interpretation is not without point. This does not explain away that he went on conducting for the Nazi regime in and outside of Germany, whenever he was given the opportunity. He never wavered to start his concerts with the "Horst Wessel Lied." ... It does not suffice, in this writer's opinion, to find extenuating circumstances in the fact that Mr. K. used to set music above everything. He is a mature and highly intelligent man.... It seems absurd to assume that such an intelligent man should have been completely unaware of the meaning and consequences of becoming a party member.

Col. L. K. Ladue, Chief, Information Services Branch, took Lothar's recommendations to heart. Here is his memo to his chief, Special Branch, U.S. Forces in Austria, June 20, 1946: "[Karajan] is the outstanding conductor in Austria, and his presence is greatly desired at the Salzburg Festival.... his presence is not essential to the success of the Festival, although a certain brilliance will be lacking by his absence. This case must be treated individually in view of the fact that the individual concerned is undoubtedly one of the great recreative artists, and as such tends to live in a music world of his own."

Col. Ladue went on to recommend that Herbert von Karajan be turned down for the festival, and indeed he was the next day, June 21, 1946. But the dictum concluded with a typical Austrian compromise: "In this case Karajan may be permitted to appear in public pending the final decision of the quadripartite Internal Affairs Division."

Karajan (and the festival) apparently took advantage of the confusion. On August 6, 1944, Lothar wrote the following memo: "Breach of Agreement re. Mr. v. Karajan: 1. The following letter was sent to Baron Puthan today. 2. Dear Baron Puthan: ... I have to tell you that I received information from several participants in the Festival to the effect that Mr. von Karajan is taking part as artistic advisor in the rehearsals of different operas ... not just as a spectator, but as a stage director whose remarks were put down in writing by assistants. I then pointed out that Mr. von Karajan should not show up in any capacity at the Festival, in which he was banned to take part. I have orders to ask you to put an immediate end to these very unfortunate activities."

So Karajan, who had basically put the festival together in 1946, had to step down, though not all the way down. "I sat in the prompter's box, helping with the words," he recalls. "It didn't matter. I had done everything. I said, 'if not this year, then next. If not next, the year after. It doesn't matter. I can wait.' "

Through the long and drawn-out denazification proceedings, there is not the slightest sign of contriteness from Karajan. One may question his ethics, but not his toughness, his strength of purpose, his self-assured single-mindedness. He told the authorities what he had done, and he told them with his head held high and his voice in full timbre. He voiced no apologies, no regrets. Here is the story: so be it. And when he was challenged, he didn't defend himself; he attacked. "There was one young American officer who interviewed me during this time," Karajan says. "In the middle of our conversation he said to me, 'When you were sitting in your hotel room in Paris, couldn't you hear the cries of the people being tortured at Buchenwald?' And I said to him, 'When you thought I could hear the cries from Buchenwald, do you know who I was sitting with in my hotel room? The ambassador to Germany from the United States, that is who. Why did you leave him on station if he could hear the cries? Why don't you think about that if you are going to be arrogant? I am telling you the truth, you can take it as you like.' But leaving the ambassador there was a sign. As long as he was there, I could conduct. And we were great friends."

Slowly, it seems, Karajan's aloof, uncompromising attitude—or at least the consistency of it—began to defuse the opposition. As the Theater and Music Section (ISB) report of August 31, 1946 summarized:

The artistic success of the Salzburg Festival is partly due to the activities of the Austrian conductor Herbert von Karajan. Before he was banned from appearing in Salzburg ... he had worked in Vienna with a number of singers whom he had selected for the Festival. Thus ... he had laid the groundwork for The Marriage of Figaro, and, to some extent, for Rosenkavalier and Don Giovanni when these works went into rehearsal in Salzburg. Apart from that, he was instrumental in choosing the right cast and advising the directors of the Festival on different artistic matters.

When the Quadripartite Commission turned him down ... Mr. Karajan nevertheless look it upon himself to go on with his preparatory work, and to step down at the moment when other conductors were appointed.

Whether he did so to ingratiate himself with the authorities who had banned him, or out of sheer idealism, remains a matter of speculation. However that may be, it seems fair to recognize the merits of his activities.

But even if Mr. Karajan had nothing to do at all with the Festival 1946, it is felt by this section that his punishment has lasted long enough, and that his talents are urgently needed to rehabilitate Austria's musical life.

It was progress, but it wasn't clearance. A break did come the next year, when Karajan was invited to conduct the Lucerne Festival. The Allies were furious, but powerless. "Lucerne said this has nothing to do with politics," Karajan recalls. "It is music, and we have decided that you will conduct. The U.S. and the Russians were giving them hell, but Lucerne didn't care." Karajan's appreciation for Lucerne's invitation has lasted forty years. He continues to conduct at least one concert each year at the Lucerne Festival.

Meanwhile, members of the Quadripartite Commission continued to argue their way through 1947, keeping Karajan away from Salzburg once again. Dr. Lothar had come around, as he stated in a memo of March 4, 1947, acknowledging Karajan's indispensability to the festival and his favorable reception by the *New York Herald Tribune* for his behind-the-scenes contributions.

But a month later Col. Ladue updated the situation (April 1, 1947): "all efforts to obtain any agreement on the case of Herbert von Karajan in the Sub-Committee for Press and Entertainment failed. After discussion at three meetings, the French Element refused to grant any clearance." As Oliver Rathkolb surmises, "the French apparently couldn't forgive that Karajan had conducted at the Paris Opéra in 1941 and played the 'Horst Wessel' Lied as an introduction."

Buoyed up by his Lucerne invitation, Karajan meanwhile was in the St. Anton mountains, waiting it out. A letter he wrote to Henry Alter on June 1, 1947, reveals his state of mind:

Your letter was a great joy to me, a message from another human being who approaches his work with the same seriousness as I do mine, and who has consequently suffered as much under the insanities of our time.

But it is good to know that that which is one's sole and ultimate purpose in life still echoes in a receptive heart. I have not let myself be deflected from my straight course, and in the end everything will return to normal. I believe one must be capable of great suffering in a cause to know how deeply one loves that cause.

Even though public appearances are not yet possible, I was able to do quite a number of recordings last fall in Vienna, and they turned out extremely well, restoring my confidence in myself. Then, early this year, I secluded myself up here for a life of quiet, concentrated study and meditation, rediscovering myself in the vastness and solitude of the mountains. I feel wonderful inside and out, it has been the most productive period in ages, and one day I'll need my sound nerves more than ever.

For the moment, let the others decimate themselves in the Viennese battle of all against all—my time is sure to come and I await it, calm and confident.

I am glad to hear that you seem to be doing so well, better than back in Vienna, the city that has such great potential, but keeps on ruining itself again and again.

I do hope we will see each other again one day—my own plans are still totally up in the air, except that I am sure to resume my work when the new season gets underway—and then I am just going to make music wherever I am offered the best conditions for it. . . .

P.S. Excuse the pencil—we are a primitive people and my fountain pen rests under the monumental tomb of the erstwhile Esplanade Hotel in Berlin.

Vienna's Musikfreunde, the leading society of musical life in Vienna, was next, after Lucerne, to actively recruit Karajan before he was cleared.

In 1947, the Musikfreunde asked Karajan to be their artistic director for life. "They lease the orchestras that play there," Karajan says. "The Vienna Philharmonic and the Vienna Symphony. They have these orchestras on contract. This led to six or eight concerts a year for me. When the other forces wouldn't let me conduct, they took up for me, saying, 'he is our concert director and he will sit in the box whether it pleases you or not.' They had backbone. They said, 'we want him and we need him.'" Karajan's first project at Goldener Hall was a recording of Brahms's *German Requiem* in October 1947.

Later that autumn, Karajan was finally cleared officially and permitted to work however he wished. He celebrated his reinstatement with a performance of Beethoven's Ninth with the Vienna Philharmonic on December 20, 1947.

It is a measure of Karajan's loyalty that his attention to the Musikfreunde has never wavered in nearly forty years. "When I was making records and the Allies wanted to stop me, the Musikfreunde said, 'When he makes records he does so as director of this house, and you have nothing to say in the management of this house.' The President of the Musikfreunde then was Hryntschak—Hotel, Romeo, Yankee . . ." (Karajan spells it out using the international phonetic alphabet, something he often does when he wants to make certain a name or word is spelled correctly.) "This man is ours, he told them, as was Brahms. The Musikfreunde have the highest standard. They are noble spirits with the best intentions. Theirs is an aristocratic view of life."

His scorn is as quickly forthcoming: "Furtwängler's opening concert, after he was cleared, was with the Vienna Symphony Orchestra—not the Vienna Philharmonic. There was a demonstration outside when he conducted. *Then* the Vienna Philharmonic came to him: 'Oh Doctor, we have always been behind you.' Ha.''

Furtwängler, in fact, seems to be the only one who opposed Karajan whom Karajan didn't attack in return. As early as 1946, the Theater and Music Section (ISB, U.S. Army) was reporting on Furtwängler's activities in Vienna, regarding a proposed Vienna Philharmonic tour through Switzerland, France, and England. Never mind that the plan was presumptuous, with no one, including thirty-five members of the orchestra, having been cleared. But as de Pasetti wrote (February 23, 1946), "Here, too, Furtwängler interferes. Von Karajan was suggested to be conductor of this tour. When F. was informed of it, he stated that he would never forget that another Austrian conductor would come with this Austrian orchestra into Switzerland when he is there and cannot conduct them. (Note: F. is a German).... Reliable evidence was given to writer that F. started his intrigues against Karajan, which means that the same picture we observe in Berlin, where F. fought Karajan, is repeated now in Vienna."

One can only surmise the reason for this uncharacteristic defensive lapse on Karajan's part. Certainly Karajan admired Furtwängler. To this day, he says that Furtwängler and Toscanini had the most influence on his own approach to music. As Karajan told the *Saturday Review*'s Herbert Pendergast in 1963, "[Furtwängler] was the first conductor who divided the responsibility for interpretation between himself and the orchestra.... Although I have not tried to change this style of playing, I have attempted to superimpose on it some of the precision which Toscanini with his absolute control imposed on his orchestras."

Karajan says he first came in contact with Toscanini when he was at La Scala. Karajan was fifteen years old. "Toscanini was at La Scala eight years, it was his greatest period. But the managing directors were glad when he left. He once rehearsed *Don Giovanni* for three months, then dropped it after the dress rehearsal, saying 'it can't be done.' But for me he was as far away as the moon. He was colossal. His were the first recordings I knew. I first met him at Bayreuth (I was at Ulm at the time). He was doing *Tannhäuser*. It was a shock for me to hear *Tannhäuser* done with such perfection. At the time it was unbelievable.

"I went back to Ulm and did *Tannhäuser* to open the season. When I went before the orchestra I had a whole different sound picture in my mind. I said nothing, but that little orchestra played a whole class higher than usual.

"Toscanini worked for the perfection of sound, for precision. Furtwängler was contrary to Toscanini in every respect. Toscanini was strict. Furtwängler was very free. Furtwängler wasn't great with opera, he never mastered the craftsmanship of opera. But he was great with the classics. He was the best with the symphonic classics. He created contact with the orchestra which led to common music making.

"Toscanini was a dictator. If he was not good during a performance, he blamed the audience for not being prepared. Walter Legge once said that Toscanini played everything as if it were written by Rossini. Where did Toscanini get his knowledge? At the piazza at noon when local wind bands played. Those first impressions are the strongest. I was lucky. I heard only good music as a child. Toscanini never felt at home with Beethoven. He played the Ninth correctly, brutally, but something was missing. He knew it, and fought it. He always had trouble with Beethoven, Wagner."

When Karajan speaks of Furtwängler, as he does occasionally, it is without rancor. It is with an amusing anecdote, usually, which seems to be how Karajan remembers those he was most fond of. He will tell the joke about the anxious Furtwängler rushing into the concert hall late to conduct a performance, and asking a startled usher, "Have they started yet?"

"His favorite word was *j'ein*" (a contraction of the German words for yes and no), Karajan says, "because he could never make up his mind. I had the concertmaster who had played for Furtwängler when I took over the Berlin, and once he told me of a performance Furtwängler conducted, and when they arrived at a slow transition passage in the symphony, Furtwängler looked at this concertmaster with sadness in his eyes because he hated to give the next sign to go. So the concertmaster went on, and he said Furtwängler was greatly relieved. He didn't want to make the music so clear that it lost the imaginative quality. It all had to be in mist and doubt.

"Someone once asked a player in the Berlin how the orchestra knew when to start with Furtwängler, and this man said it was easy: when the orchestra members first saw Furtwängler appear in the wings, they would count forty beats and begin." Perhaps Karajan laughs best because he laughs last. There doesn't appear to be any other way to account for his benign attitude toward a man who obstructed him the way Furtwängler did.

Karajan had to have known of Furtwängler's continuing manipulations against him. Austria is a small place, and gossip there ranks in importance right after food, clothing, and shelter. And yet as soon as Furtwängler was cleared, Karajan invited him to conduct at the 1948

Salzburg Festival. According to Karajan, the two had dinner to discuss the details, just as one might meet over dinner with any coworker. But Furtwängler was scheming. As Walter Legge wrote about that Salzburg season, "My attempt to arrange an armistice between Furt- wängler and Karajan was a disaster. The rivals, with their wives and myself, dined in a chambre séparée in a Salzburg hotel and vowed eternal friendship. Early next morning, Furtwängler summoned Egon Hilbert, then director of the festival, and dictated a contract under- taking to conduct every year at Salzburg on condition that Karajan should be excluded from Salzburg as long as Furtwängler lived. He agreed to Karajan's being allowed to conduct the two concerts in 1949 for which he was already engaged. Only days later did Karajan discover how he had been duped."

Karajan spent several seasons without a summer festival job. He missed 1950, then conducted in Bayreuth in 1951 and 1952. Karajan had long dreamed of appearing at Bayreuth. When he was at Aachen, he told the opera chorus master William Pitz, whom he held in high regard, that if the day ever came when he was engaged at Bayreuth, Pitz would go with him. When the invitation came, sixteen years later, the loyal Karajan didn't forget Pitz. But he hated Wieland Wagner's staging conceptions to the extent that two Bayreuth seasons were all he could stand. The egocentricities of the two men clashed as well. So until Furtwängler died in 1954, and Karajan again became active at Salzburg, he had to seek other work. He seems to have done so without expending much effort.

"My first big step was La Scala in Milan," Karajan says. "They had always wanted me. I had conducted a single concert there in 1936. They had told me later on, when I was in Milan after the war, that the moment all the occupation business was finished I should come back.

"So I did, and I began a long and happy association with them. It was there that I first stage-directed productions. I had always wanted to do that, and at La Scala I realized this ambition. It was where I first had control of everything. Wagner, Mozart, Verdi, *Lucia* with Callas. All in Italian, and the German operas in German. This was a change. It was a happy time for me then."

Karajan was still recording in Vienna at Goldene Hall with Walter Legge during this time, and was getting involved with the London Philharmonia Orchestra that Legge started after the war. It was Legge's opinion that more orchestras were needed. He had been head of a committee in London during the war which organized free concerts at noon each day. The players were in the British Army.

Every musician who came through London was required to report in and say how long he would be there. Legge would assign them to concerts.

"This gave Legge great knowledge of the musicians in Britain," Karajan says, "even foreign musicians. He had a great book on all of them. Then he made a calculation. Since he had the recording company, he could record an orchestra's performances at will and use record sales as a way to build a budget to maintain the orchestra. So he put it together. He had some wonderful players."

It was Karajan who trained them. He received high praise for the job he did. He led them during numerous recording sessions and even took then on tour—although the first tour he was supposed to do with them ran awry. The plan was for Karajan to take the orchestra to South America in 1948. At the last minute, Karajan told Legge it was off, he was taking the Vienna Philharmonic instead. Legge appealed to Edge Leslie, who was spending quiet time with Karajan in St. Anton, to talk sense to him.

"It was the only quarrel I ever had with him," Leslie says. "We had breakfast together. I told him he couldn't do such a thing. 'Oh yes I can,' he said. 'The Vienna is a better orchestra. At the moment my only ambition is to make money.' I showed him out, furious. Two months later he felt guilty about the whole thing, but he explained to me that as the war ended, he was broke. He had to rely on Anita. He swore he wouldn't rest until he was financially independent.

"The following Christmas, Karajan invited us to stay in St. Anton. When we arrived there were plates with cakes and cookies, and holly and greens hung here and there. Anita said that Karajan had done the decorating. The next day while Anita was out, Karajan spent an hour stringing recording tape all over the place. He told Anita that if she followed the trail of the tape she would find her present. It was a fur coat."

So within a year after he was cleared, Karajan was already on the move, making music wherever he was offered the best conditions—and making money. If his progress before the war had been noteworthy, his postwar rise to musical prominence was breathtaking. The postwar Karajan was seasoned, toughened by the fire, more self-assured than ever, and ready with a solid plan for whatever came his way. In 1950, Walter Legge named him chief conductor of the London Philharmonia. It was also that year that Karajan engaged André von Mattoni to help handle his affairs. And it was in 1950 that Karajan had his final confrontation—indirect, as usual—with Furtwängler.

The conflict arose over a performance of the *St. Matthew Passion*, which the Musikfreunde wanted done as part of the International Bach Festival in Vienna. Furtwängler had been asked to conduct this work with the Vienna Philharmonic, but his response was so long in coming that the Musikfreunde asked Karajan to do it with the Vienna Symphony Orchestra. Rehearsals began. Two months before Easter, Furtwängler contacted the Musikfreunde, saying he would do the *St. Matthew Passion* outside the Bach Festival as a subscription concert. Furtwängler was too late, and was told so. Karajan held nearly one hundred rehearsals of the work prior to its unveiling in what was called a "unique musical experience" of the 1950 Bach Festival.

Antony Griffiths, an esteemed recording engineer at EMI in those days, recalls the Karajan–Furtwängler conflict. "Furtwängler and Karajan would be in to record on alternate days. Furtwängler was principal conductor of the Vienna Philharmonic, Karajan of the Vienna Symphony. Furtwängler was doing a Bach Mass. Karajan withdrew the choir at Furtwängler's last rehearsal because he wanted them for his Bach Festival performance in July. So Furtwängler and the Vienna Philharmonic withdrew from the Bach Festival. There were headlines in the newspapers: 'Latest in war between Furtwängler and Karajan.' They were deadly enemies. They demanded that pictures of the other be removed from wherever they were working, or eating, etc. They argued over who got the loudest and longest applause."

Furtwängler struck another blow by arranging to have an upcoming Karajan tour with the Vienna canceled. Furtwängler was unable to do the tour, but he arranged for another conductor to take Karajan's place.

Was all this simple blind jealousy on Furtwängler's part? Perhaps, but one suspects the jealousy might have been amplified by Karajan's apparent willingness to let the Nazis use him against Furtwängler. Furtwängler's position during the war was a delicate one, that of an elder, prominent musical statesman who sought to function from within. He never joined the NSDAP, and at the end, he defended his position emotionally and articulately. That he would have resented Karajan for what Furtwängler had to regard as his willingness to be manipulated seems obvious.

There is a story from the Salzburg Festival of 1936 about how enraged Toscanini was that Furtwängler had been asked to conduct Beethoven's Ninth. In Toscanini's eyes, Furtwängler was consorting with the Nazis, and Toscanini, the fanatic anti-Nazi, was appalled. There was nothing to be done about it, however, so Toscanini agreed to do the festival as long as he didn't have to see or speak to Furt-

wängler. One day during the festival, Furtwängler walked into Toscanini's dressing room. As Hyman Howard Taubman tells the story
in *The Maestro*, "Toscanini glared at Furtwängler and said, 'I don't
want to see you.'

" 'Why?'

" 'Because you're a Nazi.'

" 'It is not true,' Furtwängler, who towered over Toscanini, protested.

" 'Yes, you are,' Toscanini insisted, 'whether you have a party card
or not. In London you lunch with Jews to make a good case for
yourself so that you won't lose your position in the West. In Germany, you work for Hitler.'

"Toscanini turned his back on the tall man, who slowly walked
away.

"When asked to return to Salzburg after the war, Toscanini said no.
'I would not mingle with Furtwängler, Karajan, and others who had
worked for Hitler and the Nazis.' "

So perhaps in Furtwängler's mind there was justice in passing on
some of the scorn the older man had suffered from Toscanini and
others. If so, the stoic Karajan afforded Furtwängler little satisfaction
by his response. He simply forged ahead in his own way, grabbing
every good opportunity that came along, and with a shrug, being
willing to wait patiently for those things that were as yet unavailable.
At the same time, he was reinforcing the foundations of his rapidly
expanding business establishment. As early as 1951 Karajan had a film
company headquartered in Liechtenstein. He was taking care of his
pleasures as well. In 1952, to avoid the Allied ban on flying (the Allies
wouldn't officially leave Austria until 1955), Karajan went to Switzerland, where he earned his first pilot's license.

His work schedule was bursting with La Scala, his recordings with
Legge, his engagements with the Musikfreunde, his commitment to
the London Philharmonia tours, and guest appearances. And whatever
he did, the reviews were sensational, the superlatives piled one on top
of the other. Surely Karajan paused briefly to read them, but (surely)
with tongue in cheek, because who knew better than he what was
good and what was not so good? He would leave quickly after concerts, avoiding the parties and postmortems, and go home to study,
prepare, and calculate while others celebrated. Edge Leslie says that
Karajan wasn't interested in what other musicians had to say about
his music. "There wasn't much they could tell him. He had learned
from Toscanini, and from Furtwängler, and he could learn from
Legge. He wanted the views of expert listeners. He thought I was

one. So he would send me the trial matrices of his recordings. Legge would bring the matrices of new recordings to Zurich, where I was stationed. Sometimes he would play them at my flat. I remember one recording of the Schubert C major. I told Karajan I wasn't impressed. He said I was dead right. 'The trouble is I have so many ideas. What is on this record are my ideas, not Schubert.' It was never issued. And he would hold back, refuse to do things that he wasn't certain of. I recall that Lucerne contacted him, said that *Otello* was a favorite at the festival, and would he do it. He told them they would hear *Otello* from him one day, but he wasn't ready yet."

At Walter Legge's home he would listen to records from Legge's enormous collection and study scores. Legge: "He studies his scores propped up on his elbows in bed, or lying like a relaxed Siamese cat on the floor. I have watched him observing how Siamese cats relax themselves, and he had learned even from them how to relax his body completely so that the mind is free to do what it wants. He never makes a mark of any kind in a score, but absorbs, memorizes, and hears in his mind's ears what the printed notes convey to him as what the composer intended, and how beautifully it can be realized."

Karajan had established his pattern from the outset. Now, as he gained prestige, it was being set in concrete. The mission was music (or vice versa), and it was obsessive. He would do what he wanted, where he wanted, when he wanted, and how he wanted to do it. That was his credo. Control was the essence. Preparation was the key to control; preparation and the iron-willed self-discipline necessary to resist distractions.

Again, Walter Legge: "In 1947, he made his debut at the Albert Hall with the Philharmonia with Dinu Lipatti—the Strauss *Don Juan*, the Schumann Piano Concerto with Lipatti, and Beethoven's Fifth. On the morning of the concert he had his last rehearsal, which lasted probably not more than eight minutes. He said, 'I want to know how much fortissimo I can expect tonight. Give me the last two chords of the Fifth with all the force of which you are capable, but still retain an absolutely beautiful sound, but the maximum of force.' The stick came down like a whiplash and he did that about twenty times until he really had the maximum that he knew he could expect—because until then he had not let them play a fortissimo. All the rehearsals had been, 'keep the dynamics down, we'll wait for the occasion'—and then—'now I want to know what you have, now show them.' And it came out."

"In those days," Edge Leslie says, "it was his intention to conduct every note. Later he let the orchestra play, 'conducting' as little as possible. But back then his whole life was calculated. Even his holidays were designed around rest, or study time he needed for a specific piece of work. A lot of his music then lacked depth. It was too calculated."

Antony Griffiths echoes Leslie's sentiments. "I remember once in Vienna, an evangelist was in town. Sort of an Italian Billy Graham type. His program was being relayed to various halls in the neighborhood. Karajan had a session with us that day, and he left wearing morning clothes, with a flower in his lapel. We asked him where he was going. He said to hear the evangelist preach. He said the guy must have something to draw the large crowds. He wanted to find out what it was.

"A lot of what he did on record was very calculated." Griffiths says. "He was always wondering, 'what can I do to hit them right between the eyes.' There was a bit of Hollywood in his technique. I remember he did Bruckner's Ninth with Legge. Legge asked me what I thought. I said it was cold, it didn't move me. Legge said, 'Karajan is his own worst enemy. This is the thing he will have to watch.'"

Of course, it wasn't all study and calculation. There were distractions. The first in a series of medical problems that would plague Karajan was infected tonsils. But even his approach to this unpleasant bit of minor surgery was academic. It's not every day one has the opportunity to watch a surgical procedure at close hand. Not too many people would want to watch a surgical procedure, especially their own. But medicine had always fascinated Karajan. In later years he has often compared the intensity of the face of a surgeon at work with that of a conductor, a reference that is missed by those who opt gratefully for general anesthesia. But Karajan wouldn't dream of missing such a chance. With the tonsilectomy, he requested a local, and had mirrors adjusted so he wouldn't miss a snip. Afterwards he said it had been most interesting.

And of course there were women. People say that Karajan had two categories into which women who interested him were placed. On the one hand were those he considered true beauties, and for them he constructed pedestals. On the other hand were those who were available. (In later years a third category would be added: loyal functionaries, like Salzburger and Runne.)

Edge Leslie tells a story about helping Legge and Karajan raise money for one European tour. "I knew this disreputable east-west trader," Leslie says. "He had made so much money underhanded that he was trying to buy himself rehabilitation as an English gentleman. I knew he would contribute to such a cultural venture. Legge said we couldn't do that. But the idea appealed to Karajan. He said in the old days kings sponsored orchestras. Now why not business kings? Legge said he supposed it was all right as long as the guy stayed out of jail until the tour was finished.

"So we took this fellow and his gorgeous blonde female companion to a concert. Afterwards they went backstage and Karajan gave them a big welcome, but he paid no attention to the beautiful woman. Then, when we started talking business with the guy, Karajan took the woman into the back and talked to her.

"For the next concert, Karajan asked me to prepare a picnic basket for him and the woman. So I did. He told me to put her right in the front of the orchestra so he could be playing only for her. The next day he didn't show up at the scheduled press conference, and he cut a rehearsal. He had taken the woman flying. Legge was so mad at me for helping Karajan that he didn't speak to me for eight years. He was like that.

"The woman told me later that she had gone somewhere with Karajan and they had checked into separate rooms. When she returned to her room, Karajan was in her bed. He quickly got up and left. He said he had just had to sleep in her bed for a while. He told me he wasn't interested in sex with her. It was only a flirtation. He said he could see her soul. She was a romantic ideal. Like paintings and flowers, such women were there to be looked at."

Karajan has a definite preference for tall blondes with straight, long hair. (His third wife, Eliette, fits that description.) It was a preference that became obvious in his casting of *Lohengrin* for an Easter Festival in the 1970s. In the wedding scene, all twenty handmaidens were tall blondes with straight hair. Those who knew him had been betting on it.

IV
The Star Ascends

When Furtwängler died on November 20, 1954, the final encumber-
ances upon Karajan were removed. Usually, when a man of
Furtwängler's stature passes on, the power base he has established is
diffused by the crowd of aspirants who have been waiting impatiently
for their shot at the various positions he had held. In this case, Karajan
was in perfect position to step into Furtwängler's shoes in the broadest
sense. Not only did he have the talent, but conductors were scarce in
Austria and Germany at the time. Many of those who had emigrated
had not returned. And given the deep foundation of German and
Austrian classics upon which the Berlin and Vienna Philharmonics are
built, it is difficult to imagine a principal conductor of either orchestra
who was not born and raised in that tradition. Of those available at
the time, Hans Knappertsbusch was not interested in a permanent
position. Erich Kleiber had reduced his desirability by the work he
had been doing in the Soviet Zone of Berlin. Josef Keilberth, conductor of the Hamburg Philharmonic and the principal conductor at
Bayreuth, was probably too young to be seriously considered.

For nearly twenty years Karajan had been dreaming of the Berlin
Philharmonic, and now it could be his. His anticipation was fueled a
full year before Furtwängler's death when the Berlin Intendant, painfully aware of Furtwängler's failing health, approached Karajan about
doing the American tour scheduled for 1955 in case Furtwängler wasn't
able.

There was competition, of course. There had to be for such an
exalted post as the Berlin artistic director. But it wasn't much. In
1945, a man named Leo Borchard took over the rebuilding of the
orchestra. Upon his death, Sergiu Celibidache, a conductor of the first
rank, led the orchestra until Furtwängler returned in 1952. Celibidache,

a Rumanian, was a serious contender for the job, the only one who could rival Karajan for both talent and showmanship. But he had the temerity to remark at Furtwängler's Heidelberg graveside that Furtwängler's death was probably timely, in that his hearing was practically gone. Furtwängler had been taking a prescribed drug that had adversely affected his hearing, but in the spiteful politics of music, Celibidache's remark was used to weaken his position. That, combined with Karajan's nationality, his political foothold in the Vienna-Berlin-Salzburg triangle, and the support afforded him by the American sponsors of the 1955 tour, landed him the coveted job. He was chosen to do the tour, elected artistic director by the players on March 3, 1955, while in Pittsburgh, Pennsylvania, and confirmed in the position by the Senate of Berlin on April 5, 1955—his forty-seventh birthday. When he first stood before the orchestra as its new leader, he told the players, "We will make music as you have always made music."

A plum like the Berlin, the project of rebuilding the war-ravaged orchestra and shaping it to his proportions, would have been more than enough of a challenge for most men. For Karajan, liberated now both as citizen and musician, it was only the beginning. Events moved rapidly. Shortly after he had taken the Berlin directorship, he was approached by the Vienna Philharmonic to be their principal conductor (the Vienna has no permanent conductor). The Vienna emissary explained that while Furtwängler was alive they had to honor their commitment to him and his wishes, but now they were free to enlist Karajan. He had to refuse them, but from this point on his relationship with the Vienna Philharmonic was a close one.

Then in March 1956, less than a year after taking over the Berlin, Karajan signed a four-year contract as artistic director of the Salzburg Festival. Negotiations here were just a little sticky. The Salzburg directors, aware of Karajan's reputation for controlling whatever he did, explained to him that the law of the festival required that unanimous decisions be made by the Festival Committee. "I told them that was the simplest thing in the world," Karajan recalls. "I told them I would put before them a proposal, and they would agree to it." Negotiations over, contract signed.

That same month, conductor Karl Böhm was adding his name to the list of those who have had terminal disagreements with the Vienna State Opera. Böhm outraged the Viennese by announcing that his opera directorship was interfering with his international career. Böhm was out, and Karajan was approached. In June, Karajan made a guest appearance at the Vienna State Opera with a production of *Lucia di Lammermoor* that featured Maria Callas. He did the stage direction as well as the conducting. A month later, Karajan signed a contract making him artistic director of the Vienna State Opera. Berlin officials were heard to grumble at the news. His schedule, one would have to say at this point, was full to bursting.

As *Time* magazine summarized in October 1956, "As impressive as [Karajan's] musical domain is his travel schedule. Last month he visited the Salzburg Festival, darted over to Lucerne for another festival (he conducted a Mozart program), then flew on to the island of Ischia in the Bay of Naples, where he rested for a few days. From there he sailed his 50-ton yacht (crew of three) to Portofino, motored to Genoa, hopped a plane to Zurich, got into his waiting silver-gray Mercedes 300 SL and soloed at a breakneck 90 mph back to Lucerne for rehearsals and a concert, then caught a plane for West Berlin for three days of rehearsals with the Philharmonic. Last week, with the orchestra following by plane, he embarked on the *Queen Mary* for New York, to begin the Berlin Philharmonic's second U.S. tour."

The money, obviously, was now arriving in substantial quantities. Karajan's life was full of work, but since a large part of his repertoire consisted of music long since committed to memory, life was also full of sports, cars, boats, airplanes, and a growing collection of gorgeous homes. The war years, combined with a traveling profession, had rendered "home" an abstract concept for Karajan. Mainly what he wanted from a "home" was convenience, and of course beauty.

In the October 1957 article in *High Fidelity* magazine, "The Operator," Berlin correspondent Paul Moor compared Karajan's rise to musical power with that of the compulsive Sammy Glick, archetypal hero of Budd Schulberg's novel *What Makes Sammy Run?*. "His drive has been no mere desire to excel: [from childhood] it was a life-and-death necessity to be one up on his associates.... But while Sammy's rise and his unlamented fall were based on a reputation built by lying, cheating and flattering, Karajan's position today as virtual lord of all European musical creation, while perhaps as lonely as Sammy Glick's, has been built through years of hard, unrelenting work and represents the just deserts of one of the most flamboyant musical endowments which this century has revealed. Furthermore, Karajan shows not the slightest indication of falling ..."

The deserts were copious. The permanent positions alone made a head-spinning list: chief conductor of the London Philharmonia; artistic director of the Berlin; artistic director of the Musikfreunde; artistic director of the Salzburg Festival; head of the German wing of La Scala; and last, but certainly not least, artistic director of the Vienna State Opera.

The Berlin marriage was what Karajan had most lusted for, but Vienna remained an irresistible temptress. Hardly had his relationship with the Berlin been consummated than he was in the arms of his nemesis.

Karajan's affair with the Vienna State Opera began as a child, when he would attend performances there with his family. The association matured during student days in Vienna, when he and his classmates saw many operas there for the first time. Then in 1937, there he was, on the podium, learning that one's expectations tend to exceed the realization. "The Vienna Opera!" Karajan says, looking back. "It was unreachable to me as a boy, as a student. As a boy all I wanted was to direct there. Then when I got the post, it faded. Things are never what you dream. The first time I was invited, I said I naturally need a number of rehearsals, three with orchestra and the normal ensemble rehearsals with the soloists. They conceded me three orchestra rehearsals. I arrived and was met at the station by a functionary of the orchestra, who said I could only have two of the three rehearsals because of a program change which otherwise occupied the orchestra. Three days later, after we had begun our piano rehearsals, another official came and said unfortunately, and there was nothing to be done, a Philharmonic concert needed another rehearsal, and now there was only one. As a young Kapellmeister I didn't want to make difficulties, so I let them take that one too. Then one day before the rehearsal, an orchestra member I knew came and said 'Look, you only have one rehearsal; in that one rehearsal you don't get anywhere at all. Give up that rehearsal and we will play as if it had been for Mahler.' So there it was, without rehearsal. I had one 'multi-informational' rehearsal. The singer who was supposed to personify Isolde came to the meeting, gave me a curt nod as greeting, and then throughout the entire rehearsal caught up with her correspondence."

So he knew how it went at the Vienna State Opera. But how soon one forgets, especially when the challenge comes from on high (following in the footsteps of Brahms, Mahler!). If opera was the question, Vienna was the answer.

Whether Vienna could be considered opera capital of the world today is uncertain. Surely the Viennese think so, and perhaps one can concede that romantically it remains at the center. But in the 1950s and '60s, opera in Vienna was at the heart of everyday existence. As Mattoni said, "In Vienna, people discuss opera in the subway." Mattoni's remark is typical Viennese understatement. They don't "discuss" opera in the subway in cities like Vienna and Milan. They argue heatedly about it, reliving performances note by note, having violent

disagreements about star singers and tempos, hanging on the latest
news from inside. When the offer came, Karajan could no more turn
it down than he could give up flying.

"My first period after the war was a multiple of activity," Karajan
says. "In the second period I saw what was important and what was
not. Why go to La Scala when I can do it better in Vienna, with a
better orchestra and chorus? When I first took over, I had a key that
no one else had. I lived nearby, so I would slip in and listen to what
went on. Then I would call people the next day, much to their
amazement. I had a whole year to study the situation before I conducted. Except when Toscanini died in 1957, I did a concert on that
occasion—the *Masonic Funeral Music* by Mozart."

When Karajan went to the Vienna State Opera the finance minister
of Austria assured him of support in case Karajan encountered snags
with changing attitudes about budgets, labor problems, etc. "He told
me," Karajan says, "that if I took the position he would give me
anything, but he would not make the same offer to anyone else."
Karajan was fortunate to have such a well-positioned backer. The
Allies had only recently departed, and Austria was in the complicated
internal throes of "new" independence. Political stability was tenuous.
Anything could happen.

The war years had brought about a change in attitude toward
music, and Karajan was the right man to be in the forefront. As
Bruno Weil explains it, "the prewar years, dominated by Furtwängler,
were characterized by a humanistic approach to music. Furtwängler
was intellectual, philosophical, emotional. He knew Goethe. His father
was an archaeologist. He had an understanding of history. Musically
he was in quest of the big, great idea. World War II issued in a cold,
modern approach to music—neutral, unemotional. The old German
tradition became suddenly old-fashioned. Karajan changed later on,
became more humanistic himself. But in the 1950s, he was aligned
with the mood of the times."

Musical business was also in flux, as singers began to take advantage
of jet travel to broaden their careers (and fees), making up for lost
time. This had the effect of breaking up the ensemble companies
within opera houses that for years had formed the basis for smooth-
running, if unremarkable, seasons. This suited Karajan, who much
preferred the Italian *stagione* system.

The *stagione* system lent itself to the importation of star personalities
for key roles, and this had been a Karajan trademark since his days at
Aachen. But of course that approach to opera cost more money. A
top singer received $2,000 a night for a guest appearance at the Vienna

State Opera in 1960. A sold-out performance which netted $4,000 would lose money if two or three guests had been booked. And the travel and expense budget of the jetting Karajan was also a considerable addition to the left side of the ledger.

Musically, things were not smooth either. His first season as boss *in absentia* was reported as lackluster by critic Joseph Wechsberg. "Karajan may have been trying to run the house by long distance," Wechsberg wrote, "but in this he failed. During the winter there were dreary stretches of uninspired conducting, poor staging, second-rate singing, and bad acting." Wechsberg was enthusiastic about the first production Karajan undertook: "Things pepped up considerably when Karajan made his debut with a supercharged, shockproof production of *Die Walküre*," but even here there was criticism. "When you hear the same opera performed under him several times, the dazzling effect seems to wear off in later performances and there remains a curious vacuum." Overall, the Wechsberg marks were not so good on the year: "Of Karajan's singing imports, few were good; many were fair-to-middling, and some were bad. . . . The Staatsoper was never at its best as a star theater, and always outstanding for unity, tradition, and integration of artistic elements. Of this there has been little evidence under Karajan."

Five years later, he was still not getting rave reviews. The *Saturday Review*'s Robert Breuer wrote, "What, with all the publicity, is the true picture of Herbert von Karajan? In the opinion of some, he is World Conductor Number One because he typifies the conductor of our time who—in contrast to Furtwängler, the 'conductor of poets and dreamers'—is the 'conductor of mathematicians and engineers.' He is not, as Mahler says, the apostle of a musical work, but its interpreter; dynamic rather than impassioned; imposing, but not overly creative."

A book published at the time, *Conductors, Stars and Bureaucrats*, by Viktor Reiman, former director of the press department of the Austrian State Theaters Administration, offered the refined, Viennese view of the Maestro: "Fascinating as the Karajan era may be, it is uninteresting. It consumes much money, but demands little spirit."

Karajan was also taken to task for the steady diet of Italian operas he fed the Viennese audiences (". . . to the detriment of Mozart and Strauss performances which are steadily declining," one critic wrote)—in Italian, of course. One of the more amusing passages of Reiman's book describes a "snob-studded" audience listening to an Italian-sung performance of *Falstaff* with such somber faces that they might have been attending a performance of some grim, Wagnerian piece.

"They said I destroyed the ensemble idea," Karajan says today, with vintage bitterness coloring his words, "and that I violated the German language tradition. It is common today to have opera sung in the original language. And the ensemble company is nothing more than an excuse for laziness. Opera has changed in my time." Karajan has helped change it, of course.

In addition to his idealistic demands about the nature of sustained rehearsal time, and for a prerecorded performance (with his own cast) that could be used as the track for blocking out the staging—as finally realized with the creation of the Easter Festival—he has had firm ideas from the outset about how singers should look. This emphasis on more physically appealing singers was mainly an extension of his own personal aesthetic, but it was a condition that would be reinforced by television in later years.

He went to great lengths to fit a singer's persona into roles. When he did *Don Giovanni* in Milan in the early 1950s, he cast an average singer in the role of Giovanni, mainly because he was 6'8" tall. The idea was that while Giovanni doesn't dominate musically in the opera, he dominates physically. He gave the man special coaching for six months until he was adequate for the part. The rest of the cast were singers of the first rank, and the production was a success.

"His eye was on the stage as much as his ear was on the music," Edge Leslie says. "Leontyne Price sang *Trovatore* with Karajan in Salzburg, but he dropped her when he took the opera to Vienna for televising. He said simply, 'a Spanish Countess isn't black.' "

He takes infinite pains to get the visual and musical effects he wants. Before he did *Boris Godunov* in Salzburg, he spent a week in Russia soaking up the atmosphere. In the performance, he supplemented the Vienna Chorus with some Slavic singers, putting them in the front row—much to the annoyance of the Vienna Chorus. But Karajan avowed that only the Slavic singers had that particular tang to their voices. They could sing the Russian properly.

His general ideas about staging—lighting, movement of singers, sets—were very particular, as we have seen. Karajan says that in Milan, a La Scala administrator told him the story of how Toscanini met Picasso in a restaurant. Toscanini was planning *Don Giovanni* at the time. So he said to Picasso, "why not paint the scenery?" Picasso thought it was such a good idea that he pulled out a black crayon and sketched out the scenes in ten minutes on the marble tabletop. Karajan was planning *Carmen* (for La Scala) when he heard this story, and it was suggested that he ask Picasso to do the same for him. "I said to this man, 'if the sketches do not please us, who will tell him?' " Not even Picasso got carte blanche from Karajan.

When he could arrange it, he would control the entire production, often with mixed results. As *Variety* wrote about a production of *Götterdämmerung* at the Vienna State Opera in 1960, "As manager, the great man is not up to himself as conductor and musician. The staging was neither revolutionary Bayreuth nor traditional Wagner. Despite the 60 light rehearsals it was impossible to see a single singer's facial expression." Twenty-two years later, in Salzburg, the same thing could have been said about the lighting in *The Flying Dutchman*. Lighting, in particular, is something Karajan is quite stubborn about.

Joachim Kaiser, the Munich critic, has called Karajan a "naïve musician," and it is in his work as stage director that this naïveté is most apparent. As Kaiser says, "If Wotan is there with his spear, for Karajan it is not a phallic symbol, it is a spear. Musicians do tend to take the literature literally. Karajan is very conservative." But he was always looking for the best effect on stage, and often his literal approach achieved it dramatically, as well as musically.

"In *Tosca*," Karajan says, "in the first act, Scarpia, who is head of the police, enters during a dance of celebration over the victory that has been won in the war. He is looking for an escapee. Traditionally, the music comes to an end, then he tries to sing stronger than the orchestra has played. This is simply not possible. When I did it, I told Scarpia to come in, the music stops, everyone is still, now he doesn't sing; he doesn't move. His eyes sweep from left to right, sinister. Then he begins to sing very quietly, with viciousness in his voice, with one eyebrow raised."

The effect was praised by opera writer Edward Greenfield in the book *Opera on Record* (edited by Alan Blyth): "The 1963 recording [of *Tosca*], with Leontyne Price as the heroine and Herbert von Karajan conducting, provides admirable instances of a new perspective that can be revealed by gramophone performance. Thanks largely to Karajan, but also to the engineers, the Te Deum scene has an impact rarely achieved even in the theater. After the enunciation of the Scarpia theme, the pivoting ostinato of the bells, B flat to low F, starts not only pianissimo but really from afar—'come da lontano.' Against this the sinister muttering of Giuseppe Taddei as Scarpia . . . is the more tense. The main ominous theme with its relentless triplet rhythm enters extremely slowly. Karajan observes Puccini's *sostenuto molto* added to *largo religioso*, and—with an eerie reverberance that immediately takes one atmospherically into Sant' Andrea della Valle— the music sounds at once still and beautiful yet profoundly ominous for the future. Karajan's crescendo to the climax of the Te Deum is remarkable, the total impact the more powerful because of the slow speed and the bigger contrast of dynamic."

Karajan's controversial preference for lyrical voices is well established, and along with that goes his penchant for new talent. The latter is not totally selfless. Karajan would rather train someone in his ways than struggle with established stars who have their own ideas— unless, of course, the talent is extraordinary. Even then he tolerates a minimum of deviation from his mark. When the great Maria Callas decided she wanted more money for the work she was doing with Karajan, he wouldn't budge. They had done several operas together, and some recordings. She was being paid 70,000 schillings (about $3,100) a night for her performances in the Vienna State Opera. She asked for 75,000. Karajan said 70,000. She said she would get 72,000 or never sing in Vienna again. Fine, Karajan said. Never again. "One was either part of Karajan's benign family, or one was not," Edge Leslie says.

The trouble is that it takes a gentle (but firm), considerate leader to maintain a benign family. The picture one draws from Karajan's Vienna days is more of a brusque, irritably efficient military commander whose schedule was strung so incredibly taut that there was barely time for salutations before the work frenzy began (meetings in airports between flights; rushing to catch the 10:40 train from the Zoo station in Berlin while applause was still ringing in the hall). "It was incredible," says Peter Busse, who traveled with Karajan then. "We dashed endlessly among Vienna, London, Berlin, Salzburg, Lucerne, living out of suitcases.

"Those were terrible days," Busse recalls. "Karajan was fierce, bitchy. There were no laughs. He was respected, but feared. When he would return to Vienna, word would pass along the hallways of the opera house like an ice-cold wind: 'the boss is back—Karajan is here.' He hated the casual, Viennese attitude; couldn't bear the nonprofessional approach to work, the laziness he saw. People were afraid to go speak with him, mainly because he was impossible to approach. His theory was that every day was a new day, and it had its laws. What he was doing ran against the tradition of how it had been. So what, he would say; this year we are a year older and a year wiser."

"He was away much of the time," Albert Moser says, "but he kept his head in Vienna." Moser is a ranking member of Austria's music establishment: he is general secretary of Vienna's Musikfreunde and president of the Salzburg Festival. He and Karajan have been associated since 1949, when Moser was a music administrator in Graz. "I invited him to come to Graz with the Vienna Symphony Orchestra,"

Moser says. "He came by train because his car was in bad shape. A friend had an open Jeep I borrowed to pick him up. He insisted on driving, tearing through the streets of Graz. Seven years later he again came to Graz, this time with the Berlin Philharmonic. He invited me to Vienna to work at the Staatsoper.

"People were afraid of him in those days because he got reports about who sang, who conducted, who was bad, who was good. It boded ill for certain people on his return. Then there were strikes against the ministry (by technical personnel and stagehands). The problem became insoluble, so Karajan walked out. Then they struck to get him back, because he spoke for them, worked intensively to get them what they wanted."

That was in 1961. Technical personnel wanted a raise and new regulations for overtime. The strike caused rehearsals for Wagner's *Ring* to be canceled. The singers had to be released. When the problem continued into February of the next year, Karajan left for Switzerland. That's when the technical people struck in force (not just a slowdown) to get the Boss back. After much wrangling, Karajan agreed to return, but as usual, he had demands: a codirector would be hired to handle administrative work; and the State Opera would enjoy more independence from the National Theater Administration. He also wanted more attention paid to his grandiose plan for coordinating the productions of the great opera houses of the world. He returned in March 1962, in time to take the Vienna Philharmonic on tour through Russia, Sweden, Denmark, Germany, England, and France.

After that tour, Karajan suffered from a kidney infection, another in the chain of medical problems that would plague him. A year later, his doctor would force him to take time off because of fatigue. Then in 1963, during the final, heated conflicts with the State Opera, he would be down again with circulatory disorders. One would have to say that the pace was beginning to catch up with him.

"I never argue with unions," Karajan says. "To this day in the Festspielhaus I talk to the people directly and find out what they want and there is never a problem. I want to know, 'what do I owe you— what do I get.' Then it is simple. In Vienna I would slip into the house at queer hours. People often didn't know I was there. Once I was sitting in the rear listening to a rehearsal. It went on too long. When it was five minutes past the time, I walked down the aisle, because now there was arguing and shouting. I said to them it is not the fault of the conductor, it is my fault. I should have intervened at the stroke of the bell. You know that I usually stop ten minutes early.

I asked them if they thought their tone was appropriate to the dignity of the house. Then I went away. Later they came to apologize.

"The State Opera orchestra was paid by the state. They have three hundred required performances a year plus a hundred rehearsals, all in ten months. In their free time this orchestra is the Vienna Philharmonic. One of their regular services is a Saturday concert at 3 P.M. and a Sunday concert at 11 A.M.—as the Philharmonic. So their committee came to me and said they needed a free day every week. I said of course. I will back you. I too must have free day. I will take Saturday noon until Sunday noon. And they said, but the concerts! It took me nearly forty years to learn how to handle big groups of people—how to train an institution—but now I know how to get them to do anything for me."

The story of the prompter may be the best illustration of Karajan in his role of "trainer." It happened toward the end of his time in Vienna. Peter Busse tells it: "In Italy, a prompter is a conductor who conducts on stage from his box in coordination with the conductor in the pit. Karajan was doing a new production of *La Bohème* in Vienna and was told that all the staff he needed, including prompters, was available. But he insisted upon hiring an Italian maestro. Since he was the artistic director, he engaged this man. During final rehearsals, the Vienna State Opera went on strike because of this. They said, 'We have our own house prompter; he has been here forty years.' It was like the clarinet player: a struggle of wills. So we rehearsed without a prompter. But then we had to replace a singer, and we asked a prominent Viennese singer to take over the role. She hadn't sung the role (Musetta) in many years, and said she needed a prompter. I said I would go into the box to help out, but I was pulled by the Viennese. Karajan got fed up, said that the Italian prompter was in. Now it's opening night, and there is a general strike. The audience arrived and just sat there. Karajan had to come out and announce that the staff was on strike, and that the opening would be postponed. He sent the audience home. A week later the opera opened without a prompter. Karajan got the greatest ovation in his life. Any other man would have been hissed and booed off the stage. But he had turned it around, taken a 'show must go on' approach, and got credit for finding a way to give the Viennese their *La Bohème*. But it was the beginning of the end. Or one of many such beginnings."

In 1964, Karajan left Vienna and the State Opera. It was not a congenial parting. It was full of anger, bitterness, with newspaper headlines and innuendo, the final scene in what Robert Breuer had called "the endless conspiracies and machinations relentlessly accom-

panying the affairs of a state-subsidized institution." Or as Walter
Legge wrote, "Ministerial interventions, political cross-currents, factions, and irresponsible gossip have long plagued Austrian musical
life, but rarely so intensely as during the Karajan era. The Austrian
newspapers ... made hay and headlines of every wisp of gossip at the
whims and prejudice of every scribbler—and the dictates and politics
of their paper's financial backers."

Karajan's final forays in Vienna (including the prompter affair)
seem to have been an escalating series of conflicts with a man named
Egon Hilbert, who was general manager of the State Opera. Hilbert
had for years been a principal authority at the Salzburg Festival. It
was Hilbert with whom Furtwängler had forged the contract that had
eliminated Karajan from the festival. Hilbert could not have been a
favorite of Karajan's. And yet it was Karajan who hired Hilbert as
State Opera general manager, the person he would have to work
closely with in terms of programs, schedules, and the booking of
singers. Karajan couldn't have made a more ill-fated choice. The
partnership quickly came apart, with Hilbert making unilateral decisions that Karajan didn't like, and vice versa. Quickly the two
refused even to communicate, and the situation became untenable.

A summary of the events leading up to Karajan's resignation from
the Vienna State Opera gives one a glimpse of what Breuer meant
when he spoke of "endless conspiracies and machinations":

—November 21, 1963: Hilbert and Karajan meet in Munich. Hilbert demands Mattoni's resignation because Mattoni was keeping
dates and plans secret from him. Hilbert offers to resign, but Karajan
won't let him, saying that the public wouldn't understand a man
whom Karajan has chosen resigning in just a few months.

—Karajan ill with circulatory problems. Hilbert refuses to speak to
or acknowledge the presence of Mattoni in Karajan's absence.

—January 1964: Hilbert again says he will resign. (Karajan's second
daughter Arabel born at this time—January 2. Berlin Philharmonic
named as "godparent.") Hilbert's resignation not accepted by the
minister. Karajan and Hilbert communicate only by telephone when
Karajan returns. During one conversation, Hilbert hangs up on Karajan when the two can't agree on a date to engage a particular singer.
Karajan waits for an apology that doesn't come. After that, Karajan
and Hilbert communicate only by letter.

—Hilbert schedules *Tannhäuser* on a date that is already taken for
Karajan with a Berlin Philharmonic concert. Karajan is furious,
because he has long established that only he will conduct *Tannhäuser*.
Hilbert refuses to budge, engages another conductor.

—Karajan signs exclusive contract with Deutsche Grammophon. The Vienna Philharmonic is exclusive with Decca, so it appears that the two can no longer record together.

—Karajan announces that all between him and Hilbert is smooth. All he wants to do is get on with his work.

—April 2, 1964: Dr. Josef Klaus becomes chancellor. Karajan meets with him shortly thereafter to tell him of his intention to resign from the State Opera. Karajan writes to other ministers of his intention, and meetings are held between various government ministries and Hilbert to try to find a basis for a workable solution.

—May 8, 1964: Karajan announces that his health demands he give up the artistic leadership of the State Opera. He says his continuing association as conductor and producer depends on whether or not they are willing to hire a new director and guarantee him artistic freedom.

—May 11, 1964: Karajan's resignation announced, but he is bound by contract to Hilbert and the opera until June. Hilbert makes plans and a budget without Karajan's approval. Karajan sees this as a breach of contract and absolves himself from all responsibility and duties.

—June 23, 1964: Karajan announces that as of August 31, he will no longer continue to work in Austria. Ghiringhelli (from Milan) and director Franco Zeffirelli cancel contracts with the State Opera for future productions, saying they were to work specifically with Karajan.

—Karajan is in Salzburg preparing *Elektra* for the festival. He is asked to be on the Salzburg Board of Directors. He is about to accept, when the move is vetoed by a government minister. Karajan says there is no point in his staying in Salzburg. After much meeting and negotiating by festival officials and other government ministers, Karajan is invited to be on the Festival Board. He accepts.

Why did Karajan select Hilbert? "He was director of the Vienna Festival. The critics loved him. Everyone wanted me to take him. If I had not, everything would have gone to pieces," Karajan says. But perhaps Water Legge had the best answer: "Most probably [Karajan] was bored by the job and saw no stimulating future in it."

In 1962, Robert Breuer suggested the impossibility of Karajan's association with the Vienna State Opera: "His goal, always to be in full command, to play the role of superman, is the reason he had to learn to live with some complexes he can no longer shrug off. He had admirers, adversaries, business partners, and people eager to serve under him, but since he himself cannot be anybody's friend, no friends." And from Viktor Reiman: "He became so overestimated that he is forced to live in a cloud."

In retrospect, Karajan sees his mission in Vienna as having been an impossible one. "When I got to Vienna, I thought I could oversee three hundred productions a year, but now I know it is not possible. I could only do one or two productions a year myself. For the rest I had to be there, and I was not in agreement with most of the other things that were done. Normally when I was in Vienna my full day ran twelve hours. When I finished rehearsal, I would train singers in the evening. Then I would sit for ten minutes in the performance. I remember one time, and it was a second class conductor, they told me he had arrived from Argentina at 4 P.M. No rehearsal. He was doing it just for the money. This was shocking to me, doing it just for the money.

"I went to Vienna wanting to create a festival in permanence, and I saw it was not possible. If we did three hundred performances a year, we could do seventy very well. The second seventy would have a diminished return, and the rest, nothing. But even if it could be done, it would not be desirable. If people were confronted every day by excellence, they could not stand it. It would be like dressing up. If you do it on Sunday, it feels good, festive. You do it every day and it loses the thrill.

"It was not intrigue that put me out," Karajan says today. "I did not resist. It was the birth of the Easter Festival in my mind. Now I can do three operas a year and do them right."

Karajan returned to Vienna in 1977, after a thirteen-year absence, to conduct once again at the Vienna State Opera. In an interview on Austrian television with Fischer Karwin, he succinctly (if unintentionally) summarized why his Vienna years had been so storm-tossed. "I was born to command and I can't change myself. That is the difference in this profession, that those organizations who, so to speak, engage me are really under *my* control."

On the surface, it would appear that the Vienna years were all-consuming. That would be far from the truth. Karajan had dropped a few of his commitments along the way—his activity at La Scala was reduced to the occasional guest appearance, and he gave up his principal conductorship with the London Philharmonia—but during the seven years he was at the Vienna State Opera, Karajan made over a hundred and twenty recordings. Some of these were with the Vienna Philharmonic, but the Berlin Philharmonic and the London Philharmonia got equal shares of his recording time. Karajan enjoyed working with Walter Legge, who wrote in his introduction to *On and Off the Record*, "Our way of thinking about music was in complete harmony." Karajan and the tough, uncompromising, self-taught master of taste were a good match for one another. (Antony Griffiths called Legge "the rudest man I ever met.") Like arrogant television quiz-show champions with fingers poised over the buttons, they undoubtedly brought out the best in each other.

Once they argued over the tempo of Ravel's *Bolero*. Legge thought Karajan was taking it too slowly, and referred Karajan to Ravel's markings. Karajan fired back that he had read a letter Ravel had written on the subject of *Bolero*, in which the composer said he would have marked it slower if he had thought orchestras were capable of playing it that way.

And Legge got in his jabs. After the war, when there were threats against Karajan in New York, Anita Karajan asked Legge with wifely concern, "Who could want to hurt my Herbert?" And Legge: "Oh, it could be Brahms, maybe Beethoven." But when Karajan's courtship of Eliette Mouret began, it was at the home of Legge and Schwarzkopf where the two had their first "date."

According to Eliette, she and Karajan met in St. Tropez in the mid-1950s. She told the story in Karajan's offices in the Festspielhaus one evening in 1982. The Karajans had been to a presentation in the Maestro's honor—a book showing all the stagings for all the opera productions he had ever done had just been released. It must have been important; it was the only time I ever saw him wearing a necktie. In the pause between presentation and departure, they stopped to chat in Lore Salzburger's office. Salzburger was there, so was Busse. The banter was quick and light. Eliette was dressed in a navy blue leather suit. She frequently tossed her golden mane of hair, and was being expansive if not totally accurate: "I was seventeen. He arrived with his second wife. We all ended up on the boat of a friend for the day. In the evening we had dinner. During dinner my escort said to Anita that he thought his friend was in love with her husband. Then we talked about the next day, what to do. Someone suggested miniature golf at 6 P.M. The Maestro was looking at me. I think he had a dirty mind."

Karajan: "Of course."

"Two years later I was at a concert in London with a man friend. He asked me if I knew Karajan, said he seemed to be looking at me. I said I had all his records. He said we should go and get his autograph. Meanwhile Karajan's blue eyes were piercing at me, indicating I come around during the break. He told Mattoni that if he saw a blonde with long hair he should send her to him. So I went to see him for my companion, who wanted an autograph. He asked me out that week, but I was busy. In two weeks? I was busy. Finally we made a date for dinner. The big love came that evening with Legge and Schwarzkopf."

Karajan: "I remember when she came to see me backstage, the orchestra buzzed. The first cellist looked at me and gave me a thumbs-up sign. She was in all the posters in London, life-size. She was the most beautiful girl of the year."

Among today's highly organized, big-money agency set, Eliette Mouret is not remembered as a star model, when she is remembered at all. In fact it is difficult to find many signs of her work in Paris and London in the early to mid-fifties, let alone life-size posters. Marc Bohan, the Dior designer who is among Eliette's close friends today, suggests that her lack of renown in the agency world has to do with sloppy record keeping. And, as Bohan says, "modeling in those days, as now, was often a springboard for 'other things.'" But there is no doubt that she was a beauty—early photographs confirm this—and only an emotional miser would be cruel and thoughtless enough to begrudge the myths of love. So one desists. Besides, the alliteration is too perfect: the Maestro and the model. Let it be, let it be.

Eliette carried on, that evening in Salzburger's office, gesturing and posturing with the complete French repertoire, telling parts of stories, being flirtatious. Karajan watched Eliette with the rapt attention he would give the oboe in a long solo passage. In addition, an unmistakable expression of love came over his face. His blue eyes were suddenly soft, his face relaxed, his lips parted in a warm smile of contentment. (I wondered if maybe his necktie was too tight.)

Eliette tried to bring Karajan into the conversation: "Now you tell what happened that evening." But he resisted: "Oh, no, it would take three hours."

Even before they met (the story goes), Eliette was sending Karajan red roses, one at a time. Everywhere he went, there would be another red rose. "Then they met, and he found out," Lore Salzburger says. "He forgot but she remembers. In the Green Room, in the bedroom when he is there—always there is a rose."

Anita knew of Karajan's attraction to Eliette, but was not worried. "He will never divorce me," she said to Edge Leslie. But Leslie knew Karajan's rationalization. "He told Anita it was more moral that he marry Eliette and have Anita as a best friend." It was a rationale that worked. Those who remember Karajan's courtship of Eliette (and vice versa) say that Anita helped Karajan secure the relationship. Upon their divorce, Karajan willingly bought Anita a house and had it redecorated. He rang her up frequently, especially on the occasion of the births of his and Eliette's daughters.

The children were an important element in these marital complexities. "He and Anita couldn't have children," Leslie says. "He felt something was missing in his manhood. One reason he married Eliette was in hopes of having children."

Karajan and Eliette Mouret were married in October 1958, at Megève in France. André von Mattoni was best man. Eliette's ski instructors were witnesses.

Karajan was busy in 1958. Just trying to keep up with him on paper gives one shortness of breath. It's like trying to keep track of two or three people, not just one. In 1958, *Time* magazine ran a photograph of him leaping, literally, from the cockpit of his 300 SL Gull-wing Mercedes, next to a story about *his* Salzburg Festival. *Time* put Karajan in the "topmost level of the world's conductors" and praised his production of Beethoven's *Fidelio*: "Festival visitors and critics generally agreed that not even the late Max Reinhardt ... had used the tricky space [of the Rocky Riding School] to better effect." But as usual, the review was mixed: "To Karajan's Beethoven, the musical reaction was reserved. Recalling Wilhelm Furtwängler's last Salzburg *Fidelio* (1950), critics complained that elegant, speed-loving Karajan did not have his idolized predecessor's warmth. Wrote one: Karajan's brilliance has the shining translucency of a perfectly formed icicle."

Also in 1958, Karajan met Ernst Haeusserman, the man who had emigrated to the U.S. with Henry Alter twenty years before. Haeusserman had attended school in the States. His theatrical interest had taken him to Hollywood, where he became assistant to Max Reinhardt, one of the several European directors who were weathering the war in Hollywood. Then he was drafted into the U.S. Army and assigned to a secret Army program to reeducate German prisoners of war who were being held in camps in the United States. At war's end, Haeusserman applied for civil employment overseas. Through the office of War Information, he returned to Austria in 1946 and took over the Red and White Radio Network.

Austrian nationals like Haeusserman (and Alter), who returned to the political and social vacuum of war's devastation as redoubtable civilian functionaries of the Allied Occupation Forces, were in excellent positions to profit from the rebuilding and rehabilitation of their country. As the cultural organism was nurtured back to health with newspapers, theaters, film companies, and radio stations regrouping under new ownership, the various applications were processed through their authority. Alter was primarily interested in concluding his postwar assignment in Europe and returning to his new life in America. In fact it was Alter, who, knowing of Haeusserman's desire to return to Austria, requested him as his replacement.

The crafty, soft-spoken Haeusserman, an inveterate deal maker with well-established connections in theater circles (his father had been an actor at the famous Burgtheater in Vienna), dug gleefully into the business at hand. He wasn't greedy; just comprehensive. It wasn't long before he became director of the Burgtheater, and he did own part of one of Vienna's largest daily newspapers, but mainly he established his power in Austria's cultural life in a more benign way: by the calculated dispensation of favors. He sowed well, and so did he reap.

His was a well-considered approach in a country like Austria, where the old-boy network is unbreachable. Austria is about 350 miles long and 160 miles across at its widest point. It is a bit smaller than, and about the same shape as, the state of Idaho. The population is only seven and a half million. And it is isolated geographically and to some extent linguistically amid Switzerland (to the west), West Germany and Czechoslovakia (to the north), Hungary (to the east), and Italy and Yugoslavia (to the south). Such positioning makes for narrow channels upon which to navigate a career. The options are few, no matter what profession one has chosen. And given the Austrian tradition of importance placed upon family and title, *whom* one knows is critical to career progress.

In many ways, Austria is an island. After spending some time there, one gets the sneaky suspicion that everyone is related by either birth or marriage.

With his Cheshire cat smile and perfect, Viennese manner, Professor Doctor Haeusserman staked his claim after the war and managed it deftly until his death by cancer of the stomach and liver in the spring of 1984. He was not by job title the most powerful cultural figure in Austria. But when one checked on how this or that minister or president had attained (or fallen from) his position, one would usually find the guiding hand of Haeusserman behind the scenes. He unfailingly sent cards of congratulation to political leaders on their birthdays, or their children's birthdays, or to take note of special accomplishments. And when these leaders discovered beautiful, richly deserving young women who (they were convinced) had great potential as actresses, they would of course call Haeusserman.

Haeusserman took these calls at one of the two "Stammtische" (regular tables) he held: one at noon, at Cafe Gerstner, where he lunched on light fare; the other, which began around 9 P.M. at Cafe

Grünwald, where his dinner would be accompanied by half a bottle of vodka on the rocks. This, three hundred and sixty-five days a year. The Stammtisch is the accepted way of doing business in Vienna's cafe-oriented society, but Haeusserman refined it into a media event. Here is where he would wring his hands in sarcastic glee over his "friends'" misfortunes, discuss his schemes, joke and gossip amid a constant stream of actors, musicians, theater officials, and Austrian political leaders, all of whom provided a satisfying audience for him as they came by to have a little coffee and do a little business.

Haeusserman says he met Karajan at a party in Vienna in the mid-1950s. "Dr. Polsterer, head of the Vienna *Kurier* newspaper, invited my wife and me to a party in honor of Gary Cooper, who was in Vienna. I met Karajan. We spoke about the Vienna Opera. I asked him if he had ever been approached to be director. He said no. I had the feeling he would be interested."

I spoke with Haeusserman in the summer of 1983 in his office in the Festspielhaus in Salzburg. I had been told by visitors to his Vienna office that his inner-sanctum door had no handle. His secretary kept the handle in a desk drawer, they reported, and used it to admit people after they had been screened. In his Festspielhaus office, the door handle was in place. The walls were hung with heavy, dark draperies. He was a small man, round of face and body, and a bit round-shouldered at the age of sixty-seven. His thinning hair was gray. He wore an old black velvet blazer, and squinted like a mole behind his eyeglasses. He spoke softly and smiled frequently. He said that from his first meeting with Karajan, he had found him open and easy to talk to, "not nimbus-wise, as legends made him appear.

"People around him always tried to make him look better so they would look better. I remember that he came to visit the Burgtheater in the '60s, after he became artistic director of the Vienna Opera. Mattoni called, said the chief would come to visit for one hour. He would like to eat. Just a little steak would be fine. The next time he came unannounced and by preference ate a peasant dish of smoked meat and dumplings.

"He didn't mind if his people kept others away from him and put him on a pedestal. The only thing he didn't like was if you didn't tell him the truth. If you rearranged the facts, and later he heard the real story—even if you had done so to make it easier for him—he couldn't understand it."

By all accounts, Karajan and Haeusserman became good friends. There is no question that they became good business associates. Karajan quickly (1959) put Haeusserman on the five-man Salzburg Festival board when Baron Puthon retired. This coveted position gave Haeusserman a quantum leap in terms of power, while it helped solidify the political side of the festival for Karajan. But there is no doubt that Haeusserman was one of the few who took meals with Karajan and spent evenings with him and his family. At one point, he lived close enough to the Karajans in Anif so that he would stop by their house on his bicycle. He gained enough of Karajan's confidence to write a book about him, *Herbert von Karajan*. It is a pat sort of biography that contains a useful and detailed listing of dates and events (concerts and reviews). It was obviously done with Karajan's close collaboration, but that Karajan would trust anyone in the music business enough to let him write a book about him is remarkable. Further testament of the two men's friendship came when Karajan visited Haeusserman when he was first hospitalized in Salzburg, a few months before his death. Haeusserman had demanded no visitors be admitted to his room, but Karajan strode purposely through the halls, fending off intervening nurses by telling them that his father had founded the place. Haeusserman was reportedly overwhelmed by Karajan's visit, and it was, in fact, a rarity. Karajan simply doesn't make hospital visits. He would sooner sit soaking wet in front of a January draft.

Karajan finished off 1958 by leaving Europe and flying to America to conduct the New York Philharmonic. A year later, he set off with the Vienna Philharmonic on a world tour that included concerts in New Delhi, Bombay, Manila, Hong Kong, Tokyo, Honolulu, Los Angeles, Salt Lake City, Chicago, Cleveland, New York, Boston, Atlanta, Washington, and Montreal.

Meanwhile, back in the recording studio, he was tackling Tchaikovsky, Richard Strauss, Brahms, Beethoven, Haydn, Mozart, Johann Strauss, Verdi, Dvořák, Handel, and Sibelius (all in 1959). It was the second recording he had made of Sibelius's *Finlandia*, and not long after that session Karajan went with Walter Legge to hear Bernstein play Sibelius in London. According to Edge Leslie, Legge suggested that Bernstein should have another look at the score. Karajan supposedly told Bernstein that he had spent ten years trying to popularize Sibelius, and that Bernstein had undone all his work in one hour. One doubts that such a confrontation took place. Such forthrightness is not the usual way of the music business, nor is it Karajan's way. Firings, dismissals, saying no, and other forms of unpleasantness are jobs that Karajan eagerly delegates.

Karajan probably spent more time making records than on any of his other endeavors, and no one gives a clearer picture of Karajan at work in the studio than John Culshaw, the late Decca producer who often worked with him. In his autobiography, Culshaw writes, "It was not easy to get to know him, but it was very easy to fault him about his seemingly casual manner. What one had to accept with Karajan was his impatience, and in time I came to understand, even to respect it. His own command, his sheer musical ability, his capacity to sight-read almost anything and get it right the first time were special qualities, which, I suspect, were not God's gifts so much as the result of years of hard work ... Karajan's main problem, and it was a minor issue, was that he always thought himself smarter than anyone else in matters not concerning music; and to keep on the right psychological terms with him we had, occasionally, to show him that was not always the case."

During the recording of *Otello*, Culshaw says some rescheduling was required because of the firing and hiring of singers. An evening session was planned, and everyone but Karajan could make it. Culshaw pleaded with him to no avail. Karajan said he had scheduled a choral rehearsal outside the city and it could not be altered. The evening paper betrayed Karajan with a story about the opening of a cinema in Vienna that was showing a new projection system, "Cinemiracle." It was to be a closed event that included the Austrian chancellor and a raft of dignitaries. Listed among them were Dr. and Mrs. Herbert von Karajan.

"There was, of course, only one thing to do," Culshaw writes. Culshaw called Karajan to make a final plea to make the session, and was told it was impossible. So Culshaw arranged for six seats to the "Cinemiracle" opening. "I reckoned he deserved what was coming to him—the sight of the six of us waiting for him at the foot of the ceremonial staircase which leads into the cinema. It was the only time I ever saw him aghast; it was perhaps the only time his impregnable security barrier had ever broken down. He shook hands with us sheepishly; and then—which was an insult we had certainly not planned—found that the seats he had been given were inferior to ours."

Culshaw's point is succinct: "The undeniable triviality of such an incident diverts attention from its single important aspect: you cannot keep on proper terms with someone like Karajan if you ever allow him to score points off you."

It is evident that EMI engineer Antony Griffiths was never a fan of Karajan's. Having watched Furtwängler invite principal players into the control room to hear and discuss tapes during sessions, Griffiths deplored the fact that Karajan excluded his players, preferring to listen alone and make unilateral decisions. And Griffiths can still chuckle over the time Karajan took it upon himself to fix an unruly piece of equipment, stuck his finger in a socket, and got a good shock. But what upset Griffiths even more was the "cult of recorded perfection" that was fast becoming the status quo in the industry as early as the 1960s.

"The sessions became so scientific, so serious—every note had to be perfect. I put the blame on the music critics. Everyone, even Sir Thomas Beecham, who was the greatest, fell prey to it. I remember one session we had with Beecham. It was a magic take. But there were a couple of very small mistakes. 'We've got to do it again to please the critics,' Beecham said. And he did. The next time it was perfect, but there was no magic. No one was willing to suffer the mistake for the good of the whole. But I saw Karajan do it with Richard Strauss's *Symphonia domestica*. He did it in one take. He was honest enough to try for spontaneity."

Despite the pressure of his many commitments, it seems that Karajan always took time to indulge his general curiosity and enhance his musical knowledge. When the possibility arose to acquire another fact or consider a new piece of research, Karajan the musicologist dropped everything. During rehearsals of Debussy's *Pelléas et Mélisande* at the Vienna Opera in the early 1960s, one of the singers mentioned that his teacher had been a friend of Debussy. Karajan halted the rehearsal and urged the singer to contact his teacher, whom Karajan subsequently had flown to Vienna. As Edge Leslie says, music is not just a profession for Karajan; it is a mission. Karajan's always fervent need to continue digging and learning often brought magic into his work.

Karajan didn't record *Pelléas* until 1978. When the recording appeared, it was received with the kind of enthusiasm registered by Felix Aprahamian in *Opera on Record*: "It is a curious fact that in so much classical music Karajan has given the impression of a super-Svengali manipulating the music marvelously, but at one remove, controlling it from outside, as it were. Here, the orchestral music, though played as immaculately as ever, seems to well up as a more deeply felt emotion, yet without the least exaggeration or contradiction of Debussy's expressive markings." The recording was the result of years of thought and study, as Aprahamian noted: "[Karajan] is the hero of the set, in a better sense than the most obvious, for it represents, as I hear it, the culminating point in his long-standing love-affair with French music."

By the 1960s Karajan's life and career pattern were well established. The breakneck pace continued, the outpouring of work was phenomenal. The concert schedule, the tours, the opera productions, and the recording sessions were jammed against one another like books on a shelf. Only the pieces, the cities, and the guest artists changed. The orchestras, for the most part, remained the same: the Berlin and Vienna Philharmonics. By the mid-1960s his "Generalmusikdirektor" phase was over. He was still artistic director for life of the Musikfreunde, and of the Berlin Philharmonic, and he had his recording contracts. But he had absented himself from administration. Milan, London, Vienna, and Salzburg (although he remained on the Salzburg Board of Directors) were no longer under his official direction. And yet, in spite of what seemed a withdrawal, the crescendo of his power showed no sign of faltering. He continued to direct Salzburg even without the portfolio. For the rest, his name was magic. His was a true attainment of power; without being in charge, he was running the show. Why? Because running the show came naturally to him, first of all. As a leader he was no pretender. He was self-styled, and he knew what he wanted, which are the best attributes a leader can have. And the public wanted him. He sold tickets. He had become a superstar, an idol. In Salzburg they built the best opera house in the world for him.

Superstars do not develop on talent alone. Immense talent is a prerequisite, but it is a unique and fortuitous combination of other elements that merge with the talent to produce the superstar. In Karajan's case, the unique and fortuitous combination is nearly as extraordinary as the man.

First of all, he had a captivating look about him, handsome, with an underlying fierceness in the eyes. And he combined the dash of a wealthy sportsman—with his fast cars, his big boats, mountain climbing and skiing—with the steely self-discipline of a Buddhist monk. He drank very little and he didn't smoke. His small stature and less than reliable good health induced an initial touch of sympathy that captured people's imaginations and was immediately converted to a perception of courage by the tough-guy stance he had carried through life. Whether he was being questioned by the Nazis about his Jewish wife, or the Allies about his Nazi associations, or harrassed by Furtwängler, or beleaguered by festival boards or opera house administrators, or confronted by prima donnas—anyone who interfered with his doing what he wanted, when and how he wanted to do it—he held with tenacity to his guiding principle: namely, that his musical mission put him essentially beyond reproach.

That is, of course, a classically outrageous attitude, one that never fails to attract public support when it is cast within a benign form

(music, sports, etc.) and features an otherwise well-intentioned pro-
tagonist going against the system, because it is an untenable attitude
for most people. When someone appears who has the talent, resources,
and arrogance to pull it off, whether Mohammad Ali or Herbert von
Karajan, he provides us with vicarious satisfaction, or at least amazement. Karajan gave as good as he got (mostly better), he apologized
to no one, and he never looked back in his obsession to get on with
the work at hand.

Sometimes Karajan really did take it beyond the limits, but such
instances just add to the myth. In 1969, for instance, there were some
difficulties with the complex negotiations among Karajan, the Berlin
Philharmonisches, and recording companies. Karajan saw problems
coming and hastily contacted business associates asking if they could
arrange for him to be principal guest conductor of the Paris Orchestra.
There was a flurry of telephoning that reached the highest levels of
the French government: it was necessary that General de Gaulle himself agree to an ex-Nazi leading the Paris Orchestra. Somehow it was
done, de Gaulle agreed, and Karajan was called with the news. He
acted puzzled. But you wanted it! his caller said, incredulous. No I
didn't, Karajan said, and went on to say that if the Paris Orchestra
wished to engage him, they should send a personal emissary to him
from de Gaulle. On another occasion, when a concert at the Vatican
was under consideration, Karajan demanded an emissary from the
Pope. (After three years of preparations, the concert at the Vatican
took place on June 27, 1985. "The public relations man from the
Vatican said, 'we announce this thing as a Mass of the Pope, and it
becomes the Herbert von Karajan show,'" Karajan said with obvious
relish. "And it was! The cameras showed the Pope whenever he was
in action of course, but when the music was on, it was us. It was too
bad: so many couldn't see him. So many couldn't see me! The Pope
kissed me. He did! He took me to his breast and kissed me.")

Karajan may have been calculating on all fronts, but he took
enough losses to certify his basic, defiant, self-centered posture as
natural and ingrained. And of course, most of the battles, both wins
and losses, were well documented in the press. So his notoriety spread.
Karajan may not read reviews, but he has always understood the value
of the press and has never hesitated to use it to advantage. As a media
manipulator, he ranks with the best. One can't control the news
stories, but on those occasions when the tide was against him, he
would become totally unavailable for comment. This behavior would
tend to make the stories harsher on him, and conjecture would take
the place of fact. The effect? Sympathy from the reader.

He used the press conference as a deadly weapon. He was so withdrawn from the press in general, so violently opposed to photographs
of himself taken without his permission and editing approval, that
when he called them, the press came in droves. (Once when he was
on tour in Oslo and saw the flash of a camera in the audience, he
stopped the concert until the violator was apprehended and his film
taken from him). And when the magazines called, they agreed to play
by his rules or not at all. Consider this idyllic rendition of the Karajans
"at home" from *Paris Match* in 1963 (the setting is the Karajans'
country house at Buchenhof, outside Vienna): The day begins with
yoga at 6 A.M. Breakfast is frugal. "We eat like peasants," says Karajan.
Breakfast is followed by a walk through the countryside. Then he
rehearses his conducting. They "eat a fruit" halfway through the
day. Then he relaxes with Eliette and the children, after which he
goes out to shoot a reindeer, or takes out his tractor, watched over
by Eliette. In the evening they have their only real meal of the day.
When they have finished their dinner, they sit by the fireside the rest
of the evening, while Karajan checks recording proofs against musical
scores.

Marvelous, really.

Herbert Breiter, a painter who lives in Salzburg, provides a more
realistic version of Karajan's home life. Breiter is an easygoing, affable
man, and earthy. His landscapes are memorable for the remarkable
quality of light he captures. Eliette, an aspiring painter, had engaged
Breiter as her teacher. She liked Breiter and his wife, and suddenly
they received an invitation to spend a few days in St. Moritz with the
Karajans. They accepted, and their presence in St. Moritz became an
annual event.

"Karajan was like a little boy at times," Breiter says. "Once he
picked me up in his four-wheel drive car. He had a box with him
containing an airplane model. He asked me to hold it so he could
whip the car up the mountain full-tilt without having to worry about
it.

"We didn't ever talk about music. But I did want to make it clear
that I didn't have a secret ambition to sing, and that I wasn't even
angling for tickets. So I told him what I really wanted to do was
conduct the Berlin Philharmonic. He looked sideways at me. 'What
piece?' I named a Mozart that I liked. 'How does it start?' I sang a
few bars. He joined in. 'Alright,' he said, 'you can do it.'

"He likes to be home, but it's part of his life to come and go. I was
at his house once when he arrived from Tokyo. Eliette was painting
something. He walked in, and it was like he had just come from the

store. Eliette looked up and said to him, 'Do you think this blue should be darker?' They travel a lot, sometimes on the spur of the moment. They decide fast, pack in fifteen minutes.

"There is no music in the house. They spend time with the TV or the video recorder. Karajan loves movies. He liked *E.T.* He loved *Tootsie*. Eliette plays music when he is not around. It's often complex, modern music that is hard to listen to or to understand.

"He likes a good joke. The mezzo-soprano Leontyne Price had a T-shirt made for him with his photograph on it. Under his photo she had printed, 'The King.' He loved it. People are important to him. If there were three violinists, all equally excellent, Karajan would want the one with the personality he liked best. With Karajan, the personalities must match, too.

"He never plays games at home. No cards, no backgammon. Luck is involved with games, and I think he is afraid he could lose."

From the practical side, it was the recordings that laid the groundwork for Karajan's superstardom, and that made him a familiar enough personage to the music-loving, record-buying public so that they were predisposed to respond eagerly to further information about him. According to the Karajan discography compiled by Antony Williams and published by General Gramophone Publications Ltd. (England, 1978), Karajan first recorded in 1938 (the Overture to Mozart's *Magic Flute* with the Berlin State Opera Orchestra).

"In 1938, doing those first recordings," Karajan says, "we recorded in a church outside Berlin. It was near the airport. We recorded in the afternoon, and at around 3 P.M. each day, planes would take off. We tried to plan, but sometimes the planes would go over in the middle of a piece and we had to start again. We made ten-inch, 78-rpm discs that ran four minutes to a side. Once we loaded a plane with wax masters. It landed in Frankfurt and got fogged in. There was a frost that night, and seventy-five percent of the waxes broke in two. It was three months' work." But even in its primitive state, Karajan felt the recording industry was where the future of music existed. It was an attitude that not many of his contemporaries shared.

By the mid-'50s, he had been recording nearly twenty years and had hundreds of records to his credit. His discs were almost impossible to avoid in the stores in the 1940s and '50s. And by design, he recorded pieces that people wanted to hear. Toscanini was lured back to the United States in the late 1940s to take over the NBC Symphony Orchestra because he wanted to reach millions of people with his music, and NBC offered him a way to do it. From the outset,

Karajan's ambition was similar: he wanted to reach the mass audience. A look at his first records indicates his choice of popular classics: Verdi's *La Forza del destino* Overture; Tchaikovsky's Symphony No. 6 (*Pathétique*); Wagner's *Die Meistersinger von Nürnberg* Overture; Dvořák's *New World* Symphony.

Karajan is a little sensitive about the "popular" designation that is often tagged to many of his recorded works. On the way to see him at his house in St. Tropez in 1982, I heard Saint-Saëns's Symphony No. 3 (the "organ symphony") by Karajan and the Berlin Philharmonic, on the car radio. It is a grandiose piece full of familiar melody that builds to a roaring climax punctuated by full-throated organ chords. When I mentioned this to Karajan he looked just a bit defensive, despite the obvious pleasure I had gotten from hearing it. The Saint-Saëns, it seems, is regarded as a bit of a show piece and is sniffed at somewhat by the cognoscenti.

My mention of it caused Karajan to recall his student days when Toscanini brought the La Scala opera company to Vienna. "The first opera they did was Donizetti's *Lucia di Lammermoor*. This made a big impression on me because *Lucia* was regarded as second-class music. Because Toscanini was coming, we studied the piece and played it in class, and I thought, 'how can such a great man play this music?' Then I heard Toscanini play it, and I knew that there was not much bad music, only bad conducting and playing. It was incredible. The secret was to play it so that it didn't sound vulgar.

"I have recorded the Barcarole from *Tales of Hoffmann*, a much-maligned piece. There has been a duel, a man has been killed, and now there is a funeral march, only it is written like a lullaby, rocked by the waves of the channel which are the same as always. It is a tragic piece in perfection. I told the orchestra, 'let yourselves be dragged like a woman by the hair—try not to play completely together, let that come later, and try for a rich sound.' And I succeeded in this. It is the same with waltzes, the clichés one hears all the time. I admire Strauss for his waltzes, but moreover for the introductions to those waltzes. He had Wagner's gift for introductions. I recorded the *Delirium Waltz* just to do it without the usual banalities. I feel it is my duty to do the great repertoire and distribute it to the great majority."

Karajan the scholar, the amateur scientist and technician, appreciated the miracle of recording. He made it his business to understand what was going on inside those big wax master machines and followed the progress of the craft with intense interest. In 1950, he made his first LP, a ten-inch disc of Mozart's Piano Concerto No. 21

in C major, K. 467. "Tape was invented by the Germans during the war," Karajan says. "They used it to scramble messages by sending them ten times faster than they should be played. The British discovered the tape capability after the war. It was incredible. At first they needed a five-second pause between notes in order to make a cut. I had it written in my contract that I would be in on all cutting sessions. Usually that is in the hands of experts. Then came stereo, with new tricks and difficulties. Then quadraphonic, which was a flop. All it did was help people who made sofas and chairs, because to hear it you had to be in the center of the room. And now there is the laser."

Karajan says he listens to all final versions of his recordings on a Sony Walkman cassette player. "Never do I listen to the disc. You have to subtract a little quality, but if it sounds good on the cassette, then I know the disc will be perfect. When the last correction is made, when it is perfect, I don't listen to it anymore. Only if I will re-record the piece. Then I go into a room for two days and listen to it and think I must have been drunk when I did it."

Recording was a two-sided miracle for Karajan, because therein was the key to his goal of reaching the masses. Today Karajan reviews what he calls "the explosion of music" with the quiet pride of a man who was astute enough to buy a quantity of Ford Motor stock in the 1930s for ten cents a share. "The early records were poor, they lasted only a short time, and they had a bad sound. First, people bought popular music. Students especially. When most students leave college they have with them seventy or eighty discs of symphonic music. We know this. I have made eight hundred titles, sold close to a hundred million records. When we started, we would sell fifteen hundred copies of a record. Now we have the explosion. I am so happy to have taken part in it.

"We can bring music to almost anybody, and that is a great achievement. It is amazing how very simple people react to music. I sometimes go outside Salzburg amid the beautiful landscape where I run upon a peasant on a tractor. He recognizes me. I ask, 'do you listen?' He says, 'oh yes, when we know you are on, we sit there very quiet.' And it makes an impression, no doubt. Music is a counterpoint or a necessity to replace the other values which have been lost. Even in the theater side, most of what you have is the reenactment of the misery and uncertainty the human race suffers. The theater doesn't relieve you of it, it reinforces it. The plays are about drunks and suicide. Whereas music—I know of only two pieces in music that end on a completely negative vein: Sibelius's Fourth and Mahler's Sixth, which ends with total destruction."

Karajan's emphasis on orchestral sound made him a perfect match for the rapidly advancing quality of the recording industry. Diamond styluses, transistorized electronics, component systems, silent-running turntables, and crystal-clear speaker systems with precise division of decibel ranges—"high fidelity"—that began to appear on the market in the 1950s suddenly made home listening a more intense experience than the concert hall. At home, there would be no one coughing during the pianissimo solo violin passage, no annoying acoustical oddities of a less than satisfactory hall. And while the spontaneity of live performance bowed to cutting and splicing, much more was possible. In the concert hall, one could not hear the sound of real cannon firing during the *1812 Overture*, as one could on the recording. In the studio, Karajan the technician took full advantage of the possibilities.

John Culshaw writes about Karajan's 1961 recording of *Otello*, in which the opening scenes called for thunder, a cannon shot, and (by Karajan's request) a wind machine for storm effect. Culshaw tells of the difficulty of finding an organ of sufficient magnitude to produce the required deep notes (C, C sharp, and D) of the lowest register that had to be sustained for more than fifty pages (eight minutes) of the score. Finally an organ with a real sixty-four-foot pipe was found at the (then) incomplete Liverpool Cathedral. So a tape was made, at night, because of the daytime construction noise. "Nothing was quite as spooky as Liverpool Cathedral, empty at the dead of night and throbbing to the sound of Verdi's sustained organ pedal," Culshaw writes. "Karajan was so pleased with the result that we gave him the tape to use in the theater, where he blew all the speakers on the first attempt."

Sound was what Karajan had to sell, and high fidelity was the perfect, custom-made marketing tool that appeared as if on cue. As Peter Busse once remarked about Karajan, "in addition to everything else, he is a lucky man." Sound was suddenly a most marketable commodity. Because aside from the better musicians and schooled listeners, the vast majority of the listening audience—even the classical buffs—are not all that perceptive. The easiest element to appreciate in any recording is the sound of it. One can enjoy the sound sensuality of a recording without the brain even being engaged. So while the critics, serious listeners, and collectors argue over subtleties of interpretation, the buyers most often go for the sound. The challenge of hi-fi, which will faithfully reproduce even a misplaced heartbeat, suited Herbert von Karajan. He was equal to the task.

"He is unique in the entire world of music," Ron Wilford says. "He was born in Salzburg, he overcame his provincial beginnings, learned languages, became an international figure. From the public's perception, he is the greatest in the world. He is accepted in all repertoires. The core repertoire is German and Austrian music. And he is at home with the Russian, the Italian, the Romantic repertoires. And since World War II, Karajan has had thirty years of constant, uninterrupted work, whereas Toscanini's career was interrupted by a war. In that time there has been a media explosion because of communications, and records, stereo. He was in the vanguard of recordings, and when the medium improved, he did the whole repertoire over again. Many new markets have been opened up—Japan, South America—and Karajan has been there."

Karajan became an international figure, as Wilford suggests, but at the same time he put down strong anchors at his Austria-Germany base. He probably could have had New York, or wherever else he wanted, but never with the kind of control, prestige, and power he developed in the Vienna-Salzburg-Berlin triangle. He was one of the old boys, after all, and the network was his. Why should he have left that foundation, or the rich and popular tradition that he was continuing right there on the hallowed ground where Brahms, Wagner, Mahler, Bruckner, Strauss, and Furtwängler had worked before him? Where else would he find such entrenched, enthusiastic audiences for his operas? Where else two orchestras side by side that could equal the Berlin and Vienna Philharmonics? Why should he have left what has developed (thanks in large part to him) into the biggest and best summer music festival in the world? Then there were the mountains he had loved since childhood, the skiing, the summer home on the Mediterranean, the sylvan setting outside Vienna, the winter lodge in St. Moritz, all easily and quickly accessible by his private jet and helicopter. He could buy the best cars in the world at his local factories, fully customized for him. He brought his music to the world via records, tours, and later on, films. Once established, he stayed at home and let the world come to him. For many years it was a perfect situation. Only in 1984, when Karajan's long-simmering argument with the Berlin Philharmonic flared into open hostilities, was he a bit trapped by his self-imposed geographical limitations. During that final set-to with the Berlin, he was unable to use quitting as a threat. He knew where his power lay. If he quit, where would he go at age seventy-six?

As early as 1960, Karajan decided he wanted to "give something back" to up-and-coming young conductors and suggested that a conducting competition be held. Willy Brandt, who was then mayor of West Berlin, quickly turned Karajan's idea into a city-sponsored event. Sixty competitors gathered, all expenses paid. It was this competition that produced Seiji Ozawa. His prize was twelve private lessons with Karajan at the rate of one a month. It is difficult to imagine the City of New York indulging such a conductor's whim.

But by 1960, the Grosse Festspielhaus was in progress, and that was a much more expensive and politically dangerous indulgence. Karajan conducted the opening performance in 1964 and caused a considerable stir by refusing to allow the event to be televised throughout the country. It was a hall for the people, it was argued, therefore the people should have at least televised access to the opening performance. But Karajan refused on the grounds that in his opinion, television wasn't aesthetically capable of handling the job. The point is, he refused, and he made it stick. No TV. Imagine *that* happening in most major cities.

The advent of the Easter Festival in 1967 practically did put Karajan beyond reproach in Austria. Not only was the venture a success musically, but Karajan was solely responsible for filling up Salzburg's hotels, restaurants, and shops for ten otherwise moderate business days. The people he filled them with were triple-A visitors, the champagne set. And because he used the Berlin Philharmonic, he got credit for putting more kudos (not to mention a lot of cash) in their already brimming basket.

There was big satisfaction in it for Karajan, too, because after all those years of complaining about how opera was produced, and all those years of outlining the proper way to all those who would listen, Easter Festival was his chance to do it his way. Such moments of truth are dangerous—putting up or shutting up, it is called—but Easter Festival was sweet. He did it his way, and it worked. The Wunder Karajan indeed.

The following March (1968), Salzburg expressed its appreciation to Karajan by presenting him with "the ring of the land"—the key to the city. Karajan countered in statesmanlike fashion by announcing the opening of two foundations in his name: the Herbert von Karajan Foundation in Berlin, for "the promotion of scientific musical activity, and for spreading a consciousness for musical feeling"; and the Research Institute of Herbert von Karajan, a foundation for experimental music/psychology in the Psychological Institute of the University of Salzburg. The timing was perfect, Karajan's status having been cranked up several notches in both Berlin and Salzburg by the festival. The foundations were more dreams realized for Karajan, and were exactly what one might have expected from him in the way of philanthropy: musical, with emphasis on the scientific.

Naturally, the ever-curious Karajan was at the heart of the initial

experiments. Who would be a better or more enthusiastic test subject? During one rehearsal in Salzburg, he had measuring instruments
similar to those used by astronauts attached to his body. His brain-
waves, cardiogram, pulse, air intake, and emotional state (measured
by static electricity on the skin's surface) were recorded and coordinated with a film of the rehearsal so the measured effects could be
matched with the music score. "The results," Karajan says, "made it
evident that the emotional load on the body is greatest *before* something happens. It was no accident that two conductors who died on
the podium did so during piano, not forte passages." It wasn't exactly
hot news, but he was enthusiastic about it.

He spoke to *High Fidelity*'s Paul Moor in 1969 about how the
foundations came about: "I felt a need to give something back, something of the enormous, inner good fortune and direction which music
has given me all my life. So I said, what can I do? First, how much
do we know about music as it influences a human being—the physical
and psychological aspects? How much do we know about the perception of music by the ear? How do we translate a sort of physical thing
into an emotional thing?

"I want to know the psychological distinction between a coordinated sequence of notes and what we normally call melody—melody
which has emotional value. I also want to know, as an interpreter,
where my work begins—where my influence on a sequence of notes
begins and ends.

"All we know that can be varied are the tempo and the dynamics.
Perhaps we can conclude what the effect of a single artist is. Has the
transmission of his personality an effect which can be actually
measured? We have to find out.

"I am quite convinced that the nucleus of music making is the
rhythm. We will discover how music of a certain meter and tempo
will influence the heartbeat.... Rhythm, for instance, may be closely
related to two-thirds or four-sevenths of your heartbeat. I know that
from the way, sometimes, when I attack the beginning of a piece of
music and it comes out of myself, I feel it is right. At other times,
you fight yourself—it's a little too fast or a little too slow—and I'm
convinced that this happens on a day when the tempo is not in
concordance with your heartbeat."

Karajan said he hoped that his foundation would get at the roots
of how music affected people in order to use it as therapy for the
mentally dislocated.

Nothing so momentous came out of the foundations. After an
unsuccessful effort to convert the Salzburg foundation into a school

for singers, it was discontinued altogether in 1980. All that remains of the original concept are the "Salzburg Conversations" that take place each year during the Easter Festival among various scientific-minded and musical personalities who are invited to participate.

The Berlin foundation still exists, with its purpose being the support of conductors and orchestras. For several years competitions sponsored by this foundation provided talented people with well-deserved recognition, but of late they have faded. "They are not very important any more," says one who has watched their progress. "They are not well attended, there are no big names." Conducting contenders come mainly from the East, from Iron Curtain countries, and Karajan is not interested in putting on a competition exclusively for this group. In the last three years, he has witheld the awarding of first prizes for conducting because he saw no one with sufficient talent. The orchestra competition has stopped altogether.

A third foundation was begun in Vienna, on the occasion of Karajan's seventieth birthday, in 1978. It sponsors a two-to-three-day music symposium every other year that is of a scientific nature.

The master classes Karajan held at the Mozarteum during the Salzburg Festival weren't always as advertised. One student who attended in the late 1970s reported that Karajan appeared only twice out of forty-seven meetings, and then he did little but make disparaging remarks about the quality of the students. The tuition for the classes was $7,000.

The success of the Easter Festival seemed to reduce Karajan's activity, when in fact it served only to centralize it further. From this point on, his guest conducting virtually stopped. "One is never given enough time to prepare the new orchestra, so why should I do it?" he said. And his tours became infrequent. He had gotten out of his provincial little town, made his mark, and now he was back, reunited with Salzburg in his own way, on his terms, with the town gratefully paying its respects to him.

Once during the summer of 1983 I drove with Karajan to a high vantage point in the mountains outside Salzburg, where we sat and talked. "Life is not pleasant here," he said, looking through the windshield of the big Mercedes at the town stretched out along the valley below. "It has to do with the weather. It changes quickly. The sirocco comes from on high, the air gets heated, the temperature rises. People couldn't bear it. People who are experts on animals know that the young and temperamental horse will lose his vitality here. So people used to say to me, 'don't stay here too long.' It is a narrow-minded place. All the good guys from here have been treated poorly. Mozart was treated like a coachman, and ultimately kicked out. I have had to pay. People know I depend on being here. I have no other theater. 'He won't leave,' they say, 'let him pay.' I have paid. What I have paid for the Easter Festival in the last fifteen years I couldn't tell you. Maybe $10 million. But I am not complaining. It is my pride. My joy."

I suggested that he must have got some of the money back in recording royalties. He looked sideways at me with the faint trace of a smile. "Oh yes, of course," he said gruffly.

"It has taken me a long time to like Salzburg again. I never go into the town. When I go from Anif to the Festspielhaus, I always drive around the mountain and come in the back way. You will never catch me in the center of town."

While he stuck close to his various home bases after 1967, with a few exceptions, like the tour of Japan in 1977 with the Berlin Philharmonic, and the U.S. appearance in 1982, his work load was never decreased. His productivity can best be appreciated when one looks at the record output. In 1967, he made 16 recordings; in 1968, 8; in 1969, 27; in 1970, 15; in 1971, 31; in 1972, 21; and so on. Each year's recorded works included a complete opera that was taped in the fall preceding its live production at Easter Festival the following spring. And he was working hard at putting music on film, a long-time fascination of his.

In 1977, thirteen years afer his terrible row with the Vienna State Opera, Karajan returned to that venerable institution to do nine performances of an opera production. The opera he selected for the occasion was Verdi's *Il Trovatore*, in Italian, of course. At the time, an interviewer said that it was expected he would conduct twelve to sixteen performances, given the wide interest his appearance has generated. And it was only nine. "Wasn't it possible for you to conduct more performances?"

"No," Karajan told the interviewer. "I believe there is one decisive factor. It's always the same here: far too many rumors are spread around—what will and what won't happen. Why didn't anyone ask me? I knew I couldn't accommodate more than that."

And he was clear on why he had come to do a production in Vienna: "My activity here is for the purpose of creating a foundation upon which a really adequate TV transmission, a live transmission of an opera conducted by me, can take place. I told the Federal Chancellor this. For I don't understand that when a country which is relatively small and really, to the admiration of the whole world, raises this sum [the Vienna Opera House has by far the largest budget, more than any other opera house has, or probably ever will have] why so many people should be shut out from the pleasure."

This was certainly a turnaround in attitude from the anti-TV stance Karajan had taken at the opening of the Grosse Festspielhaus in 1964. But having assessed the problem—inadequacy of technique on the part of the medium—he had been working on it. And he lectured the Viennese in a most belittling manner, with ill-concealed glee: "I believe we have now developed a new kind of technique which in the meantime we have tried out in Japan, to see how it functions. This is naturally not the usual fumbling about with the senseless moving around, backwards and forwards, but a long-prepared affair which needs four or five days' rehearsal.

"You see, we have been doing this for about eight years. I am now on my thirty-second TV music production either of concerts or operas . . . and we have naturally amassed a lot of experience and have the know-how. So far we have worked mainly in film studios—*Otello* was made in Munich, with all imaginable splendor, and that is where the great public begins to be interested."

Leontyne Price sang Leonora in *Trovatore* with Karajan in 1962–63 in Vienna, and she returned with him in 1977. Karajan could take full credit for her appearance. She had been absent from Vienna for as long as Karajan. "I have a terrible habit," Miss Price says today, recalling both productions: "loyalty to those who have been kind to me. When Karajan left Vienna, I left too. Thirteen years later he asked me to return with him to do *Trovatore*. In 1962 it had been a great cast, a great theatrical experience for me. So when he called, I said, 'I'll be fifty.' He said, 'You have taken care of your instrument. You have sung on the interest, not the capital. At fifty you will be as good if not greater than you were at thirty-seven.'"

Price's memories of Karajan are fond. Many singers have dropped by the wayside, or have been dropped by Karajan. Leontyne Price has gone the distance with him. Her ability sustained, as Karajan pointed out. But that could be said about some of the others who fell from grace. Perhaps Price lasted because she has a sense of herself that is strong enough to match both her talent and her ego. Her marvelous sense of humor, combined with a charming haughtiness, seems to have complimented her great talent in a way that was irresistable to Karajan. "If you are an American Beauty Rose," Price says, "don't try and be a lily. Stay in your own artistic firmament. My mother told me that. And if you are fortunate enough to have a genius who likes your instrument, you can't let that make you forget your own individuality. You can relate to your desires, but never at the expense of who you are.

"I auditioned for him in Carnegie Hall in 1955. He called me 'an artist of the future.' He came to the stage, waved my pianist away, and played with me. The chemistry was there both for the music and the friendship. He still gives me artistic advice. I hold him in profound admiration."

Price made her debut in San Francisco in 1957, after which Karajan brought her to Vienna, where he used her frequently for seven seasons. She calls Karajan one of the kindest men she ever met: "concerned, and full of humor. My southern accent amuses him, as it does most Europeans. He tells me, 'it is amazing you can sing the way you do and speak in such a way.' He says I am like two people-'one of those nice, relaxed Americans.' He likes me because of my approach to work. I'm not into the trumpets. No entrances and exits are necessary. I just plunge right in. His vocal advice and new reading of *Trovatore* [in 1977]—his awareness of my own capabilities in a more mature stage—was like having a series of vocal lessons from someone who knew my voice as well as I do.

"No one tells him no, but I do. I am not the least bit afraid of him. I looked into those mesmerizing blue eyes, those hypnotic, penetrating eyes that are never told no, and I told him no to *Salome*. He was furious. And he might have been right. It probably would have been great. But I never lost my priorities. And I said no to *Carmen*. The year he did it I was asked to open the Met season with *Cleopatra*. The timing was wrong. But it was a privilege and an honor to open the Met. I had earned it. I had to choose the most important, and opening the Met was an historic occasion.

"He got his *Carmen* [1963], and I got my *Salome* at age fifty-six. Music has been my whole life, but you can't lose yourself along the way. In music, in marriage, in love affairs, you can't give it all. You have to save some for you. The priorities must be you. He has respect for that. He wasn't really mad—just disappointed. The great conductors have egos that are indescribable. They have no business being on the podium if that is not the case. I adore the few who get a kick out of it, and who are prepared to do it."

There have been a few times when Karajan's ego has receded momentarily, when the bravado that carries him through has failed in the face of something that threatened to touch his core. The occasion of his honorary degree from Oxford University was one such time. Oxford first contacted Edge Leslie and asked him to get Karajan's response to the notion of a degree. Oxford likes to keep such matters secret until the potential candidate has let it be known that he will accept. Leslie called Karajan. "We spoke for thirty minutes," Leslie says. "He said he was so flattered he hardly knew what to say. The idea of a ceremony frightened him. He asked me a dozen questions: would it be a large affair? Would he have to make a speech? He said if he didn't have to speak, he would accept."

Karajan received his honorary music doctorate from Oxford on June 21, 1978. The citation read (in part): "A consummate conductor ends our procession, a native of Salzburg, who as a ten-year-old boy is said to have hidden himself behind the organ pipes when Toscanini was conducting a private orchestral rehearsal, to eavesdrop on the proceedings: to think of organ pipes no longer voiced but, as it were, sharp-eared!"

That fall, Karajan was in Berlin, rehearsing the Philharmonic prior to recording Verdi's *Don Carlos*. He was seated on a high stool with his feet on the base of the music stand in front of him attending to the business at hand, when he suddenly pitched forward, landing on the floor in front of the first violins. It was thought that the music stand had broken, causing him to lose his balance. The public was told simply that he had had a fall. In fact, he had suffered a stroke. He was rushed to the hospital, where he stayed four weeks. A tour was canceled, and it was two months before he was back at work—a speedy recovery given the serious nature of the problem. But the stroke had attacked the right side of his body, and some of the effects would be long-lasting. That Karajan had a stroke was never announced or discussed outside a close circle of acquaintances and coworkers.

The harborfront of St. Tropez, the town made famous by Brigitte Bardot, perhaps the greatest cinematic sex symbol of them all, is shaped in a long, sweeping curve, like the inside of a horseshoe. On the shore side, it is lined with outdoor cafes and shops. Across a wide promenade, the water ends at a stone bulkhead against which yachts park perpendicular, stern-to, Mediterranean style. In July of 1981, the sleek racing sloop amid the lavish, Italian-styled motor yachts—the 77-footer with the wide, three-part, red horizontal stripe along its gray hull, and the white spars—was the yacht of Herbert von Karajan. Designed by the well-known race-boat architect German Frers, it is a so-called maxi, the largest boat that can race under the International Offshore Rule. Its name, *Helisara*, is a contraction of Herbert, Eliette, Isabel, and Arabel. Karajan says he gave a lot of thought to the red stripe. "It had to be just right," he says. "The object was to make the boat look even bigger and more fearsome than it is."

Those who go sailing on *Helisara* board the boat in town. Captain and crew then motor the three or four miles along the coast to the east and pick up the yacht's mooring in a small cove off Karajan's house. This, at about 2 P.M. on days when the Maestro has decided to go sailing. Gary Jobson, who had been hired by Karajan to help him organize and understand his highly strung thoroughbred, and I did this, and watched as Karajan walked down his narrow dock and got into a small rubber boat. Josef was with him, driving the boat as he does the cars. Karajan had been limping noticeably as he walked, and it was with considerable difficulty that he negotiated the unstable steps that had been lowered over *Helisara*'s side. One of his feet got tangled in the lifelines. He quickly made his way to the helmsman's seat, and settled himself with obvious relief behind the wheel of leather-covered stainless steel which is six feet in diameter.

He spoke to his crew in French, and soon sails were raised, the mooring cast off, and we were moving in the light summer breeze. Karajan wore a jogging suit and faded blue-visored cap with the word "Goodyear" embroidered across the front. Under his jogging suit top he wore a shirt from the twelve-meter *Freedom*, winner of the 1980 America's Cup, that had been given to him by *Freedom*'s skipper Dennis Conner, another of his sailing teachers.

His approach to the boat was much like his approach to his jet aircraft: serious. His face was set in a frown of concentration. This was to be work, not play. There were maneuvers to be practiced and mastered, boat-handling drills to be coordinated and refined among this crew of twenty men. One might have wondered toward what purpose, if Jobson had not already settled that question, because even the helm of a maxi boat under anything but the most moderate conditions is a workout (the deck jobs are best attempted by large, muscular young men in good condition). Karajan's age and health would surely prevent him from undertaking anything but the shortest helm tricks during a race. Even the more accomplished maxi owners have no qualms about yielding to professional sailors when the action gets hot, such is the level of competence required to handle the huge boats safely. But Jobson, who likes to know what the goal is in such situations, had it figured: "Making von Karajan happy is the only goal," he said. "His kick is seeing maneuvers done perfectly."

For two hours Jobson ran the boat through various drills, with Karajan following his directions from the helm. Once Karajan broke off in mid-stream when he encountered another vessel, a ratty-looking cruising boat in the fifty-foot range. "Wait until I beat this fellow," he told Jobson, sliding down to the low side and concentrating with more vigor. It was like a Ferrari taking a Ford, but Karajan got satisfaction from it.

Jobson took the helm at one point to demonstrate a certain technique. He sailed through a maneuver, and it was a bit sloppy. Karajan pointed this out to Jobson. "Let's try it again," Gary said. "Don't release the sail until I give the word." The second time it was smooth.

"Very good," said Karajan.

"You're my coach," Jobson told him.

We were invited to dinner at Karajan's villa, *La Palme*, an honor reserved for close associates, heads of state, and sportsmen. The house is modest, elegantly comfortable. The decor is white, with accents of off-white and silver. One of Eliette's paintings, a muddy, ill-defined landscape, hung on a wall of the sitting room. We ate a simple but tasty meal on a large, flagstone porch that was glassed in on the two sides facing the water. It was cooked and served by Francesco, a twenty-year employee of the Karajans. Eliette did not join us. Karajan barely touched his food. He drank half a glass of wine with his left hand. When he did use his right hand it was with some difficulty. And when he moved around the house, he lurched from chair back to table for support. But he was a good host. Conversation was lively. He spoke with enthusiasm about the boat.

"Before the maxi was created, I was after the fastest boat there was," he said. "Then came *Helisara*. The first afternoon I took the boat out there was a good breeze. The boat vibrated with power, force. I couldn't sleep all night thinking about it." Mainly it is the orderly process that absorbs him with a boat of *Helisara*'s size and complexity. "In what other sport must you coordinate twenty people? The orchestra is more or less the same. People responding to a common will. It is a synchronized process that runs like film. Like the rhythm of flying, or driving. When it is right, your grandmother could be riding in the back with no fear. With sailing, it is the coordination of people with me and the boat. When it is right, the boat feels as if it moves by itself. Of course it works best in a smaller boat. On the maxi you pay for it by having a crew of twenty."

Jobson wondered about the crew. "They talk to one another sometimes, but rarely as a unit," he observed, and wondered why.

"Here, everybody attacks everybody," Karajan said, waving his arm in a wide arc. He shrugged, and with a grimace of exasperation said, "They are French!" He paused, smiled. "My wife is French. It has been my good luck not to have to beat her."

The boat obviously frustrates him. "If I could have two months working with the crew," he said, "it would be possible." But he does not have two months. If age and health did not prohibit it, his work schedule would. He cannot race the boat, but if he lets the boat go to race with a hired skipper, then it is not in St. Tropez for him to use. But if it doesn't race, the crew quickly loses interest. So the crew comes and goes, and he hires the Jobsons and the Conners and rehearses the maneuvers for the perfection, the pleasure of it—a most Corinthian, lonely, and expensive undertaking.

The next morning Karajan arrived at my motel at 7 A.M., as promised, in his new red Renault GTL Turbo. He said that he often drove the hilly back roads around St. Tropez in the early morning, and offered to take me along. He may have suffered a stroke, but in the car he was competent and totally at ease, like a crippled diver whose body is restored by returning to the depths. Soon we were tearing up the twisting, narrow mountain road. Karajan's back was pressed firmly against the seat. His arms were outstretched, his hands at ten past ten on the cushioned wheel. His feet, clad in Italian driving slippers, deftly worked the pedals. The rpms never dropped below 3500. It gave one hope to see a man of seventy-three drive with such practiced gusto.

At the top we got out to contemplate the wide-angle, aerial view of the Côte d'Azur simmering in summer haze. The only sound was of birds, and the car ticking cool. Karajan spoke about driving with Austrian auto racer Niki Lauda, and about a factory training session he had done at Audi, where he was shown the intricacies of driving on ice by breaking and accelerating at the same time. "In twenty minutes I learned more about driving than in my whole life," he said. "In summer one judges the quality of a driver by the number of flies he kills with the side windows."

He spoke about how his fascination with cars had paralleled his love for boats. He started small. "Then they came out with the Mercedes Gull-wing. Remember that one? It was very fast. When I stepped into that and put the wings down I said, 'why not before?' What fascinates me about such things is, am I worthy of it. Am I on the same level as the machine? It gave me a challenge, and if something gives me that ... ahhh ...."

V
Vienna Again

⸎

May 1983

Karajan has come to Vienna to put the finishing touches on his recording of the Richard Strauss opera *Der Rosenkavalier*, which he is conducting in July in Salzburg, and to record the *German Requiem* by Brahms. He will do both pieces with the Vienna Philharmonic. His first recording of *Rosenkavalier* was done in 1947, on 78 rpm, although his name did not appear on the label; the orchestra was the Vienna Philharmonic. Ten years later he did a complete version of the opera with the London Philharmonia for Walter Legge, to reviews that praised both orchestra and casting. It is like Karajan to repeat works he likes (he has recorded Beethoven's Fifth five times). In the case of opera, there are new singers to be exposed, and with any piece there are always new interpretations to consider. Karajan is also likely to redo a piece when a technological advance makes his previous efforts obsolete in terms of sound. "Sometimes people say to me," Karajan explains, "'don't you have this piece up to here?', and I tell them I sometimes feel I don't even know it. One of the signs of a great piece of music is that it will never come to the end of interpretation. It is like a deep well. You can dip and dip and never come to the end of it."

Musikfreunde Hall had been turned into a recording studio. Thick clusters of black cables ran from the myriad of microphones in the hall proper, along the hallways, and into the two rehearsal rooms that had been crammed with tape machines, mixing boards, all the electronic complexities of modern recording techniques. The entire second floor was bustling with orchestra members, singers and managers, technicians, hall officials, Deutsche Grammophon executives, and members of Karajan's retinue, including the ever-present Papier.

Once the session was underway in the hall, the singers were sequestered behind large, lucite baffles to protect their microphones from the orchestral sound. Kurt Moll, a bass, was singing the demanding part of Baron Ochs. Anna Tomova-Sintov, a soprano, was singing the Marschallin. Mezzo-soprano Agnes Baltsa was singing Octavian, and soprano Janet Perry was singing Sophie. Karajan was sideways on his stool, ministering to the orchestra with one hand, attending to the singers with his eyes and other hand. He looked relaxed and was obviously enjoying working with the opera he probably knows better than any other.

Insiders refer to Musikfreunde Hall as "Goldene" Hall, and once inside, one understands why. If King Solomon's mines had a performance hall, it would look like Musikfreunde Hall, a glowing, golden room from ceiling to floor—offset by trim of maroon and tan—and breathtaking for its ornateness. It is a long, rectangular room with a fifty-foot ceiling that is elaborately paneled around a sequence of ten large, central paintings of robed, floating female figures. At the orchestra end of the room, organ pipes set into a columned, Parthenon-like facade form a high backdrop at balcony level. Four white, long-necked birds and two reclining figures decorate the pitched roof of the facade. The facade, and the rest of the narrow balcony, is supported by columns cast in the form of large-breasted, Amazonian figures—Caryatids—that are naked from the waist up. They are gold, of course, and altogether there are thirty-six of them ringing the hall. The faces of these otherwise imposing women are passive; their shoulder-length hair falls in ringlets.

Above the balcony, there is a row of high windows, which give the room its spacious feeling. Below them, a row of doors open onto the balconies. Above each door there is a pitched roof adorned with reclining figures in white. Between each door is a bust of a prominent composer or musician, lit from below by a large wall sconce. The balcony front is adorned with a repeated winged horse and lute motif. Five large and glittering chandeliers hang above each of the two aisles that split the audience into three parts. There is no wall or elevation that comes between audience and orchestra. The excellent acoustics of the room are enhanced by the feeling of intimacy one has with the players.

Musikfreunde Hall is a spectacular room, but surely what has taken place there since the first concert in 1870 has endowed it with a patina that no master craftsman's brush could have achieved. The director of the Musikfreunde's 1872–73 season, for instance, was Johannes Brahms, who was forty years old at the time. The fact that many of his original manuscripts, along with those of Robert Schumann, Franz Liszt, Johann Strauss, and Richard Strauss (to name but a few), repose in temperature- and humidity-controlled security in the Musikfreunde's library on the third floor makes all that gold within the hall seem so much deeper.

Musikfreunde Hall is typical of the grandeur one finds in Vienna. It is a city of parks and elaborate monuments, fountains, and structures like the "town house" palace of Franz Josef, that truly extends one's credulity. Strolling through Vienna, one comes upon this "dwelling"—the Hofburg palace—as one might pass the mayor's home in New York City. The imperial family's summer palace at Schönbrunn has a thousand rooms, ample enough quarters, one would think. But the Hofburg is an extravaganza of 2,600 rooms, 54 stairways, 18 wings and 19 courtyards, a complex of stone and copper, of reflecting pools and heated greenhouses that would compare favorably with any of the world's larger parliamentary compounds. The palace and grounds are now a tourist attraction that would take the better part of a week to explore thoroughly.

It is in Vienna, with its broad thoroughfares, its expansive squares that were designed with pomp in mind, and its abundance of cafes where an endless procession of stern waiters in black tie and white apron serve demitasses of delicious coffees and *schokolade* with the most tempting of pastries and cakes, that the Habsburgian shadow is strongest.

In her book *The Emperor and the Actress*, Joan Haslip describes the Vienna of the late 1890s: "The great families stayed more and more on their country estates and the 'Second Society' took over the town. The finance barons had consolidated their position by their open-handed generosity to charities with aristocratic patronesses and the splendor of their entertainments. It was the era of the Rothschilds, of brilliant balls and cotillions with expensive party favors, and musical soirees of superlative quality, for talent was not lacking in a city in which Brahms and Bruckner, Hugo Wolf and Mahler were all living and working at the same time. It was a world in which the brothers Strauss were still conducting the orchestras at the court balls when Gustav Mahler was appointed director of the Opera House; in which Otto Wagner was planning the most modern estates in Europe, while Hasenauer was completing the baroque entrance to the Hofburg, designed by Fischer von Erlach two centuries before. It was a world reflected in the Ringstrasse which more than any other street in

Europe conveyed the atmosphere of a hybrid affluence typical of Vienna at the time. The Gothic Rathaus, the Renaissance museums, the classic Parliament house and the baroque theater all had their place on the Ringstrasse, which a Viennese wit summed up as 'a menu of various dishes served up in stone.'"

In many ways, today's Vienna resembles any other center of business, finance, and culture. It has a better than average system of public transportation and the usual problems of traffic and crime. It boasts a cosmopolitan collection of people, and therefore an interesting selection of good restaurants. A closer look reveals an underlying attitude that is at once arrogant and apologetic, superior and insecure, and wrapped in a protective overcoat of manners. But as poet T. S. Eliot wrote, "after such knowledge, what forgiveness?" The Viennese are stuck with their extraordinary legacy. One can understand if the care and preservation of it makes them anxious.

Performances of the Vienna State Opera continue to be served up three hundred nights a year from the impressive stone edifice on the Ringstrasse. Surely this institution continues to enjoy Viennese patronage, but the evening I was there to see and hear *The Magic Flute*, foreign tourists comprised the bulk of the audience. There were lots of Americans in the full-house crowd, some bright-eyed with anticipation, their beleaguered husbands in tow. One woman, eye-catching in a hot pink, clinging sheath of a dress that was gathered at one hip and trimmed in white fur, with matching white fur pillbox hat, raised on her tiptoes and began waving madly as she squealed to her husband, "there are the Helgers! Helloooo!" It made one feel like speaking French.

The decor of the place is a touch gaudy. The many-tiered balconies are done in off-white with gold filigree. The transparent bulbs that project refracted light through jeweled wall sconces make the place look like a collection of headboards from bridal suites. One performance doesn't make a season, but the *Magic Flute* production I saw was a remarkably poor one. Many high-school theatrical offerings have better lighting effects. Several times one could sense the clack of switches as lights went on and off, and occasionally the long beak of a stage spot would peek beyond its protective side curtain. Both the singing and orchestral playing were a step below what one might expect even from production-line opera. The trio of Genii from the forest who appear in Act I looked more like Sino-German killer moths. I had obviously been spoiled by Karajan's Salzburg approach to opera, and left after Act I.

One Sunday while in Vienna I was invited to the home of a Vienna

Chorus member I had met for an "afternoon musicale." It sounded casual, so that is how my companion and I dressed: jeans, turtleneck, boots, her hair in braids. We walked in on thirty or so people in jackets, ties, and cocktail dresses, squeezed into a relatively small apartment. To our surprise and dismay, we were the guests of honor. Chairs were arranged, and the music began at 3 P.M., with forty minutes of violin playing by a young woman who hit every single note of the concerto she attempted with grim determination—every one a millimeter off the mark. Tonally, the low notes were bearable; the high notes were torturous. Sympathy struggled with the urge to flee. The woman, we were told, had studied for years. It was an agonizing, if unnecessary, reminder of how difficult it is to play the violin.

She rendered a second piece, after which the hostess rang a little bell to announce intermission. Orange juice and pastries were served— stronger stuff was called for—after which the musicale continued. An American from Kansas who was studying piano in Vienna was next (not bad), followed by the hostess's understandably reluctant eleven-year-old son playing the cello. Then her nine-year-old son, a sparkly-eyed child with musical promise, played the violin. The hostess herself sang an obscure aria, followed by a final concerto by the lead-off violinist. The hostess was flushed with pride over the afternoon of music she had provided, obviously pleased to display that she was holding up Viennese proprieties. At 7 P.M. I mumbled lies about a dinner appointment, and we escaped into the comparative joy of a drenching spring rain.

It is this side of Viennese life that drives Karajan crazy. He hates the pretentiousness. I had heard that the famous photographer Jacques Lartigue had once taken a portrait of Karajan and asked him about that. The question set him off on a tirade about the images represented in the work of Lartigue, whose best-known photographs document France's Belle Epoque, or Gilded Age—1890 to 1910—a time of fancy, fashionable dress and unabashed frivolity, of dedication to the pursuit of pleasure. "How I hate all that," Karajan said finally. "It was like a big lie, the women in their huge hats and frills ... I could never stand the opera *Lulu*, the unfinished work of Berg, because it was set in that time."

Karajan has never been much of a social animal. He took in his share of parties during the postwar period, when his career was booming. But even at those times he was never known for his gregariousness. Ernst Haeusserman shared a number of social occasions with Karajan. "Even at parties he would be focused, purposeful," Haeusserman said, "like the true workaholic he was. He didn't have a 'party face.' He would always pick out one interesting person, someone who could teach him something, and spend all evening talking to him. Once it was the actor Curt Jurgens. Another time it was race driver Niki Lauda."

Edge Leslie says Karajan has always refused to dress up. "You would see him dining in some fancy Paris hotel in sports clothes. Eliette would be in a Dior creation, eager to join some snobby party. She would go off, and Karajan would go upstairs to his room. He has German traits in his character, but he also has a good shot of what the Austrians call 'Gemütlichkeit', which is best described as a desire to be comfortable, with the feet up, cozy, at home."

Vienna, for Karajan today, is a restricted path that leads from the airport to his house in the country an hour outside the city, to the Musikfreunde, a long-time refuge. When he arrives at the Musik-freunde, the large wooden doors at street level are swung open, and Josef wheels the Mercedes into the building's covered, interior alley to the private entrance. Even the crowd on the second floor are friends or trusted associates, or in the case of the sturdy woman with the gray hair dressed in the green, Tyrolean manner, an ex-wife—Anita von Karajan.

She had come to hear the recording session, by Karajan's invitation, of course. One doesn't enter the hall without it. She had been im-movable on the telephone: she would absolutely not speak about her "husband," as she refers to the Maestro. A pity. She could provide so much, fill in so many gaps. But she was adamant.

I asked Karajan if he would intercede with Anita on my behalf. He said he would, as long as I didn't ask her too many "personal" ques-tions. I agreed. I reminded him several times of this during a particular week when I was in Salzburg. He said he had tried calling her several times, but that she must be traveling. I later learned that he had spoken with her several times that week. It seems he had never in-tended to intercede for me; but for some reason he couldn't tell me that.

Henry Alter mentioned that he had been in Vienna the previous month. He had been at a Rosenkavalier session at the time and had been introduced to Anita, whom he had never met. He said she had thanked him profusely for his help with Arabel's admission to the Parsons School in New York, and for finding Arabel an apartment. "It was strange," Alter said. "She kept referring to Arabel as 'Her-bert's and my little girl.'"

Eliette was also in attendance, in white UFO jeans and white, karate-styled sweat shirt. She was two boxes over from where Anita sat, although the two often chatted during breaks. Eliette was again unable to sit still. She kneeled on her chair, or stood behind it leaning on its back, and shifted into half a dozen other positions as the rehearsal and recording proceeded. She said her back was bothering her, that she had been taking an aerobic exercise course.

The Vienna Philharmonic was at full strength, and that was a pleasure. If the Berlin is articulate, self-assured, crisp, deep-throated, steely, explosive, massive, stentorian, the Vienna is eloquent, elegant, lyrical, deft, pink of cheek, rounder of edge, mellow. A tale of the two cities. Listening to the Vienna play any of the core repertoire is a treat, but they shine brightest when they can apply all their rich tradition to the task at hand. Strauss's *Rosenkavalier* gives them that opportunity. As Roberto Paternostro said as he took the chair next to mine, his eyes burning with excitement, "Have you heard them play the waltzes? Just wait." Every time they came to one of the all-too-short waltz themes that are scattered throughout the opera, Roberto would cue me as if I were the violin section. He was right. There is nothing quite like listening to the Vienna Philharmonic play a waltz.

The Vienna Philharmonic is an orchestral tradition. The very music sheets they play from have been marked by the hands of Brahms, Toscanini, Furtwängler, Richard Strauss. They use special horns (brassier, less bright) and oboes that are made in Vienna. Many of the instruments—including a complete set of strings—are the age-old property of the orchestra and are passed from player to player. John Moffat, a young violist from Canada who had just been admitted to his probationary year with the orchestra, said he had been studying in Vienna for seven years, playing in chamber groups and learning to play "the Viennese way," which he described as "no harsh attacks— we sort of sneak in, and sneak out again." He said that playing in the orchestra, one listens, becomes flooded by "the way," until one learns by osmosis. And always, he is accompanied by the imposing immensity of tradition, which rises grandly on all sides, and which is honored the way an initiate bows to the mores of a monastery. "At a rehearsal the other day," Moffat said, "the chorus thanked the orchestra for 125 years of working together. The two have played over 225 concert performances."

All this explains in part how one hundred musicians can sit together and play a waltz the way the Vienna does, with the introductory ritardando in exquisite unison, and the famous way in which they hurry (together!) the second beat of each measure just a little so there is a slight hesitation before the third beat—a technique that unfailingly provides the listener with one of the true musical thrills. But it does not explain it all, by any means. Such phrasing cannot be conducted. Even Herbert von Karajan lets the Vienna have its head when it comes to such moments. Surely there is magic involved, for the effect inspires awe.

At the break, Karajan adjourned to the control room with Kurt Moll and Anna Tomova-Sintov. He sat at the center of the control board with the singers on either side. His eyes were closed and one hand moved with the music. "Halt!" he would bark from time to time, a command that would be carried over an open mike into the neighboring room where an engineer was starting and stopping the tape. Then he would work on a section, singing gently to Moll, talking, praising the good parts, polishing the sticky places, with Moll mouthing the words, nodding as the tape rolled and Karajan pointed out improvements he wanted. Then with Sintov, he took an even softer approach, sensual, flirting with her and touching her arm, working on one word over and over, laughing at the silliness of it, then over and over until she had it right.

"I'm not sure we can finish today," Karajan said quietly after the singers had left. He addressed a smallish man in a green velour turtleneck pullover. An exotic-smelling, tapered cigarette in a beige wrapper languished upon the man's heavy lips. His face was sad-eyed, expressive, his black hair in working disarray. His offhand demeanor was quite unlike that of the other members of the recording crew, the polished German fellows from Deutsche Grammophon in Hamburg. This was Michel Glotz, a somewhat controversial Frenchman who is one of Europe's top artists' agents. He has been Karajan's collaborator for recording for more than twenty years.

"Do you see me nervous?" Glotz said to Karajan. Later he told me: "I must be completely calm, no matter that it is costing DG plenty if he doesn't finish. If I wanted to be devilish I would say, 'there is no point trying because you simply can't do it.' Then pride would take over and he would do it. If it was a crisis I would do it."

Karajan chuckled. "It is like the story about the boat that is in flames. The owner runs to the captain. The captain says, 'I'm not nervous—it is your ship.'" Then he told the story, apropos of nothing, about the two boatloads of Jews who pass at sea. One boat is full of Jews who have fled to America before the war and are returning. The other is full of Jews who have been hiding during the war, now going to the United States. In mid-ocean they look at each other and touch their temples, indicating that the other boatload is crazy. Glotz, a Jew whose promising career as a concert pianist was interrupted by the German occupation of Paris, laughed heartily.

Back in the hall, Karajan called Glotz on the phone: "To give you a hint, we will start at the point where the curtain goes up. Maybe you will find it." Glotz smiled, opened his score, rolled tape. "If we weren't pressed for time," he said, "I would call him back and ask where is it." There was a pause. Karajan was straightening something out in the hall. Glotz used the moment to complain about the poor service. "I can't even get a liverwurst sandwich here." "We are not in Berlin, you know," one of the crew told him.

"I know," Glotz said. "They are not civilized here."

Karajan worked about forty minutes before the next break. Halfway through the take, Agnes Baltsa, the mezzo-soprano who was singing the role of Octavian (a young man's role which is always played by a woman), had missed a high E flat. It wasn't a big thing—Baltsa is a rising star, a strong presence, a Karajan favorite who works frequently with him at Salzburg and on record (her *Carmen* with Karajan was applauded). She is a young woman of good humor with a marvelously sexy, frizzy-haired look about her. Her eyes are dark, quick, and she seems always on the verge of a funny remark. Karajan brought her into the control room to hear her flub.

"You really missed that one," Glotz told her. Baltsa hid her face in mock despair. "But it was fantastic otherwise." Baltsa smiled, curtsied to Glotz. "Sometimes," Glotz said as if surprised, "you are good." Baltsa straightened up, sneered at him, tossed her head.

Karajan put Baltsa next to him at the control board. The tape they had just made was played. Karajan tilted his chair, leaning his head toward Baltsa and looking into her eyes. He entwined his left arm in hers, while his right hand moved in the air. He hummed with the music, his eyes on her face. When the flub came she grimaced. Karajan laughed, ran his hand through her hair. They sat together quietly, listening and talking for ten more minutes.

Eliette came in and the banter began. She said she was hungry. "Well, then, we will get something to eat," Karajan said. There was no place to sit in the control room. Eliette kneeled on the floor and began talking to one of the recording crew. Karajan and Baltsa left.

The man who had reminded Glotz he was not in Berlin returned with a liverwurst sandwich. Glotz, touched, joked about its inferior quality. An executive from DG came in to see Glotz. "There won't be time to finish," he said, looking serious.

"It is outstanding," Glotz said. "Everyone sings well."

"The losses will be outstanding."

Eliette stood up, complaining about how hot it was in the little room. She removed her sweatshirt, rearranged her thin silk blouse, and stretched provocatively. She looked at me and winked. "You must be the new one," she said to the man next to Glotz. Glotz had been unavailable at the outset of the *Rosenkavalier* sessions because of his mother's terminal illness. A producer from DG has filled in for him. Glotz introduced the man to Eliette. "I'm hungry," she said. "Where is he?" Her question was answered by the ring of Glotz's telephone. The Maestro was on the podium, ready to continue. Soon the room was flooded with music.

Glotz says that his family never was keen on him being an artist. "They were too bourgeois," he says. Moreover, his crucial formative years had been spent in hiding. It was too late to pursue piano seriously. So he went to college after the war and ended up in administration at EMI. When a colleague was sick, he substituted at a recording session and quickly swung to that side of the business. When Beecham came to Paris, Glotz was assigned to work with him finding singers and making recordings. Then he met Callas, and in 1958 she asked him, as a friend, if he would produce her records. Along the way he was introduced to Karajan. "I met the biggies one after the other," Glotz says. "I wasn't hunting. It was coincidence."

He first got to know Karajan over a stereo installation. Glotz was asked to go to St. Tropez and make sure everything was in order. "We discussed music," Glotz says. "He got interested in me. We saw each other frequently after that. He was at the Vienna State Opera at the time. But it wasn't until 1965 that he asked me to be his collaborator. I had to leave EMI, but he said it was OK to manage artists on the side in a small way."

Only Karajan could have gotten away with bringing in his own producer for recording sessions. It was alright with EMI—they knew Glotz. But when Karajan went to Polydor, there was resistance that didn't break until 1974. Glotz calls himself "artistic coordinator." With EMI he was "record producer for von Karajan"; with Polydor, "director of recording for von Karajan."

"I am his real music critic," Glotz says. "He says that my ears are the same as his. My job is to produce the correct equilibrium of sound. I follow the score, we talk on the phone. He calls, 'How was it?' If I hesitate even for a second, he says 'What?' He wants to know right away, this, this, and this. No blah blah. He wants facts. The only way to survive in this business is never to lie to any artist. You don't have to be brutal; say it nicely, but tell the truth. Go to the point.

"He is a bit of a tyrant, sure. You cannot achieve such perfection in music without being a tyrant. You've got to push people. Human nature is made of laxness, permissiveness.

"We have had our problems over the years. Mainly because of this business. The Germans have an expression: '*Schadenfreude*.' It means the pleasure of turning people against one another. That's how it is in music. Last summer I was not in good shape. I was doing some recording with Mr. Maazel. Someone told Karajan that I was making *Carmen* behind his back. In bad health, I left Salzburg, and the rumor was that I was fleeing him. First, one must never panic, never be afraid. Never lie. Then pick up the pieces and put it together again.

"People think of me as a shark. They attack because they are jealous. Karajan says I am not suspicious enough. I keep falling into traps. I resent the fact that Karajan is so suspicious, but maybe he is right and I am wrong.

"He is a superprofessional, but he can be impatient from time to time, and impossible with his wife, his children, and me; to singers and instrumentalists. Once I called him on the phone while we were recording. He was enraged. He threw the phone down: 'Leave me alone!' So I put my coat on and prepared to leave. But he has a sixth sense. He called for a break and we crossed paths. He wanted to know where I was going. I said 'to my hotel—you said to leave you alone.' He told me *I* was impossible."

Glotz is Karajan's man in the control room. Karajan would be there himself if he could be two places at once. Since he cannot, there is Glotz, whose job has been to learn what Karajan wants and give it to him. "The producer is a mirror," Glotz says. "You can't take yourself as an artist. If you do you are lost. I select the tapes to be used, and then mix, trying to imagine what he wants to hear. In twenty years he has never replaced the take I have selected. Of course, he asks for corrections in the mix down."

When Glotz is criticized, it is for being more mirror than producer. "Glotz exaggerates the dynamics," Antony Griffiths says. "He raises the level of the climaxes, and changes the perspective all the time." To the occasional listener, Griffiths has a point. The triple pianissimo passages on many of the Karajan recordings I own require a trip to the amplifier to crank up the volume. Then I must run to the amplifier a few moments later to keep the glassware from shattering at a fortissimo.

Griffiths apparently had some tough years with Glotz and Karajan. "They would be angry that after Karajan approved a tape, they would send it to England and we would alter it," he says. There was a struggle, and Karajan won, of course, until *Salome* arrived in England. "That piece meant a lot to me," Griffiths says, "and I was horrified by it. It had to be cut as taped, but I made a new master anyway, because it was terrible. When it came out, it got rave notices, but I got retired a year early for doing it. Karajan is a law unto himself. That's not easy for an engineer to deal with. When he was recording Tchaikovsky's Fourth Symphony one time, a critical microphone went bad. Karajan wouldn't wait until it was fixed. He refused to stop. Glotz was at fault there. The result was a crackle. We had to fade out the tracks with the crackle, which meant no left side of the orchestra. So we added a reverb mike and went with it. In England, no engineer or producer would have let that happen. In Austria and Germany, they say 'yes, Mr. Karajan,' and that's that."

Glotz is aware of the criticisms aimed at him. "Mixing isn't manipulation," he says. "It just augments what he did on the podium. In art, the quest is for perfection, more beauty. The purists want it as it comes, not more beautiful or lush. But to me it should always be more moving, more beautiful. Would a lady in an evening gown not use makeup? It is the perfection of nature. Cosmetics are not artificial if it is part of what you are thinking while recording.

"Karajan's lush sound is made from blending all the instruments. To achieve this he takes time to make full chords, which are perhaps less precise, but round. There is almost an imperceptible delay by the cellos and double basses—hit and reverberate. It makes a deeper sound. He is a mountain man. There is no superficiality about him. His music and his personality are consistent. Music is the conception of his life.

"People think that beauty of sound interferes with the truth of the music. They make a stupid distinction between sheer beauty (static beauty) and life rhythms—that beauty eclipses the other. Nonsense. Why should a beautiful sound interfere with rhythm, drive, impulse? That has nothing to do with each note being beautiful. Often the great ski champions have lousy style—but Jean Claude Killy had both. Form and function. The beauty of the movement of a skier doesn't prevent him from going fast. Beauty does not work against efficiency."

The next day, Karajan was in the hall, running the Vienna Philharmonic through various sections of the Brahms *Requiem* that he wanted to polish. For a half hour he worked only with the bassoons, cellos, violas, and reeds, urging the cellos to enter softly, then build and fade, in and out, going for maximum expressiveness. His approach was very businesslike. He said very little, but he often sang passages to the orchestra, overemphasizing the effects he was looking for.

Watching him work with the Vienna, an ensemble so different from the Berlin in approach and attitude as well as sound, one wondered how he managed what seemed to be a smooth transition between the two. "The two orchestras show you the difference between the German and Austrian state of mind," Glotz had said. "Karajan is Austrian from Greek heritage, but he has a large shot of German discipline. The combination makes it natural for him to handle both the massive and the elegant."

Rehearsal is the best time for watching Karajan. In rehearsal he uses it all—the face, the body, the hands. In rehearsal he truly "conducts"—works. Performance, as Karajan has said, is more a concept. Performance is, after all (according to the Oxford English Dictionary), "a notable deed, a ceremony or rite, a public exhibition ..."—or—"ridiculous or contemptible behavior." The latter definition is of course reserved for the "poor player that struts and frets his hour upon the stage and then is heard no more." Karajan is perhaps the least distracting conductor to watch in performance, but even for him it is a public projection of self, with as much posturing as pedantry involved. (This is less so with opera, because then he is truly very busy, and, from the midpoint on, fatigued from the length of the effort.) Violinist and conductor Pinchas Zuckerman has commented on the stage mannerisms of classical musicians, saying "We're not actors, we don't practice in front of the mirror. I make it look easy, some make it look difficult." Be that as it may, the public exhibition factor is not to be denied. The audience is a critical mass for any performer. To a greater or lesser degree, every performer will make some extramusical effort to engage them.

In rehearsal, the conductor is making full effort to engage only the orchestra, and while a responsive and enthusiastic audience can have a magical effect on an orchestra's performance, an empty hall can do just as well if other forces are at work. Karajan himself has spoken of this phenomenon, an unforgettable moment he witnessed in Milan in the early 1940s. "The opera *L'Amico Fritz* was being revived. I was at the dress rehearsal. There is a great intermezzo in this opera, and when it came to that part, the conductor stopped, because he knew the composer, Pietro Mascagni, was in the hall. He offered the old man the baton. Mascagni was very old then, and in very poor health. He had to be helped to the stage, and it took several minutes before he was in place on the podium. He had to conduct while seated. Toward the end, he stood up, and there was an explosion in the orchestra the likes of which I have never heard. Whether or not the music was really great or not, I can't tell you. But to those of us who were there, it was unbelievable, because there was an inner tension that you cannot measure."

Karajan says he was the focal point of such a moment, again in the 1940s, after the war, before he was allowed to conduct. Oddly enough, the location was Vienna, and the piece in question was the Brahms *Requiem*. "We must have had a dozen rehearsals," Karajan said. "Then when it was time to record, I had stepped on a nail. My foot had become infected. They thought they might have to remove it. I was told I could not stand up under any circumstances. So they brought me out on a stretcher and I conducted the whole thing with one finger. And it was incredible. Magical. Mystical."

Now here he was in Vienna, nearly forty years later, with the same piece of music, and on the verge of more magic. During the previous two days of recording and rehearsal, he had seemed in good spirits, but in bad health. He was walking with even more difficulty than usual, almost dragging one leg along. His face was drawn, tight, one assumed, with pain. Perhaps that alone was creating the anxiety that one could feel whenever he was present. Much had been made the previous evening over Karajan's insistence that Glotz accompany him to his home outside the city. Glotz, a city mouse, played it for laughs, fortifying himself with sweaters and jackets as though he were trekking to a base camp high in the mountains. But it was serious. Karajan wanted his company. Something was up.

At the end of the mid-afternoon break, Karajan came out of the green room earlier than usual. The habitual line-up of people waiting to speak with him began to converge politely on his position, but he walked through them to where I was standing. We hadn't spoken since I had arrived in Vienna. "Well," he said pleasantly, "get the point?" And he spoke for a moment about the recording procedure, making sure I understood what was going on. Then he asked how long I would be staying in Vienna, a strange question given that we had a schedule of appointments arranged. I told him I would leave for Salzburg when he left in order to see him there.

"Yes, but I will only be there one day, you see. Then I will go for the operation."

I was shocked. There had been a lot of talk among Karajan's close associates about the badly needed operation, and much head shaking about his unwillingness to take the time for it. Now the decision came out of the blue. "I didn't know," I said to him.

"How could you know?" he asked, wide-eyed. Then he began

talking about the operation: "What I have is like stunt-man's disease, from taking falls. There is a spur this size"—he held up the last section of his little finger—"in between the vertebrae in my neck. It must be removed. That is why my legs are like this." He slapped his thighs as he spoke. "Please don't tell anyone this."

With that he went into the hall to work. Suddenly I was on the inside of a drama that I had only sensed during the previous two days. Many people knew about it. "That's why he made me come home with him last night," Glotz said. "I divert him, make him laugh. We stayed up half the night, raided the refrigerator at midnight. We talked about everything but the operation." And there was deep concern among the regulars. When a seventy-five-year-old person goes in for serious back surgery, anything can happen. Hence the anxiety. Hence the tension when Karajan faced orchestra and soloists and raised his baton.

The plan was for an hour more of rehearsal in preparation for the two performances of the *Requiem* (in the ensuing two days) that would be recorded. But for some reason, Karajan began at the beginning, and Glotz, always on the lookout for even a partial, usable take, rolled tape. What he got was priceless, because all the elements came together. The *Requiem* is one of Karajan's favorites, and there was no one listening who didn't consider that this cycle would be his last encounter with it. There would be the concerts, but now it was a private performance for associates, musicians, soloists—after-hours magic.

He went through the first section without a stop. Halfway through the second section those of us listening knew we were privileged to be there. Karajan played all seven sections, beginning to end. Then he lowered his baton, observing the obligatory second or two of silence for taping purposes. When the red light beside him went out, the orchestra exploded with applause. In the control room, Glotz stopped the tape and wiped his eyes. "I sensed that I could go to him, kiss him, and he would burst into tears," Glotz said later. "It was best to laugh. The moment could go either way. So I said, 'Cancel the concerts, we have all we need.' He laughed. He was relieved that there was no big sentiment."

Observing the phenomenon of Karajan's *Requiem* in Vienna added another piece to the "conductor" puzzle. It brought to mind something Karajan had mentioned earlier, during a discussion that was prompted by the phrase "play it as written," a quality most often ascribed to Toscanini. "I had a great friend, Victor De Sabata, who was a great conductor," Karajan had said. "When I went to La Scala,

he often came to rehearsals. I was doing *Tannhäuser*, and when I came
to a slow choral section I told the orchestra to go on because I wanted
to hear it from further back. Victor, who was sitting in the hall, with
a nice gesture, took my place and conducted the orchestra. Walter
Legge, who was there, told me afterwards that it was a most interesting experience. The moment this man, who was without a doubt
a great conductor, took over, there was a change in the music without
him speaking one word—just by the personality he brought before
the orchestra. The whole texture changed. For better or worse, it
doesn't matter; it was different.

"I said I now understood what the impression of the personality
means. Because of course, he had conducted this orchestra for
twenty-five years and he had worked out a general way of sound, a
way of combining notes that was his way. So the minute he took the
baton they looked up and went automatically to his way of conducting. From this time on I said it was completely useless to discuss what
is the truth in music. If we entrust someone with the playing of a
thing, we must know it is *his* playing of it.

"In Goethe's *Faust* they speak of *Zeitgeist*: the spirit of one special
time. In reality it is the spirit of the people in which they see (as in a
mirror) their own time. Spirit/time: time/spirit. It means that we see
everything in retrospect to our own thinking. It is an important term
in music. I cannot abstract myself. The music goes through me. I
become imbued with it."

His own scientific-mindedness aside, Karajan says that music is not
a science. "Written music only provides us with hints," Karajan says.
"I can play a piece in one tempo and it will sound hurried. I can play
it again in exactly the same tempo, and it will sound right. Bartók was
a precise man. In one of his compositions, *Concerto for Orchestra*, he
tried to define exactly what he wanted by making notations in
seconds. He would indicate thirty-five seconds from here to there.
Once with some pupils I played a certain section of this piece two
times. I changed everything, but both times I arrived in exactly
thirty-five seconds. What they said about Toscanini, that he is right
because he plays the music as written, this is nonsense.

"Music breathes by itself. There is a poem of Goethe that speaks of
the contrast between taking a breath and expelling it. The intake
makes a pressure on you, the exhale is a release. The poem says it is
so wonderful that life is mixed; one should thank God that he pressures you, because then he will release you. Much of yoga is based on
the different rhythms of breathing in and out. With music, there is a
natural ebb and flow. It is unbearable to me if someone cannot stay

in tempo. Then I get aggressive. I was born with natural rhythm. I tuned this even finer with the metronome. I have taken a test at the Max Planck Institute in Dortmund, West Germany. You first pick any tempo, say eighty-six beats per minute. On a piano, you first play quarter notes, then triplets, then eighth notes, sixteenths, then you work back to quarter notes and see if you are still on tempo. Now, every orchestra will try and go ten to twenty percent faster when they play sixteenths. It is very difficult, this test. Errors can be up to thirty percent. My error was only two percent. They said I must have a computer in my brain.

"Heisenberg, who was a great German scientist, had the theory that just the act of studying something—an atom, a molecule—would transform it. For instance if you want to study one crystal of snow and you take it in your hand, it is already transformed by the heat of your hand. Thus, by taking a piece of music in your hand, and giving it also to an orchestra, it is transformed by those actions. Unless one agrees with this, one shouldn't make music.

"Just the printing of music alters it. Sometimes the musicians play from very old parts. I wonder how they can see the notes. Sometimes they complain. In one instance, the Vienna Philharmonic complained about some old music sheets, so I bought a new edition. It was a beautiful new thing, very clear. And the orchestra got completely lost because it was a different visual thing, and the breaks came at different times. I said to them, 'don't forget that you have played for years from the old music. Your grandfathers and your fathers played from it. From this music you have played all your hopes, your despair, all your love—it's all there, and when you look at it, it all comes back. It is a good, well-rounded image that you see and feel. Then this new white and black page you see for the first time and everything is wiped out.'

"In one Beethoven rehearsal the orchestra always speeded up at the same place. So finally I asked to see the music. The publisher, in order to have a clean break at the page turn, had compressed the notes slightly on the page. And that small visual thing was the problem. The printing makes an enormous difference on the music.

"Then, of course, there is reading the music, transposing the black and white notes into sound, something that calls for a lot of imagination. Because if I tell you that we have a mountain, you can imagine a mountain. If I tell you the mountain is in a fairy tale, and made of green glass, I can combine the mountain with the color of a bottle. But here, in a score, there are things, mixtures of instructions, that give a certain sound. So one acquires an ability to read a score and approximate the sound. It takes a long time, this ability to take black points on white paper and change them into an emotional impression in your inner system, your soul, or heart, or whatever it is. Then the orchestra plays it and it is a completely different sound.

"This has to do with why I don't use a score when I conduct: the constant shifting between seeing and hearing is impossible. After I learn a score, at the end I try and forget what I have seen. Because seeing and hearing are two such different things. I have a feeling for continuity. When I am in the midst of an opera, basically I hear all the other parts in advance up to the end. That is why I only conduct a work when it is so in my system that I don't have to think. The average person would never think while singing his national anthem. It is automatic. If you want, my whole repertoire is the national anthem.

"I can make a comparison: you sit in a car and the road is before you. You have someone next to you who reads the map and tells you the hills, turns, and bridges before you come to them. At the end of the road you will have experienced following directions, but you will have felt nothing of the landscape. In the other situation, the driver knows the road intimately as it unfolds. He will adapt his speed, acceleration, slowing down, to the character of the road. Because he has driven the road thirty or forty times, he will drive in such a way that the car seems to go by itself. The passengers will arrive in good time without discomfort, and on the way they will have freedom to see the beauty of the scenery and enjoy points of interest. The driver will even have time to explain things to the rider. Everyone will arrive with a general impression of the whole trip, with no missed details. This is what I call harmony."

It was harmony that Karajan gave us that afternoon in the Musikfreunde in Vienna, the harmony of an old man face to face with his lifelong compatriot Johannes Brahms and the music Brahms wrote about farewell. If Karajan was at the wheel, Brahms was on the passenger side, humming along. Those of us lucky enough to be in the hall were in the back, thoroughly enjoying the ride. It was a journey I will never forget. *Zeitgeist.*

A few days later there was another journey. Back in Salzburg, Karajan's plans for surgery were less certain, but he would go to the clinic in Hannover, in any case, to be looked over. He was quite sure that after the checkup, he would go to St. Tropez, where he would relax for a few weeks prior to the beginning of rehearsals of *Rosenkavalier* in Salzburg on July 6. The plan was for me to wait for him in St.

Tropez. He said he would be flying himself, by helicopter, to Munich, where he would catch a commercial flight to Hannover. He invited me along for the ride.

The appointed morning was an idyllic one at the house in Anif. The dew was heavy on the thick grass. The Untersberg looked less menacing, though no less massive, with the early sun full on it. The fields stretching away in every direction from the house provided a comforting sense of isolation that was heightened by the silence of the windless day. To the east, several eagles that live on a high, rocky ledge that forms the backdrop for the Anif Zoo soared lazily.

Josef was feeding the Maestro's small menagerie, which consists of a donkey, a large sheep, and a white llama that was Karajan's previous year's Christmas present from Eliette (she had delegated the job of obtaining the animal to Lore Salzburger). After the helicopter arrived, the pilot joined Josef, André, and me, and we leaned on the split-rail fence, Austrian cowboy style. Karajan came out after a few moments, with Francesco carrying his coat and a small overnight bag. He joined us at the fence, where he was unsuccessful at coaxing the llama to come for a head scratch. He was in good spirits, and seemed in no particular hurry.

Karajan took the left seat in the helicopter. He bid Josef and Francesco cheery farewells and shut the door. Eliette waved from her bedroom window. Karajan pulled back on the stick and we angled off toward Munich.

Flying a helicopter is not easy. Precise coordination between both hands and both feet is required to keep the awkward machine upright and headed in the proper direction. Karajan is learning to fly the helicopter because it interests him, first of all, and because he will soon pass the age limit for flying jet aircraft. The helicopter is vastly more fascinating than a return to propeller-driven aircraft. After only six hours (at that time), Karajan was doing very well. The pilot watched him like a hawk, keeping his hand near the stick at all times, but through two takeoffs and two landings, he never had to touch it (we were required to stop at Salzburg to file a flight plan into Germany).

Karajan obviously relishes both the machine and the challenge it presents. "They are tough here," he said when the pilot had gone in to file papers. "They require you to hover down over a fence, touch it with the landing skids, and balance on it for a few moments before lifting off again."

In Munich, a yellow and black van met us on the tarmac and took us to a private aircraft customs gate, where we checked in. Karajan seemed to be on his own. I asked if I could help in any way. He shook hands and waved me off, saying he would see me in St. Tropez. Then he turned and limped off to find his flight.

A week later I was in St. Tropez, but Karajan wasn't. Having had his checkup, he was in Salzburg wrestling with the decision about the operation. On the telephone, Lore Salzburger was as distraught as I had ever heard her. "He changes his mind every four hours," she said. That he would have the operation was evident, but exactly when was not. "It was supposed to be this week, but maybe he will move it to next week, or maybe the week after, I don't know." She suggested I call him, and gave me a time.

On the phone, Karajan said he would have the operation soon, "but please don't tell anyone." He said he would definitely be in St. Tropez by June 7 or 8. But he didn't know for sure. Was the boat there?

I told him the boat looked fine; it was at the dock, with several crew members keeping things in order. I asked him when the operation would be.

"When the doctor says it will be."

"Next week?"

"I will know when I am operated upon. But perhaps you shouldn't wait for me. Save your time. I won't be in St. Tropez until . . ." (long pause) . . . "June 15, at the earliest. Then on July 6 I fly to Salzburg to begin rehearsals for *Rosenkavalier*. You will be there?"

"Yes."

"How long do you stay?"

"Until the premiere."

"Good. Stay in touch with Lore Salzburger. She will tell you when to come back to St. Tropez to see me."

"I will. I wish you well with the operation."

Karajan gave me his grimmest chuckle: "I will do my best."

VI
The Show Goes On

June 1983

Karajan was sitting up with pillows piled behind his head in the single bed of his small bedroom at *La Palme* in St. Tropez. His breakfast tray and newspaper lay on the bed. With them was a sponge rubber neck brace with velcro fastenings that he was supposed to be wearing. One leg was outside the covers, showing a long, navy blue stocking. He had on one of the America's Cup shirts ("US 27") that Dennis Conner had given him. It too was navy blue, which set off his gray-white hair and blended with the rest of the room: light blue walls and white shag rug, navy and white striped sheets, navy blanket. It was very much a boy's room, but equipped with the essential stuff. The door had been soundproofed. A miniature stereo system was stacked on the bookcase to his left, with a TV next to it. There was a Phillips VCR setup and a big Uher tape recorder. On the bedside table to his right was an elaborate, space-age flashlight, a toy gun which fired a light ray at the target across the room, and a real gun that he said matter of factly he would not hesitate to use on someone breaking in. Break-ins happen in big-money resort towns like St. Tropez. In the 1960s, Karajan suffered a black eye and a few other bruises in a tussle with a burglar he had surprised at work.

Propped up in bed in such a setting, Karajan looked very much the boy. The youthful feeling that emanates from this man in his mid-seventies is something people often remark about. It's not that he hasn't aged, especially in the face, where thick folds lead from his cheekbones to a proper set of jowls. In combination with his eyes, which are clear and blue, and his natural color, which tends toward the olive, this effect of aging is not unattractive. Perhaps it's because the youthfulness is still there, and after a study one concludes his skin is responsible. His arms, legs, and chest are hairless, and the skin has a smooth, glowing look to it that is quite amazing. It is the skin of a much younger person. Beautiful Greek skin.

It was the end of June, only two and a half weeks since he was operated on, and he looked unbelievably good, healthy, rested. "They said if I had not had the operation I would have been paralyzed in three weeks," he said, with obvious appreciation of the precision timing of it, the efficiency. "I watched the whole thing on videotape five days after they did it. It was fascinating. The drill removes one-tenth of a millimeter at a time. It is no thicker than a woman's hair. There have been 236 operations of this type. It had to happen. When I was twelve I fell seventy-five feet while climbing. Then later on I went into a train crossbar on a motorcycle. Since age four and a half I have been on skis and horses. I have been bad to my back. Six years ago I had a disc operation. When the doctors looked at the X rays they said this person must have been confined to a wheelchair all his life. Now I have a two-year exercise program, because the backbone is only as good as the muscles that surround it."

At the foot of his bed, a large window offered a wide view of the Mediterranean. Even in mid-morning, with very little breeze, the sailboats and runabouts and sailboards were out in great numbers. No doubt that is where Karajan would like to have been. In town, *Helisara* was at the dock. The crew was ready. He had kept them all on standby just in case there had been no operation, just in case his recovery had been truly miraculous. As if he was reading my mind, Karajan motioned toward the window with one of the short, abrupt gestures he habitually uses—nonverbal equivilants of his mumbling. "Shut it if you would. There is a draft."

A year before, I had sailed with Karajan in the Giraglia Race, a two-hundred-and-fifty-mile excursion into the Mediterranean from Toulon, France, around a mark off Giraglia (the north tip of Corsica), to the finish at San Remo in Italy. Karajan had despaired in advance over the light air that usually plagues the race. "I hate it when it comes time to tie shoelaces on the spinnaker and fuss endlessly looking for a wisp of wind. I would rather go below and get drunk." But it was a race, it was close by, and he had looked forward to it.

He had invited Robby Doyle and Jeff Prior from Hood Sailmakers to supervise *Helisara*'s effort. They introduced him to the intricacies of a timed start, and with their guidance Karajan put the boat over the line at the preferred end just a few seconds after the gun. There were twelve knots of breeze at the start, the most we would have all race. Within two hours we had left the small fleet astern, then we ran out of all but the lightest air for the duration. It was an uncomfortable race. Karajan's captain, a somewhat hysterical Frenchman, had established a watch system that was much better suited to a shorter race than the fifty hours we would spend crawling around the course. The crew quickly became fatigued.

Meals were served whenever the cook felt like it (dinner at 10 P.M.), and it was stiflingly hot above and below deck. Yet Karajan was in good spirits throughout. Wearing nothing but his bikini bathing trunks, he didn't seem bothered by the heat ("It is never too hot for me."). His one concession to the privilege of command—and perhaps to the ennui of the drifting conditions—was the eight to ten hours of sleep he logged both nights. Otherwise he took hourlong stints at the wheel, enjoyed sociable meals at the saloon table with the crew, and entertained everyone with stories in a most relaxed, fatherly manner. When an electronic navigation device acted up, he dug out the manual and read it through.

At one point he produced a magazine article about the new, high-tech, multihull sailboats that are popular in Europe, and pumped Doyle and Prior for information about them. Karajan said he was looking into having a multihull built—a seventy-footer, a boat that would do thirty knots. He figured he could moor it in front of his house in St. Tropez, unlike *Helisara*, and with only four or five people he could enjoy the fastest possible sail on short notice. The pros said it sounded like a reasonable plan.

Helisara beat the closest competitor over the finish line by twelve hours and won the race on corrected time. The paparazzi were waiting for Karajan as he stepped off the boat. He spent ten minutes charming Italy's infamous, intrepid reporters. Then he got into his Subaru station wagon, which Josef had driven over, and left for St. Tropez.

A week or so later, West German Chancellor Helmut Schmidt and his wife arrived to spend a few days at *La Palme*. Naturally, Karajan took Schmidt sailing on *Helisara*. Schmidt said he often sailed small boats at Kiel. So Karajan had to show off his big one. We had sailed out of the cove, and as we entered clear water, Karajan announced a turning maneuver called a jibe, in which the wind passes across the stern. Then he kept right on going in the fairly tight turn—seventy-odd feet of deep, high-performance sailboat getting into it, banking like a flying fortress, only to the *outside* of the turn, everything taking a strain, twenty-five crewmen going full tilt to keep up with the boat's demands and not quite making it, the helmsman on the extreme side—until he tacked the boat (passed the bow through the wind and off on the other side), with running backstays having to be let off and taken in on the new weather side, and the big genoa jib having to be cast off and led around the mast and taken in on the new side, with four of the strongest crew spinning the grinder handles like bike racers cranking downhill, after they had just spent major effort trimming up to the tack. All for no particular reason except Karajan's whim, the general in the field showing the commander-in-chief how the troops can perform. After all, such a maneuver just might be necessary in a race. Unlikely, but possible.

Karajan's little beach had been crawling with secret service as we had departed, and two boatloads of photographers had chased us around the Med for three hours. At the end of the afternoon, everyone had stood at parade rest against the boom and Schmidt had gone down the line, shaking hands. The next day a German newspaper published a photograph of Karajan supervising Schmidt at the helm, with the headline, "Chancellor Steers Karajan's Yacht."

The maxi boat world championships that year were in Sardinia, just a short jump to the east. Karajan had engaged Jobson to run the boat, and off he went. According to Jobson, Karajan had fun competing against the circuit regulars. Once, after a race, when Jim Kilroy's well-known boat *Kialoa* started to go by *Helisara* under power, Karajan jammed the throttle ahead, then picked up a line as if to offer *Kialoa* a tow. *Kialoa* ended up the winner that year, with *Helisara* a respectable third. But *Helisara* took the long-distance race after an all-day, all-night battle with *Kialoa* that had Karajan on the edge of his seat. "When we won it," Jobson said, "Karajan had tears in his eyes."

Jobson fell out with Karajan after that. His unwillingness to have Karajan's daughter Isabel steer during races (Isabel loves to sail) annoyed the Maestro. And when Karajan suggested that in the future he would be in charge, with Jobson in a hands-off, advisory position, Jobson bowed out.

"It was an interesting experience," Jobson says in retrospect. "Dick Bertram [a well-known yacht broker who sold Karajan several of his boats] put me on to him. So I wrote him a letter offering my services. He wrote back right away inviting me to come. He flew me over on the Concorde and had a car and driver waiting for me at the airport. During 'my time,' two to six P.M. each day, he was really friendly, arm around my shoulders, 'Gary my friend,' and all that. But the rest of the time he shut it off. He invited me to dinner just once, the night you were there. Strange guy, the Maestro."

*   *   *

The previous summer had been an active one, the kind Karajan likes, and now there he was, on the mend, on the inside looking out. But he was lucky, and he knew it. He hadn't exaggerated the seriousness of the operation, or the nearness of the miss. His surgeon, a sought-after back specialist named Professor Dr. Madjid Samii, M.D., chairman of the Neurosurgical Clinic, Hannover, Germany, confirmed the seriousness of the situation:

Mr. Herbert von Karajan was suffering from a progressive compression of the cervical spinal cord ... he had considerable weakness and spasticity (stiffness) of his upper and lower limb muscles. There had been a steep downhill course in the couple of weeks just prior to the operation when he was barely able to walk. At that time I was in New York giving a guest lecture ... and had plans to visit Boston the next day, when I was urgently summoned by telex and telephone calls to rush down to Hannover to attend to this famous Maestro. I abandoned my further engagements and was here in Hannover on 5th June, 1983. It was true that Mr. von Karajan's condition was such that any further postponement would have been catastrophic. I operated on him the next morning at 8 A.M. ... the operation lasted three and a half hours ....

Mr. Herbert von Karajan recovered from his foot drop the very next day, and his gait improved rapidly and considerably. He also feels very well in his upper limbs. I must admit that his neurologic recovery is yet incomplete being largely affected by his yet unresolved spasticity, but as I said earlier the final results depend on the extent of permanent damage done to the sensitive spinal cord.

Mainly what I saw when I looked at Karajan recovering was the absence of pain in his face. He had continually denied that it had existed, of course, but it had been plainly visible, and now it was gone. No doubt that had something to do with his looking younger and fresher. His energy level was high, and since he was confined to quarters by doctor's orders—nothing less could have kept him off the boat—he was resigned to conversation. For a week we spoke for an hour each morning in his blue bedroom. It was a time for reflection.

He said that since the operation, he no longer had to write in clumsy, block letters. I had wondered about this. When I had first spoken to him in 1981, he had referred to notes he had written that were in uneven, childish capital letters. And a map he had once drawn to lead me from Salzburg to Anif was barely decipherable. He also said he would never conduct a performance while seated. "I would give it up first," he said. But he confessed that for the past four years he had struggled to stay upright: "Every step I have taken has been an adventure, planned and executed."

He spoke of his childhood in Vienna, his early proficiency on the piano, his parents, and of merry pranks with his brother. "When we went on trips with our parents, and stayed in hotels, my brother and I loved to ride around in the elevators, which were hand-operated in those days. Some hotels didn't mind, and some forbade it. When we weren't allowed to run the elevator, we would think of ways to get revenge on the hotel. We used to go into the rooms that weren't occupied, take the big ceramic wash basins, and tap them gently on the floor until we heard them crack. We could imagine what would happen the next time a guest filled them with water."

With glee he recalled the time in New York when he and André von Mattoni were accosted by muggers as they strolled in Central Park. Mattoni, oblivious to the peril of the situation, registered annoyance at the interruption of his evening walk. Then he dug into his pants, handed each of the muggers a dollar and shooed them on their way. The muggers were too nonplussed to persist. (One could imagine their story unfolding in some downtown bar, to the intense amusement of their fellows.)

And Karajan elaborated upon the time he refused to allow the opening of the Festspielhaus to be televised. "If you can wake up the fantasy and imagination of the audience, they will follow you," Karajan said, "and TV did not have the technical means to accomplish this. Research and development were needed. When I buy a helicopter I know it will work, I don't hope it will work. And the TV would have been only a hope. So I refused. They said the hall was public property. I still said no. They had a strong case. It was taken before parliament. They said I would be taken away and another conductor appointed. The Vienna Philharmonic was solid: 'If so, we don't play.' Now we do it with twenty-three cameras, six performances; it takes three years to put it all together. But then, I said it would spoil the public's taste for opera."

He spoke about operas he will not do. *La Traviata*, for instance. "It is impossible for me to give that opera credence. A woman falls in love with a young man. They live together in a house outside Paris. Then the man's father turns up. He talks with his son's lover. He tells her that his daughter wants to marry, but her intended husband had heard that her brother lives out of wedlock. For this reason, he refuses to marry the girl. It is so stupid, to hell!, I can't believe it. I could not put my energy into this. Now the Marschallin in *Rosenkavalier*, she is something else. She is growing old, and she loves Octavian in a way that accepts and supports his love for another, and this is very beautiful."

Once again we spoke about the war, "the Nazi time," and his escape into Italy as the Allies closed in on Hitler. He spoke about the terrible hotel where he holed up, and of being in dangerous limbo between the Germans and the Allies. "And there was a man who took you in for a while, wasn't there?" I reminded him.

"Yes, there was."

"An architect . . . named Pozzi?"

"Yes," Karajan said. "Pozzi. That's right."

"And you told me he was shot?"

Karajan suddenly looked at me, through me, his eyes very wide, his mouth open, as if hearing this ghastly news for the first time. Then he focused.

"That's right! Pozzi *was* shot. He was!"

The moment passed quickly, but he had once again glimpsed the horror, this preoccupied old man in his boy's room for whom the past has been warped by expedience, shrouded in its own enormity, and is filled with surprises.

(Later, Karajan made it a point to say that Pozzi had *not* been shot for harboring him and Anita. "Pozzi is alive in Milano," he said. "You can call him up." When pressed, he did not have a number or an address, nor did his office have anything on file. And it remained that twice he told me that Pozzi *had* been shot. "It is one of those things we will never know," one of his staffers said.)

Work is the incentive responsible for Karajan's speedy recoveries from illnesses. The cliché about living to work applies to Karajan. Work is what has always kept him going. Before having this most recent operation, he had focused on the July production of *Rosenkavalier* with the ferocity of a karate champion concentrating on the space beneath the thick plank he intends to split with the edge of his hand. The operation was the plank, a detail to be dispatched as casually as possible on the way to the destination, which was Salzburg.

The plan was that he would appear at the Festspielhaus on July 8 for the first rehearsal. So naturally he left a day early just to surprise everyone, see what was going on, and pick up an extra soupçon of admiration for how fast he had recovered, for how well he looked. Again he flew the helicopter, this time to Nice, where the Falcon 10 was waiting for the flight to Salzburg. I met him in Nice. Isabel and Arabel were with him. They had been at *La Palme* during their father's recovery, at his behest. They seemed bored, listless. "We don't see him much," Arabel explained, "but he wants us to be around."

The two are an interesting pair. Isabel has more her mother's face, more her father's disposition. Arabel, the reverse. Isabel is cool, distant, preoccupied, quite self-centered. Arabel's detachment is foiled by her curiosity. She is the more pleasant of the two.

There was considerable surprise when Karajan walked into the Festspielhaus a day early. There were no singers or musicians in the hall, just the regular crew making final lighting adjustments on one of the sets which was in place on the huge stage. For people who knew only that Karajan was "having surgery" that could possibly end his career or even his life, the sight of him lurching into the hall in high spirits, with a big smile on his face, had a temporarily stunning effect. He was lurching now, not from pain or spinal pressure, but from the relief. The removal of the impaction in his vertebrae had the effect of loosening the bands of muscle that operated his lower body. Until the new set of muscles adjusted to their job, his legs were like rubber, his feet like weights that had to be swung in the correct direction and set in place (the spasticity Dr. Samii had mentioned). Karajan was learning to walk all over again, and the effort presented a curious picture, that of a man plodding carefully through thick mud, worried that he might lose a shoe. After only a moment, a nice round of applause began which increased as technicians busy at their posts peeked out to determine the cause of the commotion, then joined in.

Then without further ado, he gave his coat to Papier and took his customary seat. Soon he was in conversation with "Richie" Reichmann about a lighting detail. He didn't stay long, but his presence had created a stir. One could practically feel the place perk up. The boss was back.

So were the hard-core regulars: Schneider-Siemssen (even though the sets were not his this time), Peter Busse, Frau Burkhardt, Uli Märkle, and Baltsa, Moll, Tomova-Sintov, Perry, and the rest of the now-familiar cast. The following day they were all on hand as Karajan dove right into a run-through (in costume) of the first big scene in the opera: the Marschallin's morning interview with her attorney, cook, milliner, hairdresser, animal dealer, literary adviser, flautist, and an Italian tenor, whose business was to divert her. Karajan made some small changes—the animal dealer was to carry one dog instead of leading two—and he delighted over Busse's antics as the hairdresser. Busse always takes a small, nonsinging part for his own amusement. And there was Vinson Cole, the tenor who had last been seen nearly a year ago, auditioning for Karajan in New York's Carnegie Hall, playing the Italian tenor, and singing his heart out, tape or no tape. Karajan worked with him: "You are too humble. When you come in, you must think that everyone is there only to listen to you. You have come to sing for the Marschallin. You are the center of attention. You must think of the Italian expression that means 'I am sorry I am so good.' You have quiet satisfaction—'I am here'—nothing interests you except your voice. Take it a little slower."

It wasn't long before Karajan found an excuse to go to the stage, where he loves to be, and mingle with this wonderful crowd of characters, suggesting changes of position and timing, pondering costume alterations, adjusting the angle of a light, and mainly enjoying himself. In the spring, at Easter Festival, he had gone to the stage only when necessary because of the effort involved. During *Rosenkavalier*, he would spend half the time there.

This was the sixth *Rosenkavalier* production of his career. The first was at Ulm in the 1930s. He knows every word, every subtlety, every note of this opera by heart—or, as he would say, like the national anthem. That is like knowing a long novel by heart, including punctuation, because the score of *Rosenkavalier* is 523 pages long. Performance runs over three hours. It is not the longest opera, but its intricate, conversational nature makes it one of the more complicated ones. In three weeks of rehearsal—and the performance—I never saw Karajan refer to the score. Such familiarity had its advantages and its disadvantages.

Rehearsals were both relaxed and disorganized. Relaxed because Karajan knew the material so well, and disorganized as a result, because there was no plan. Karajan and Busse were winging it, operating from experience and memory, which left those with lesser knowledge of the opera at something of a loss. And it took time. Busse would consult with Karajan, then run to the stage and execute what had been discussed. Then he would consult again with Karajan. This would happen ten or a dozen times per rehearsal. Partly this was because Karajan is not a good initiator of action. He needs a place to begin. So Busse would block out a scene, it would play, then Karajan would adjust it to his liking, making quick, unilateral decisions to demonstrate that he was sure.

"The basic concept of the opera is set," Karajan had said when asked. "It has been played so often it has evolved into a general tradition. It all goes back to an early time when Strauss himself first conducted it. One simply follows the tradition. All the characters' reactions are in there if you can read the score. It's too bad so many can't read the score."

Rehearsals began on a high note of good spirits and hail fellowship: the boss is back and feeling good, and the gang is all together. Karajan had time for lots of jokes, like the story of the conductor Hans Knappertsbusch: "He didn't like to rehearse," Karajan said to those gathered around his seat. "So one time he was going over Tchaikovsky's Fifth with the Vienna Philharmonic. He came to the second movement, with the horn solo, and said, 'Let's start.' He did a few bars, stopped, and said, 'See you this evening. You know the piece, I know the hall.' The solo horn protested, 'I am new, I have never played this piece in concert.' Knappertsbusch said, 'It is beautiful music—you will love it.'"

Karajan's tangents always caused Uli Märkle to fiercely clutch his soft leather briefcase and look impatient. "I have urgent business with him and he tells jokes," he would sputter.

Karajan told about Otto Klemperer's daughter bringing a young conductor friend of hers back to see her father after a performance. "'Please just say two nice words to him, Daddy,' she pleaded. And Klemperer says, 'Good night.'" Karajan laughed. "One and a half years after the war I went to Graz to see Klemperer conduct and to meet him," Karajan went on. "He was angry. I didn't know why, because OK, I had been a Nazi—but we were all Nazis, Furtwängler, Böhm, me ..."

Several times Karajan lapsed into stories about Goebbels, which he related in imitative German dialogue, and about Hitler, including the one about the nervous private who had stopped the supreme commander at a stage door and asked for his identification, and how Hitler had praised the man for doing his job. And once he referred to Leni Riefenstahl ("a great woman"), who made propaganda films for Hitler. But most of the jokes and stories were old, the laughter forced.

Sarcasm, not good humor, was Karajan's principal tool. Sitting back twelve rows in the darkened hall, when he saw something he didn't like, he would pick up his microphone and with vehemence spit "*shhhht!*" into it, producing a spine-chilling clot of white noise that stopped everything on stage (some of the singers would cover their ears and grimace), causing Paternostro to lunge for the "stop tape" button. Or he would yell, "*halt, halt, halt!*" which had a similar effect. Then he would voice a cutting aside about this or that singer who had made a mistake. Busse, or Märkle, or Otto Sertl (festival director), or Schneider-Siemssen, or perhaps all of them, would be clustered around Karajan's seat, providing his essential "aside" audience (in what Paternostro referred to as "the Godfather scene"). But one had the uncomfortable feeling that his remarks carried beyond the footlights to the singer in question.

Often, his approach was even less subtle. One day at rehearsal, the stage manager, a Mr. F., approached Karajan about the position of the couches, which he said should be made symmetrical. Karajan said OK. The next day at the outset of rehearsal, Karajan said, "Can we begin, with Mr. F.'s permission?" Mr. F. was not in the house, of course. The rest were expected to have a little chuckle at his expense—the very idea of such an underling holding up the Great Man—which they did, on cue.

"Several times," one of the assistant directors said, "a singer was playing to the wrong side. We noticed, but no one bothered to mention it because it would have had to go through five people to get to him, then he would take offense, or find something wrong with the observation, so everyone forgets about it. Rehearsals are stagnant because no one has anything to do. There is no exchange with people—that's why he isn't a creative director. People only do his bidding. When attending to details he is good, but his direction is obvious. I have never seen him do anything extraordinary. He moves the singers around like robots. There is no exchange to speak of. So they don't get as involved as they could."

Karajan once said that his theory of stage direction, and conducting, for that matter, had been stolen from Max Reinhardt. "He would drill his actors, and drill them and drill them. Then after the last rehearsal he would tell them, 'You are free.' That made them feel good, but of course then it was too late for them to do anything but what they had rehearsed." The only surprise, then, was how completely he was adhering to the "drill, drill, drill" part. There really wasn't much room for the actor's input, and that was a little curious given that several members of the cast had sung Rosenkavalier more than a hundred times. That's how it is with opera. Once a singer breaks into a key role in a popular opera and does it well, he is frequently asked to sing that role wherever the opera is performed. It conserves rehearsal time if the singer already knows the part, and opera buffs demand to see the newest candidate for glory in a particular role. Singers have been known to make a career out of one part. Kurt Moll, Agnes Baltsa, and Tomova-Sintov were all at the top of their Rosenkavalier roles (Baron Ochs, Octavian, and the Marschallin, respectively), and American soprano Janet Perry was becoming well established as Sophie. Even Gottfried Hornik as Herr von Faninal, and Heinz Zednik as Valzacchi, could count a hundred performances in those roles. But Karajan has no room for singers who have their own ideas of how a part should be played. The other singers seemed pleased to be in Salzburg working with Karajan, and cheerfully resigned to do his bidding. But Agnes Baltsa went energetically to work in a more usual way.

First, in the opening scene, where Octavian plays as the Marschallin's lover, she had her shoes off. Karajan stopped, asked her about her shoes. She said they were too small, first of all, and they were very slippery on the tile floor. They bantered, argued, Baltsa pouted, Karajan insisted, so she put her shoes back on. Then in a later scene, there was conflict about what Baltsa should do with her hat and sword. She wanted to wear them into the scene, and take them off in the Marschallin's bedroom and set them on a chair. Karajan said no. If she had the sword and hat to worry about, it would distract her and ruin her exit. She insisted. Karajan shifted uneasily in his seat, but kept his cool and tried for humorous banter. "A man doesn't enter the bedroom of a lady with his hat on and his sword. Usually he has nothing on. Or perhaps he has a whip. It depends on one's taste."

Karajan went to the stage and pretended to strangle Baltsa with his foam rubber neck brace. He touched her, cajoled her, pressed his thumb on the bridge of her nose in the manner of those who tame wolves, and got her to do what he wanted.

At the end of the scene with the Marschallin, Baltsa whirled and stormed offstage. Karajan called her back. "You must walk out slowly, with military bearing." Baltsa said she was distraught, emotionally upset after her time with the Marschallin. She felt like rushing off. Karajan won that one too. "When she first came to Salzburg," Karajan said during the break, "she thought it would be easy. She wasn't prepared. Since then I have worked with her. She can be difficult, but she can laugh at herself, that is the best thing. There are no divas here. If one came and played the diva she would never last."

The disagreement with Baltsa appeared to be light. But as Peter Busse said later, "It was close. He doesn't like musical disagreement from singers. He hates to be contradicted. He knows exactly what he wants. Disagree, and there will be a falling out. One more word from Baltsa, and it would have been close. He hates opposition. You have to do what you are told. It's lucky he likes Baltsa, respects her, gives her lots of credit."

In her dressing room, Baltsa and her husband, a singer, spoke about Karajan with the help of a translator. "Karajan always tries to get her in his style," Baltsa's husband said in reference to the sword and hat disagreement. "Especially in *Rosenkavalier*. My wife has a strong temperament, and he always must persuade her."

"In *Don Carlos* he let me explode in the last aria," Agnes Baltsa said. "But not in *Rosenkavalier*. He keeps me subdued. Many say bad things about his directing, but his way is one you can be content with. With Karajan, the personalities must match. He doesn't like dumb people, or fat ones. He has a strict way of directing that doesn't leave much for actors. At first, at the beginning, he is a dictator—every millimeter counts. Then he eases up later on. He has some magic. He is able to hypnotize people. His eyes have something of the devil in them. He always touches the women he likes."

Baltsa's husband spoke up at this point, beginning a story about another singer to illustrate his wife's point. "Darling!" she stopped him with flashing eyes and a devastating smile: "Don't talk about other singers—this interview is about *me*."

Karajan's feeling about the staging of opera adhering faithfully to the music is taken to an extreme by *Rosenkavalier*. Over and over he would tell the singers, "The gestures must come from the music." The kissing of a hand would be slow or fast, depending on the music. All reactions, and every detail, had to be played with a mind to making the action flow out of, and with, the musical score. The glass Octavian throws at one point must shatter on the beat! Sometimes during the second rehearsal of the day, when Karajan was beginning to yawn with fatigue, and it was the seventh run-through of the same scene, he would shake his head and mumble, "Everything is in the music. All they have to do is read the music and they will know what to do."

Sometimes, in fact, the simplicity of the action was painfully amateurish. One scene was particularly awkward. The situation is complicated: Baron Ochs (Moll) had taken Octavian (Baltsa), who was now dressed in disguise as a woman, to a country inn in hopes of seducing her. It was a setup to dupe Ochs, pay him back for his philandering ways. Several people were hiding here and there in the inn to frighten Ochs by popping out at just the right time and disappearing again. Ochs's plight would be further confused by Octavian, who would claim to have seen nothing.

Karajan's solution to this visual problem was to have Ochs keep pointing at the various people who briefly appeared, while registering shock at the same time. Moll stands 6'4" and weighs a stocky 240 pounds. The sight of this expansive man staggering around the stage, pointing (look, everybody!) and giving cries of distress with his eyes wide and his mouth open, didn't work no matter how many times it was rehearsed. The more it was rehearsed, the wearier Moll looked. But Moll, who has sung Baron Ochs several hundred times, simply shrugged when asked about this. "Directors have strange ideas," is all he would say, his broad smile a signal that conversation on the topic was concluded. But he did say later that Karajan's use of the microphone was annoying, in that no one could understand what he was saying most of the time.

"I can understand why he tries to direct opera," Moll said. "There have been so many crazy directors who want to depart so much from the original that they have nothing. He is right: opera is first of all music. And here he is fantastic to work with. He is a suggestive force. I feel what I have to do when he takes a breath. I feel the energy coming from him. For me a lot of the conductor's power is in his breathing. The real force of personality comes from breathing normally, not huffing and puffing as the man thrashes about. When the breathing is right, the audience will feel it. If the singers are breathing right, are open, then the audience will be open.

"But if I don't feel it, I can talk with him. He is not God. At least I don't feel that he is; some do. He is a very normal man. His public image isn't right. But after fifty years, at the top of his profession, it is impossible for him to have a normal image."

The communication Moll spoke about was evident at a rehearsal with the orchestra two weeks later. In mid-scene, Moll looked at Karajan and raised his eyes. Karajan added the most subtle gesture to his flow of conducting, and Moll was directed off to fix his troublesome wig.

Moll has the ideal persona for Karajan. He is big in a gentle, bearlike way. He's good, he is always prepared, he knows his own mind, he's calm, and, as he says, "German, correct, precise," ready to take direction. Moll too breathes normally, on or off stage. He is most comfortable wearing a smile, but he says no as easily as yes. He says he too has told Karajan "no" to operas Karajan asked him to do. "It is not true that he won't take you after that. I am here." But then Moll fits the formula.

Those who don't, become toys for Karajan. At an earlier rehearsal Karajan called a halt ("*shhhht!*"), and with some annoyance, chased a singer off to obtain his proper costume. The singer returned with a report that the costume wasn't ready. Karajan called for a break and gathered those connected with costumes around him. He lectured them quietly but sternly for about ten minutes, stressing preparation, slapping the arm of his seat for emphasis, chastising them for their lateness. "The set is ready, the music is ready, the singers are ready, but the costumes are not ready." They sat quiet, contrite, until he finished. Then he began to lighten up. He made a small joke. They laughed too eagerly. Then he warmed up, telling another Knappertsbusch story: "He was conducting in Italy, where sometimes it becomes necessary to yell at the players to be heard. One old man in the orchestra had told Knappertsbusch to be careful, the oboe player had once knifed someone. A few days later in rehearsal Knappertsbusch threw down his baton in frustration and said to the oboe player, 'Kill me if you must, but you play like a pig.'" The costume crew laughed happily, and went back to work.

Later that day (a Friday) I learned that Karajan had been hasty. The costumes weren't scheduled to be completed until the following Monday. A newcomer to the Festspielhaus scene, a student who was helping out with the production, was outraged by the way Karajan continually "played" with people. "And they always give him what he wants. If he wants them to be nervous, they are nervous. If he wants them to be sunny, they are sunny. He has them on a string. I don't know why they go along with this. It's bad for their work. The organization is bad. Busse tries to find out by noon what we will be doing the next day, does tricks to work it out with Karajan. Sometimes he gets on the telephone at noon and changes everything. The people in the smaller parts are uptight because no one tells them what to do. And the singers are nervous, especially Janet Perry, from the constant repetition of that one gesture at rehearsal the other day. The problem with Karajan's way is that not everyone has been in six productions."

The young man had a point, but he seemed to be the only one voicing complaints. The rest were obviously adhering to the bottom line, according to Kurt Moll: "Karajan is a big name. Working with him is very good for my career." That, and the fact that singers and actors go through life being directed, inures them to a variety of working rigors. And they are a handful too, most of them; no bargain for any director. The struggle goes both ways. All directors have unpleasant sides to their technique. And when the compliments do come, from whom else would it mean so much? As Karajan said about Tomova-Sintov, "Toscanini never had access to a voice like hers—she can hit C sharp at nine o'clock in the morning." Or about Perry: "It is the best I ever heard the part sung; the best high piano I ever heard." The compliments mean a lot not just because they come from the Great Man, but because of the intensity of the experience some singers have with Karajan. They can feel his commitment. When they get the message that he is appreciating *their* commitment, *their* talent, then all else is forgiven.

"I feel his recognition, his approval," said Janet Perry, who in both voice and appearance has an uncanny resemblance to pop singer Linda Ronstadt. "He heard something special in my voice that he liked—

a certain timbre. I feel he is reading me. I think we inspire each
other. This is why I became a singer. Mostly it is a struggle with
conductors. The greater a conductor gets, the more he is able to
communicate.

"He allows you to sing," Perry said. "He expects a return of the
energy he puts out. He inspires singers to make music. Many fine
conductors bend you to their will. Not Karajan. He lifts people out
of their own technical problems. His meditations have given him
power. He can drop the intellectual approach and respond naturally
to situations he is in."

Heinz Zednik, who played Valzacchi (a man of affairs, a hustler),
has been singing around Europe for twenty years. He was at Bayreuth
for ten. He thought the *Rosenkavalier* production could have been
funnier, but he said that Karajan was caught up in the royalty aspect
of the opera—the Marschallin is a princess, Ochs is a baron, and it's
von Faninal. "He relates to this," Zednik said. And in fact Moll had
mentioned that he often plays Ochs in a more coarse, country way,
but Karajan wanted the character to be more a man of manners.
Zednik agreed that for a singer, Karajan was the best. "To be on
stage and have him in the pit is the greatest. Because at heart he is the
simple Kapellmeister [choir master]—he knows the old tricks. Some
conductors need the greatest orchestra and the greatest singers. If you
make a mistake, Karajan catches you with the simplest gesture and
puts you on track. He never loses a singer. Afterwards he says nothing.
But if you are not prepared, he will make you feel small. Some
conductors will help. Not Karajan. You know right away if he likes
you. He's a good old man."

The "old man" part was significant. One had to remember that
this was not just another opera production. It was a celebration of
Karajan's very presence, his new lease on life. And it was the sixth,
and probably last time he would ever tackle *Rosenkavalier*. Watching
the antics of Peter Busse over the three weeks of rehearsals, all this
became very clear. The energetic Busse knocked himself out. He was
everywhere, whipping around the huge hall with the look of a man
hustling back to the restaurant where he has just eaten dinner in hopes
of finding his missing wallet. His discussions with Karajan were laced
with good humor that often left Karajan chuckling quietly with his
head in his hands. On stage, Busse ran rampant, filling in for as many
as three actors at one time during early rehearsals, playing each part
with hilarious overstatement. It got so one never knew in which guise
Busse would next appear on stage. And he would always be
straight-faced, totally into whatever character he had stolen; playing

it to the hilt with campy extravagance. Several times each day Busse brought Karajan to a halt with laughter.

Once when Janet Perry was trying to understand Karajan while he was explaining something over the microphone, there was Busse at her side, sucking on her arm. His greatest moment was when he played all five children who were supposed to stand at Moll's feet and jump up at him yelling "papaa, papaa." The memory of Busse crouched at Moll's feet leaping up at him, arms flailing, screaming "papaa"—and Moll's astonished look (real, this time)—can still make me laugh out loud. If opera on television ever becomes popular in America, it will be because some producer has had the good sense to give Peter Busse a half-hour show before the opera, during which (with a few props), he acts out a high-speed summary of the plot. It would be a hit.

Busse the actor knew what he was about. "I exaggerate, but it is clear, no?" he asked. It was clear. He shrugged. "I try to make the old man laugh. And why not. He is so grim so much of the time. I owe it to him."

During the first week of rehearsals, Karajan had called Papier over and sent him off on some mission. Papier's exit was accompanied by a terrible crash in the seats of the darkened theater. Paternostro and several others ran toward the sound and found Papier flat on his face, blood streaming from a cut on his head. He had gone through the empty aisle behind the big speaker that was broadcasting the taped score of the opera and tripped on the cord. Karajan never moved from his seat, and rehearsal was quickly resumed. But later he asked about his faithful servant, who is close to him in age. "I can see us in a few years, Papier and me, stumbling along, leaning on each other." Four stitches, and Papier was back on the job.

That afternoon, Karajan went to the stage to work with Tomova-Sintov on the scene where she is alone in her boudoir. There was a brief pause while Tomova-Sintov attended to a costume detail. Karajan, seated at the stage dressing table, absently picked up a brush and smoothed his hair.

Arabel had been regularly attending rehearsals with her father. During one break she retreated to a settee on the promenade to have a cigarette. Sitting alone, she looked up warily at my approach, then relaxed. "It's because I smoked a long time in secret," she said. "I used to empty the butts into the fireplace. Once my father counted them. There were over a hundred from me and a friend who had been visiting. He really got mad. He doesn't mind now, if I don't smoke too much. He has one or two cigarettes at night. But his self-control! I wish I had some of it. He can do anything he wants to do, whether it is his work, or not eating, not smoking—whatever."

At nineteen, Arabel has a womanly presence. She is a handsome person, with dark, steady eyes and a full mouth. Some of her father's Greek ancestry is in her face. She is quiet to the point of shyness. She spoke of her father in the distant third person, like the daughter of Franz Josef might have spoken of her father, the emperor. She said that as a child, she hadn't seen much of him. "He had his room up there, over us, with a view, not exactly like a ruler, but sort of." Early on there were concerts to attend. "I remember one of my first concerts, it was in Berlin, Tchaikovsky's *Pathétique*. Suddenly I was so afraid. It was so intense—*he* was so intense up there. I thought that the music could kill him. Every time I hear that piece I shiver."

She said she had been coming to rehearsals at the Festspielhaus since she could remember. "Dad didn't force me to come," she said, "but there was always an open invitation. I've slept so much here. I would come to rehearsal, love the music, and close my eyes. *Don Carlos* was the first music I remember here. I went to rehearsals, afterwards I would ask questions, and always he would explain. He gave me the cassettes he made. Once I bought a symphony by another conductor. Then he played the same symphony and it was faster. I asked him why. He told me, 'It is in the score!' "

Arabel dreamed of being a singer, but she was not born with enough of a voice. A disappointment. So she was studying photography in New York, and it was obvious that she, like her father, was happy to be out of her provincial little home town. She said she was interested in putting opera on film. Her father had said she had a good eye, a sense of the moment: "She knows when to press the shutter."

Both Arabel and her sister Isabel, the actress, have been infected by their long exposure to music and the performing arts. During her senior year in school, Isabel directed the class play and played two roles—a chip off the old block. Karajan reportedly beamed his way through the performance. As children, both girls got their fill of their father's work. "It's spoiled me," Arabel says. "In New York I've gone to the Met a few times, and sometimes I have walked out."

She said that she and her sister hadn't seen much of their father while he was on the mend in St. Tropez. "He just likes us around," she said. But she was obviously enjoying being back in the Festspielhaus at rehearsals with old friends. "This is his life," she said—"not the boat, not St. Tropez. I just wish he would slow down. He talks about taking some time, maybe going to Ischia at the end of the summer. Knowing him, it will be more like October. But he needs it now. I wish he would end an hour early and go home for a massage and a swim."

On the evening before the day off, at about the midpoint in rehearsals, I drove two hours north to Augsburg to see Bruno Weil, the young director of the State Theater there who had been Karajan's backup at Easter Festival. Weil is an interesting fellow. As a student, he had been selected from his small town in Germany for an exchange program in the U.S. He spent a year at high school in Fresno, California, where he had joined the football team as one of the first soccer-style place kickers in the country. In the big game (1966), he had boomed a 48-yard field goal that still stands as a California high-school record. Homesickness had driven him back to Germany after a year, college football scholarship offers aside. Now he was a talented conductor on the rise, a favorite of Karajan's, a young man with traditional ideas about his profession. While his contemporaries were busy angling for guest appearances and TV opportunities, Weil was content to polish his technique and expand his repertoire surely in his small theater in Augsburg—Karajan style.

He agreed with Karajan's thesis that it takes thirty years of training for a conductor to come of age. "Karajan was nearly fifty before he began to become really well known," the thirty-three-year-old Weil said, "and Böhm was sixty-five." Weil's relaxed self-confidence made him good company. His sense of humor was keen, his taste formed in the German tradition. "I would rather have Furtwängler with scratches," he said one day when Beethoven was under discussion, "than Levine with lasers."

Weil had a surprise: dinner would be with Sena Jurinac, a ranking soprano (and former Karajan favorite), who had just finished a distinguished career. She was living outside Augsburg with her husband, a surgeon named Lederle, and beginning to teach. Jurinac is a delightful, welcoming woman, a woman of substance. She has big, expressive eyes set in a round face surrounded by a sculptured gray-black cap of curly hair. Her good humor bubbled quickly to the surface: her Bulgarian name, she said, rhymed more or less with "you're nuts." Her Karajan imitation was second to none.

With pride, she conducted a tour of the first garden she'd had time for in many years. Dr. Lederle followed, indulgent with camera. Then she secluded herself in the kitchen with the huge turkey she was preparing. Dr. Lederle, a tall, angular man with high color and twinkling eyes, poured wine and spoke to everyone in German, which didn't seem to matter, so eloquent was his face. Dinner was memorable. Sena had practiced some kind of Eastern European magic on the turkey. And there were potatoes, fresh vegetables, and an intriguing cabbage dish, all in copious amounts, with an unending supply of wine.

"I had a twenty-year musical love affair with Karajan," Jurinac said between bites. "But at the end, I felt he acted badly. When he was through with me, he was through. That was that. No one even came to my dressing room after the last performance. Afterwards I was in Stuttgart singing. Karajan was in the audience. He said he wanted to record *Boris Godunov* and do a film, and he must have me to sing Marina. 'I promise,' he said. I told him, 'If you change your mind I can't help it.' And I think he did. He asked me to do it on two dates when I was busy. An old ruse."

Sena stood up, sliced more turkey, paused with the knife in her hand. "What is wrong if after twenty years you cannot send a letter? Or take fifteen minutes to say face to face that you have decided to take someone else?

"But it was fantastic to sing for him." She sat down, passed the platter of succulent turkey slices. "It was like being in the bosom of Abraham. I remember singing Desdemona in *Otello*, the scene where I had to walk back to the stairs, turn slowly, and begin the 'Amen.' I turned, and Karajan was standing there in the pit, his arms folded. He looked at me, nodded—please!—I began, and the orchestra was there. How wonderful! Because the conductor has to give me support. I hate to look down and see flailing. My concentration breaks. Bernstein is sympathetic. But he is extroverted—the opposite of Karajan. I believe he is happy, and he knows his music, but he is like a dervish in the pit. Karajan is calmer. But why is it necessary to put on an exhibition of your insides? It is not. The best on the podium was Ormandy."

Dessert arrived, lightly stewed berries in a cut-glass bowl the size of a small washtub. Fresh elderberries, eisenberries, raspberries, strawberries, and wild cherries had comingled their juices over delicate heat to produce a dark red compote of irresistible dimension, at once tart and sweet. First we ladled freshly made vanilla custard into our bowls, golden yellow custard that was smooth and rich beyond American comprehension. We covered the custard with as much of the compote as we dared, then topped the fruit with generous dollops of snow-white, hand-whipped cream. We moaned as we ate.

Dr. Lederle had opened just the right wine to go with the dessert masterpiece, which we sipped while weighing the insanity of second helpings. Then he passed out little yellow pills which he said were very good for digestion—not as an insult to Sena the cook, but as a compliment to a great meal.

After a small respite, Sena and her husband herded us downstairs to the ping-pong room, where we all battled intensely for an hour. Such a workout called for just a touch more dessert, and of course Lederle had the perfect bottle of wine for winding down the evening. Still flushed from his success at the ping-pong table, Lederle suddenly lifted his glass and fixed me with his eyes. "Thank you," he said in quite passable English, "for coming to our rescue." For a moment, I didn't know what he meant. All evening he had been speaking German to me as though I were a native. I had been struggling to understand from inflection and gesture. Suddenly he had said something in English, and he had me equally stumped. Maybe a joke? No. His face was serious. "I mean it," he said, grave. Then I got it. The war. Hitler. The Yankee presence a sudden reminder as the night grew old.

Before I left, Sena spoke again of Karajan: "He lacks the human touch. I admire the perfection, but I don't love the music. I admire his technique, but after the technique is gone, he throws it away."

From the other end of the table, Dr. Lederle asked his wife what she had been saying about Herbert von Karajan. She told him. It was perhaps more explicit in German. He nodded his head several times, then looked at me with a smile. "His mistake," Lederle said in English, "is that he doesn't know how to live the baroque life."

Salzburg, ever busy with tourists in the warm months, was beginning to brim with the festival crowd. There are more than forty music festivals held in Europe each summer, but of them all, Salzburg, with its five high-powered weeks of operas, dramatic presentations, orchestra concerts, Mozart orchestra concerts, concerts of religious and choral music, solo recitals, chamber music concerts, and recitations (readings), is without question the most impressive. The opera production alone is staggering. In 1983, in addition to *Der Rosenkavalier*, James Levine and Jean-Pierre Ponnelle were doing Mozart's *Idomeneo*; Riccardo Muti and Michael Hampe were doing Mozart's *Così fan tutte*; Lorin Maazel and Leopold Lindtberg were doing Beethoven's *Fidelio*; Levine and Ponnelle were also doing Mozart's *Magic Flute*. Ravel's *Daphnis and Chloë* and Stravinsky's *Firebird* were also on the schedule. The list of other participants read like a segment of Who's Who in the performing arts: Ingmar Bergman, Otto Schenk, Wolfgang

Sawallisch, Seiji Ozawa, Claudio Abbado, Zubin Mehta, Edith
Mathis, Christa Ludwig, Dietrich Fischer-Dieskau, Jessye Norman,
Placido Domingo, André Watts, Anne-Sophie Mutter, Alexis Weissen-
berg, Christoph Eschenbach, Justis Frantz, Pinchas Zuckerman, Mark
Neikrug, Bruno Leonard Gelber, Claudio Arrau, and Klaus Maria
Brandauer.

It's no wonder that Jane Kramer, writing in the *New Yorker*, called
Salzburg "the most elegant and expensive music festival in the
world.... People who pass through Cannes in May for the kitsch can
often be seen in Salzburg toward August ... tidying up their
minds.... No one is selling rights or making deals outside the Festspielhaus. They are, rather, very conspicuously consuming some of
the best music in the world. The people who go to Salzburg are
people who can afford to pay a hundred and fifty dollars a ticket in
December and not worry very much about whether they will actually
get there at the end of August. Once the season starts, and the scalpers
take over at two or three hundred dollars a ticket, silver-haired in-
dustrialists can be seen pacing the sidewalk in front of the Festspielhaus
and waving wads of money—hoping that one of the women in emer-
ald chokers and Dior gowns will have an extra ticket to Herbert von
Karajan's Brahms concert that night because her husband has got
indigestion from too much wurst ..."

The deals, in fact, are made within the Festspielhaus, and usually
quietly, with the kind of regal, privileged, and irreproachable deco-
rum that is the Austrian way. And so it was with considerable surprise,
not to mention anger in some quarters, that as final rehearsals for the
festival got under way, the Austrian and German press published
detailed information about festival budgets. It was the first "leak" of
such information in nine years. *Profil* magazine ran a bust of Karajan
on the cover that was depicted as solid gold. "Karajan & Co. spend
our money," the blurb read. As the German magazine *Der Spiegel*
reported, "The Austrian financial bureau had determined that the von
Karajan-mastered festival celebrated away more subsidies in five
weeks than most German stages use in their entire season." It was, as
Austrians love to say, "a scandal."

The numbers published were impressive. For *Fidelio*, it was reported that $110,000 had been spent for costumes; $280,000 for sets.
For *Così fan tutte*, $140,00 for costumes; $305,000 for sets. The totals
reported were $500,000 for hair and wardrobe; $1 million for lighting;
$2.65 million for administrative and technical personnel. The 147
year-round personnel at the Festspielhaus consumed $3.6 million.
Maazel received $50,000; Sawallisch $40,000; Levine $100,000. Karajan

reportedly received $11,000 per evening for conducting, and $20,000 for producing. The soloists shared $1.75 million. Each of the Vienna Philharmonic's 147 players was receiving $7,500. The total festival subsidy was around $6 million.

"Karajan's reputation seemed damaged," *Der Spiegel* wrote. "Hardly had festival critic Herbert Moritz demanded something be done, when the board of directors of the festival accused him of slandering their honor. Karajan and his fellow festival board members all felt themselves libeled.

"Formally this quintet determined who would and who would not be in the festival. In actuality though, Karajan dictates. Even though Kaut, age seventy-nine, hasn't given any sign of retiring, Karajan wanted to replace him as a board member. The battle of succession had proceeded like an Alpinland operetta.... Former Vienna State Opera chief Egon Seefehlner was mentioned as a candidate, and as always, when important posts are at stake, Rolf Liebermann, a composer of modern music who is head of the Hamburg Opera, and former director of the Paris Opéra. Yet none of the praiseworthy group was acceptable to Karajan; least of all Liebermann, seventy-two, who is knowledgeable about the theater and who could stand up to the old, autocratic Maestro.

"So, under Karajan's goodwill, the suggestion of the board of directors and the choice of the curator was Albert Moser, sixty-two, a long-time acquaintance of Karajan." Karajan had in fact said that if Moser was not taken, he would resign from the board and the festival.

There are a number of stories that illustrate the autocratic nature of the festival, the board's desire to maintain the high-priced, aristocratic flavor, the "chilling elegance of the audience," as Jane Kramer described it. A few years ago, the well-known Italian stage director Giorgio Strehler was invited to do an opera at Salzburg. His production was a success, but he was not invited back, and the suggestion that he be elected to the board was quickly dismissed. It appeared he was too democratic. He was in favor of creating some cheap seats and opening up the festival to a broader audience, the way it is done in Verona. Exit Giorgio Strehler.

The Festspielhaus was buzzing the day *Profil* hit the street. During the morning break, several people were gathered around the soda machine in the courtyard parking area within the Festspielhaus gates. There, parked next to Placido Domingo's large Maserati, was the new, dark green Mercedes 190 SE belonging to Otto Sertl, director of the festival. Sertl had been criticized in the newspaper for his new car, and there were several jokes made about his poor sense of timing.

One man jokingly suggested that on days he knew the press were coming, he rode his bicycle to work. I recalled that discussion at 9 P.M., when rehearsal broke. Karajan had driven his Porsche Turbo to work, the gray one with the wraparound red and blue racing stripes, the rear-deck spoiler, and the high-speed driving lights. When he left the Fest-spielhaus and turned into the tunnel, it seemed he leaned on it just a bit harder than usual. At any rate, all three hundred turbo-charged horse-power seemed to pop, crackle, and roar with twice the usual clamor as he held first gear well beyond the red line. The racket was enough to rattle windows. I could imagine Karajan's grim little smile of satis-faction as the powerful car's acceleration pressed him back into the seat.

The press may get exercised about Karajan and the festival's costs to the taxpayer, and well it should. That's the job of the fourth estate. But it is doubtful there will be many changes while Karajan is around, and one doubts that the general populace feels similar outrage. Again, the idol factor is at work. Consider this: in 1967, during the first Easter Festival in Salzburg, Vienna music critic Franz Endler was physically abused by Karajan fans for writing less than enthusiastic commentary about the event. "Karajan told the public he was paying for it," Endler said at his afternoon Stammtisch at Salzburg's Cafe Bazar on the east bank of the Salzach River. He was in town to cover *Der Rosenkavalier*. "I wrote that in one or two years the taxpayers would end up paying for it because it couldn't work. And so it was. But the fans didn't like it." Endler found himself in the crowd that always gathers in the cobblestone parking area at the rear of the Festspielhaus after Karajan concerts. Up to a hundred people wait there for a glimpse of the Maestro. Sometimes people hang on his car as it starts to move, rock-star style. Endler was recognized by someone in the crowd, and several physically attacked him until he left.

"The taxpayers did end up paying for Easter Festival," Endler says, "until 1983. That was the first year no money was forthcoming from the city or the county." (Summer Festival losses, Endler says, are covered 40 percent by the State of Austria; 20 percent by the city; 20 percent by the county; and 20 percent by an assessment of the mer-chants of Salzburg.) "Now they are seeking a better relationship be-tween Easter and Summer Festivals. Because people began to ask, what will come after Karajan? What will Easter Festival be like with-out Karajan? So they are working out arrangements to connect Easter and Summer. The same opera Karajan does at Easter will be done in Summer—beginning in 1984—and that will save production costs. Because Salzburg doesn't want to lose the Easter Festival, and the money it brings in."

Endler, who once sang in a chorus in Vienna that Karajan frequently directed, has been writing about him for thirty years. "We had our great troubles when he directed the Vienna State Opera," Endler said, "but we spoke a lot. Now I never see him."

The Vienna Philharmonic was in the pit as final rehearsals began. For one rehearsal in particular, the singers sat in a line of folding chairs on the apron of the stage for a run-through of certain sections of the opera with the orchestra. As a group, in their street clothes, they defied categorization. By reason of the old cliché—largeness of girth, hautiness of manner—one expects opera singers to be readily identifiable. Most of the *Rosenkavalier* cast looked like anything but opera singers. Janet Perry, in a wide red skirt, matching red shoes with straps, a yellow tailored shirt and red scarf, with her pale, girlish face, looked like an aspiring pop singer, or maybe a graduate student in philosophy. Baltsa was in a scoop-necked yellow blouse and bright green designer slacks cut tight at the ankles. Her flats matched her blouse. Her full-bodied hair was pulled back, and she wore a lot of costume jewelry. Tanned, aggressive, with the widest smile in all of Greece, she could have been a boutique owner from Mykonos. In his bluejeans and sneakers, with a short-sleeved striped polo shirt stretched over his big frame, Moll looked like a thinned-down Robert Morley on vacation, or perhaps a seagoing chef. Tomova-Sintov and one of the other sopranos, in dress and heels and sitting erect, looked like opera singers despite their lack of girth. For the rest, I counted a Boy Scout leader, a waiter, an insurance man, a lawyer, and an actress who had just come from method class.

After they had done their work, Karajan dismissed the singers and rehearsed the orchestra. At the conclusion of the heady waltz that ends Act II, he stopped and put down his baton. "With the long notes, hold them as long as possible," he told the players. "And when the music is like birds in the beginning of Act II, please play small birds, not condors. We must try and hold the melodic line through the '*parlando*,' the talking sound. The whole piece is like conversation that is mixed in and out of the melodic parts. The line stops for conversation, but must continue afterwards. The music grows out of the rhythm of the words."

Later on, Bruno Weil, who is a great Richard Strauss admirer, spoke further about *Rosenkavalier*, of the difficulty of composing humor. "Haydn was best at it," Weil said. "But Strauss wasn't bad. If you listen carefully, you will hear the dog peeing during the Marschallin's bedchamber scene in Act I.

"Hugo von Hofmannsthal, who did the libretto, was sensational," Weil said. "He and Strauss fought it out. They exchanged many letters." At one point Hofmannsthal wrote to Strauss that he liked the music, but in parts it was too soft, too sweet. Over the years, many conductors have made adjustments to temper the sweetness Hofmannsthal mentioned. But not Karajan. If anything, he wrings ultimate sweetness and softness out of those passages. "He is more Catholic than the Pope," one knowledgeable listener commented after hearing the sections in question. "But that is like him. With the help of his producer, Michel Glotz, he is always going for the extremes."

Weil said it was in dealing with the farewell music of *Rosenkavalier* that he thought Karajan really excelled. "He is always at his best with farewell music," Weil said. "That was the story in Vienna, for the Brahms *Requiem* recording. And in *Falstaff.* Falstaff gets all dressed up because the women want him, then disaster. But before Falstaff enters there is great farewell music. And in Schubert. The music is generally optimistic, but there is great sadness in it, because we know that at thirty-one he is dying. And in *Rosenkavalier* there is the Marschallin, growing old, losing her lover. Her aria in Act I is very moving, and then again toward the end of Act III, when she bids them all *adieu* ... it's very melancholy. Karajan is the best at this. He is the only one who can teach me this.

"It takes fifty years to conduct this opera the way he can. His genius is his memory—to conduct this piece by heart is unbelievable—and for the sound he gets. The Vienna Philharmonic, in this case, brings ninety-five percent of the sound. He gets the other five percent. Other orchestras bring thirty-five percent, and he gets the rest. He must have learned this piece in the 1930s ... like a crazy man. He knows the voices, every word in the text. This is not something you can sit in the sun and learn.

"You must know inside you how the music has to sound, then be able to put the combinations together in the orchestra. With a middle-of-the-road orchestra, you have to slow it down, get the notes, then work on expression. It might take fifteen minutes to get through two bars. You can't think about this sound if you are unsure of the notes you play. But when you can make the orchestra sound the way you want, then it is because of the strength of your personality that comes through like a beam of light. We have a word for this: '*Ausstrahlung*'—a radiating of personality. This is what Karajan has.

"The conductor can't listen to the orchestra, because it will drag him. The first opera I ever did I waited for the singers and it got slower and slower. You have to have the courage to go on. This is what Karajan does—and all hundred people follow. That is how he puts it together: musicality and hard work. The hard work is what he does now." Weil nodded toward the stage, from whence came the sound of velcro tearing as Karajan once again discarded his neck brace.

He was on stage with about fifty singers and extras, running through the most massive scene in the opera for the orchestra's benefit. Ochs has come to call on Sophie, his intended, daughter of the *nouveau riche* merchant von Faninal. Ochs has, of course, brought his retinue with him, and these rowdy fellows are chasing Faninal's women servants while Ochs makes similarly crass attempts to fondle Sophie. The result is havoc. It was a complicated scene, with women screaming and clothes being torn in the background, while Sophie and Ochs carry on, center stage. It was a big coordination problem ("Listen to the music!"), and it *looked* like hard work.

Karajan kept at it for half an hour, then took a break. He remained on stage, seated in the ornate, period armchair he had taken for his command post in front of the prompter's box. The chair's back was to the audience. Karajan was slumped in the chair, his legs stretched in front of him. Only his arms were visible hanging straight down to either side in a position of complete relaxation. He must have been tired.

Busse approached him with a small package in hand. He stood in front of Karajan and opened it. It was a silver rose, the prop that gives the opera its name; that which Octavian—the "rose bearer" (*Rosenkavalier*)—is assigned to carry to Sophie as a sign of Ochs's intentions of marriage. The rose in the Salzburg prop collection had lost its lustre, so Karajan had sent to Berlin to borrow the State Opera rose. Busse handed it to him. He peered at it. It was plastic. He chuckled. The Salzburg rose was fetched. Karajan looked at it. It turned out to be sterling. It needed only to be shined. He should have known.

Baltsa approached. She wanted to skip morning rehearsal. Her discussion with Karajan was long, full of banter and jokes. Baltsa played the actress. She was alternately coy, distraught, distant, severe, cajoling. Karajan played the actor, responding with understanding and good nature. The answer: absolutely not. But no hard feelings, of course.

Having dismissed the singers for the evening, Karajan turned to the orchestra for a little more work. It was late. There was a false start. Karajan stopped, waited. "It must be like the Holy Bible," he said. "Before you play, my hand must fall down." Karajan smiled at his

conceit, and a little chuckle rippled through the Vienna Philharmonic.
But the joke was on them.

The next day, the day of the dress rehearsal, fifty photographers were
in the audience, setting up their tripods from various vantage points.
Papier and Busse were trying to watch all fifty of them at once,
because when it comes to photographs and Karajan, the rules are
strict. Generally, he wants to approve any photo of himself before it
is printed. His two trusted "house" photographers—Emil Perauer and
Siegfried Lauterwasser—had been shooting during several rehearsals.
But now the press were in the Festspielhaus and there was conster-
nation.

In 1960, when Karajan had opened the Festspielhaus with *Rosenkavalier*, there had been a pitched battle over photographic (as well as
televised) coverage. Taking liberties with the German language, the
American show-biz weekly, *Variety*, had carried the headline, "Pho-
togs Won't Heil for von Karajan; Threaten Salzburg With Boycott."
Karajan, the story went, had issued an edict that only one German
and one Austrian photographer would be allowed to cover the event.
He had planned to give free copies of the approved pictures to all the
papers. The press hit the roof. Karajan relented, said he would allow
two German, and *two* Austrian photographers. While he won the TV
blackout battle that year, he lost to the photographers, who said that
since the Festspielhaus was built with tax money, it was unfair to let
Karajan impose his autocratic will.

Since then, there has always been a "photographer's rehearsal," and
it has always been a tense situation. Exactly why, and just what Busse
and Papier were watching for, didn't become evident until the photographers were packing their gear to leave. One enterprising young
women knelt down as if to place something in her bag, and, glancing
furtively about, turned slowly to where Karajan was sitting with
Eliette and raised her camera. Just as she got in position, the sharp-
eyed Busse stepped in front of her.

Tax money or no, as Karajan once told me, "This house is my
personal possession." It would follow that, from Karajan's point of
view, pictures taken of him and his wife in the Festspielhaus would
be an invasion of privacy.

That afternoon Karajan summoned the entire cast to his office for
a meeting. It was a hot, sultry day in Salzburg. The waiting room off
Lore Salzburger's office was warm to begin with. After the cast of
thirty had assembled there, it became quickly stifling. They all waited
thirty minutes in the little room. Then Salzburger opened the door

and told them the Maestro wanted only the soloists. The rest could go.

The performance was received with mixed notices. The music and the singing were magnificent, even to one whose ear is not particularly tuned to opera. It recalled a David Hamilton evaluation of a previous Karajan production in Salzburg: "the sables-and-diamonds sound of Karajan's Salzburg 'Cinemascope Spectacular' is undeniably seductive ..." Baltsa's fierce mezzo voice and her naturally aggressive posture made her Octavian a great match for Perry's fretful Sophie, with her ethereal, captivating, high soprano. Baltsa's entrance at the beginning of Act II was spectacular. She was dressed all in silver, and carried the glittering rose in front of her like a holy chalice. Her love duet with Perry was an unforgettable rendition of exquisitely written music.

Tomova-Sintov's mature, wistful soprano provided the perfect counterpart for the young Octavian's assertive boyishness and for Sophie's girlish hand wringing. When all three came together in the last act to sing the emotional trio, it was another great event, as their distinctive voices combined to produce a compelling sound.

Behind it all was the Vienna Philharmonic at its perfect, soft-sweet, lilting best. Ahh, the waltzes. And there was a special treat. I went backstage for Act III, and there were twenty or so members of the Vienna Philharmonic, grouped together casually, instruments in hand, the way one might run into the band waiting inside a football stadium portal as halftime approached. A conductor was before them, carefully following his score and watching Karajan on a closed-circuit TV monitor. Suddenly they played, providing music that was supposed to be coming from the country inn set that was on stage. Their piece lasted less than a minute, but when one heard them play backstage, among the actors and singers scurrying around the darkened, eerie space, amid dim work lights and silent technicians at their posts in the theater's innards, the romantic piece acquired added impact from its dislocation.

The applause at the end was long and deafening. Karajan hustled backstage to take curtain calls with the singers. He was given flowers. He was beaming. At the end of the correction rehearsal the next day in his office, he told the group, "This was the most beautiful production of my life. Thank you for making it so." Then he tossed his sweater over his shoulder and retreated quickly into his inner sanctum. Karajan is a man of pronouncements, not exchanges.

As usual, with a Karajan production, enthusiasm for the staging

didn't run high. One thing was painfully evident during the performance: the audience was not laughing. *Rosenkavalier* is supposed to be
an amusing opera. Lots of laughs should be forthcoming over the
bumbling, outrageous Ochs, the deceptive, clever Octavian, from the
situation comedy of it all. But the laughs were few and far between.
Perhaps it is difficult to laugh when an idol is at the podium, an aging
idol who is bidding an opera farewell. Does one laugh at an "event"?
As Franz Endler observed: "The opening night audience is always a
status audience; they are not music lovers."

Buffs and insiders were of two minds. As one said with a shrug,
"It was the best of old-fashioned grand opera, with classic staging."
And many agreed with that. Others were simply not happy with
what they saw. "Taking all the staging from the music isn't so good,"
one of the female production assistants said. "There are many mistakes
in *Rosenkavalier*. There is the libretto too. That must be considered. In
Act I we are in the chamber of a woman growing old. There should
be special candle lights that show her to best advantage. And where
is the clock? A few mirrors? Such a woman would want these things.

"When Ochs enters, in keeping with the times, his major domo
should be with him. Ochs shouldn't open the window. He should tell
his lacky to do it. I tried to discuss these things with Karajan but he
won't listen. He tells me only that I am wrong because I don't know
the music."

Franz Endler said he thought the language in the opera was bad.
"It is not the Viennese dialect," he said. Endler's provinciality was
showing, and he was unashamed. "Everything is too international
these days. Karajan says not to think in provincial terms, but now I
can see *Idomeneo* in New York, Zurich, Salzburg. Pavarotti is OK,
but I want to hear a Viennese *Idomeneo*."

Otherwise, Endler wasn't terribly happy with what he saw. "The
sets are bland. When the nursemaid looks out the window and sees
Octavian approaching, she sings about it to the street, not to Sophie.
Von Faninal is funnier in Vienna. Faninal is important for laughing,
and Act II was not good for laughing because Faninal is not so good.
And Moll is not a good Ochs. He has a great voice, but the Viennese
Ochs is funnier."

One had to agree that the Marschallin's bedchamber was a barren
set, painted all creme color with no visual highlights or relief. And
the Marschallin's nightgown was a terrible, lowbrow, hospital green
that was neither regal nor attractive. There was an unmistakable touch
of 1940s Hollywood stiffness about the action throughout the opera.
Some of the lighting, of which Karajan was immensely proud, was

a study in first-year basics: when a shade was raised, click, the sun would pour into the room. When a candle was lit, light intensity would increase. And the embracing that went on was stagey to the point of distraction.

Sena Jurinac and Dr. Lederle were among the opening night crowd. Jurinac had sung Octavian in 1960 with Karajan when *Rosenkavalier* had opened the Festspielhaus. (He had not been the stage director in 1960.) One expected that she had been given a ticket, just for old times' sake, if nothing more. But Karajan hadn't thought of it, therefore it hadn't been done. She had paid her way. Bruno Weil said it was ever thus. He had been told at Easter Festival there was no ticket for him—and he was Karajan's official understudy. So he announced he was leaving. He got his ticket. I found on opening night that I had no ticket. I roamed around, slipping past the gray uniformed hulks of usher-guards, popping up here and there, feeling somewhat like the phantom of the opera—all in the name of Festspielhaus public non-relations. As Lore Salzburger was fond of saying, "Why should we!?" Hadn't I seen the dress rehearsal?

After the performance, I found myself sitting down to eat once again with the Lederles. Sena took charge of the table, soberly impressing upon our luckless waiter the gravity of his mission, urging him to bring the second round of drinks when the first was but half gone; pressing us to decide what we wanted, and offering free consultations.

Jurinac was spare in her criticism of the music. As a former Octavian, she was not without her prejudices, but she guarded them with dignity. "The music was good, if a bit too combed," was all she had to say. But she was visibly upset about the staging. "When Octavian comes in with the rose, she stands there motionless, stiff. And Sophie was not upset enough when Ochs was grabbing at her. To me the whole thing was lifeless. A few chuckles is all he got from the audience, and that is the proof."

Sena was distracted by the waiter's unauthorized appearance at the other end of the table, slipping her husband his second dessert, a generous portion of *Kaiserschmarrn*, a heavenly combination of custard and fluffy baked egg whites. She looked at him, frowned, rolled her eyes. He winked at her, rubbed his hands in glee.

"*Rosenkavalier* was the third opera I conducted in Ulm," Karajan said. "I have been thinking about it for sixty-five years. Never has a performance equaled this one. Especially the singers. These three voices—Tomova-Sintov, Perry, Baltsa—they are incredible. Even the famous

Schwarzkopf is surpassed by Tomova-Sintov. She is a real discovery. When I first heard her I said, 'This is a woman we must develop.'"

Karajan was speaking over the roar of the Porsche Turbo, which he had moving at about a hundred miles an hour down the Autobahn. "Come out," he had said a few days after the opening, "and I will take you to a favorite walking place." Doctor's orders were for him to walk twice a day. For this walk he had picked a place ten miles from his house. We left the highway and ascended a narrow mountain road that became nothing more than a wide logging path through a tall, quiet woods. Karajan pulled to the side and stopped the car. Off to our left on a hillside stood a dozen large cows, grazing among the trees. Directly, they ambled down off the hill toward us. Several of them wore leather collars with large brass bells that bonged soulfully as they walked. Ignoring them, Karajan set off on his walk, hands clasped behind his back, leaning forward, concentrating on each step. The cows followed at our heels. Bong, bong.

We would stop, turn to look at them, and they would stop, look at us. We would walk on, so would they. I was laughing out loud. Karajan was chuckling. I wished Busse had been with us. God knows what he would have done with the cows. Karajan took off his hat and shooed them off, laughing the whole time, whacking them gently on the flanks, dispatching them with Austrian "*kuh*" admonitions. They took the hint and returned to the green grass on the bank.

Down the road, we sat on a log to rest. I asked Karajan how he had learned *Rosenkavalier* so completely.

"I am not a fast learner," he said. "I need much time. There are different ways. Mitropoulos had a photographic memory, as did de Sabata. When Mitropoulos was conducting, the joke was that people would look at him and say, 'Now he turns the page.' I learn from different printed scores to eliminate visions of the printed page. Because the score must be part of my system.

"When I read a score I hear it. With new music I can tell you when the composer thinks in a different way—where in the score he will not hear what he thinks he has written. Afterwards it can be bent and corrected, but I mean as it plays at the first reading.

"By studying from a score, you make an ideal sound picture that is not really feasible. It is one thing when you study works of general knowledge. But when you study without hearing the true sound, you make fantasies which cannot be fulfilled. Today, of course, you can buy fifteen renditions of most pieces. But when I read Beethoven for the first time, I imagined something which wasn't realized when I stood in front of an orchestra."

Karajan said that over a period of years, pieces continue to evolve within him. "They work inside you, improve by the fact of age. At times I may think about a certain piece and feel it is not right. I come to the conclusion that something must be done. It is not thought out, this process. It is more like intuition. It comes to me the way great inventions come to people. There is a book, *The Part and the Whole*, which is dialogues between five atomic scientists. They agree that it takes about three years to prove a new theory or formula. It is the same with music.

"It happens all the time. With the Ninth of Beethoven once I got an uncomfortable feeling that certain passages were not right. Mostly these things come to me in front of the orchestra. That is when I get a sense that something is wrong. So I try something."

As far as Karajan's approach to opera is concerned, it is important to remember his interest in Kabuki theater. A Kabuki theater presentation lasts nearly six hours, and the action is slow far beyond Western limits of pleasure and comfort. Kabuki has been called "the artful use of emptiness and silence." Its traditional form and use of stylized movements, and its duration, clearly link Kabuki with classic opera. Opera breaks the silence, of course, but the action in most classic operas is slow enough to challenge one's tolerance, if not one's endurance.

Like the Kabuki plays, the same thirty to forty operas have been performed over and over again for years. They have become rites, rituals, with the pleasure derived from hearing the familiar repeated; the fascination from observing new singers in the traditional roles, costumes, and sets, and new conductors on the podium.

Karajan's enchantment with Kabuki could explain the barren sets, the stiffness of action, and the rigid adherence to musical clues that he applied to *Rosenkavalier*. As he said there in the Austrian woods, "Kabuki is my ideal. If it is perfect, why change it?"

The tone of the Kabuki plays is serious, often tragic. To relieve the atmosphere, it became a tradition to have farces performed in between the five plays that always comprise a Kabuki program. *Rosenkavalier* has its more serious moments, its melancholy aspects, as Bruno Weil pointed out. But is is mostly a farce. And Karajan's version wasn't very funny.

VII
The Monument

October 1983

Josef was working on the new gate at the house in Anif. It was a handsome gate, a latticework of wood struts powered by an electric motor that would slide it open and shut on metal tracks. It was quite a bit fancier than the gate it was replacing, which had been more in keeping with the rustic, agricultural setting of the house, essentially a bunch of planks and saplings nailed together. But with the old gate, it was necessary to get out of the car, open it by removing the stock wedged across the two panels, drive through, stop, get out of the car, and close it. The new gate would be operated by the touch of a button inside the car—gate-o-matic.

Security wasn't a factor as far as the gate was concerned. Karajan does not live in a compound. A low stone wall overgrown with brush defines the property on the farm road side. The side toward the Untersberg is wide open. The locals know that Karajan lives in their midst—the road he lives on is named after him—but Austrians are very good at minding their own business. And tourists would have to stray far afield before they came to the little sign that reads "Herbert von Karajan Strasse." Even then, they would be hard-pressed to find his place. It looks like a lot of other large, local farmhouses. If they did, the gate would simply be a deterrent. Beyond the gate would be Nero, one of those crazed-looking, loud-but-harmless German shepherds that was more Josef's dog than Karajan's. Lore Salzburger named him. Nero means "black" in Italian. Throw the stick for him and he's yours. He takes out his aggressions on automobile tires, not people.

Karajan was in the cellar with Gela Marina Runne, working on his film project. Two large rooms had been turned into work space. They were lined with floor-to-ceiling metal shelves filled with carefully labeled boxes of 35-mm film that were standing on end like books. The walls were white, and the track lighting was on dimmer switches. The Prevost three-head cutting table took up most of one wall, and there were projection machines and cutting racks and the usual paraphernalia of film editing, all in perfect order. Karajan sat on a high, adjustable draftsman's-type chair at the center of the Prevost in front of the control lever. In the same way aircraft controls culminate in a stick, the functions of the Prevost (forward, fast forward, stop, reverse), had been wired to this one lever. Once Runne, sitting to his left, found the right three takes and loaded each of them through a complex, ten-foot maze of rollers and pickups—making certain each was perfectly synched with the other—Karajan was ready to drive the thing. Runne's hands flew surely to her task as if she could prepare the table in the dark, in her sleep. Then Karajan let it roll.

The three images were projected by mirrors on three small screens positioned side by side, just above the rear of the table. Beethoven's Sixth was the piece in question. The three images were of Karajan conducting, filmed from different angles. On two cameras, orchestra members were seen in the background, playing. On the third, Karajan was framed by the rising and falling bows of string instruments. On all three screens, Karajan more or less filled the frame, or was at least the strong focal point of the shot.

Runne and Karajan were discussing cuts in German, with Runne stopping the machine to mark the film with grease pencil before moving on. After an hour, quite a lot of film had been loaded and viewed, and the three shots on the screen had not changed perceptibly: they were Karajan times three, from different angles.

At the table, Karajan was conducting the three images of himself conducting, his right hand flowing with the music, his left hand indicating the left screen, now the right. "You can't go directly left to right," he said by way of explanation, during a pause. "We are trying now to find out how many frames it takes before you don't know there has been a cut made." He was making cuts on precise beats and musical cues, as in his direction of the *Rosenkavalier* action. "Here is the shot over the violas," Karajan pointed out. "This gives good force, the movement of the bows in unison. But I must be careful. The great danger here is that my nose gets scratched." He chuckled.

"The cutting is as important as conducting," Karajan said. "We must do it every day. There must be no gags, no gimmicks. The viewer shouldn't see too much. The music is what must be heard. We only underline it. People want to be led through the piece. It must be unpretentious. Runne and I have worked together for nearly twenty years. At the beginning she didn't know what music was. Now she takes Arabel under her wing. I would say, conservatively, that she has now seen my face 50,000 times."

A few days earlier, Karajan had spoken at length about his film project. We were sitting upstairs in a comfortable living room done in Austrian country style, with white stucco walls, a low vaulted ceiling achieved with a thick center post, and unfinished wood floor and trim. The furniture was off-white and on the worn side, which made for easy relaxing. At one end of the room was an ample fireplace with an expansive hearth and built-in banquettes on either side. To the right of the hearth was a large television set that included a second, smaller screen for multichannel monitoring. A vase of fresh flowers stood on the hearth.

Out the wide French doors was a striking view of the Untersberg. Nearly devoid of foothills, this mountain juts rather abruptly from the earth. Karajan's house is so close to it that one must stand at the French doors to look up to see the summit. Towering over the house like a three-thousand-foot-high breaking wave, it is an awesome neighbor. For Karajan, who climbed all over the mountain as a boy, the Untersberg is a reassuring companion.

The house had felt lonely. Karajan was in residence with Josef and the maids. He swam twice a day. In the afternoon, Lore Salzburger would drive out with a stack of mail and business to discuss, or perhaps with a bag or two of clothes she had picked up for him. Karajan doesn't frequent stores. When he sees items he wants, he tells Lore and she brings a selection to the house. Once a day a woman came by to give him a massage. And in the early evening Runne would arrive to work on the film project. Eliette was in Paris.

Karajan didn't look very good. His hair was in disarray, and he had a three- or four-day growth of beard, which was unusual for him. On closer inspection, thin, fresh scars stood out across his hairline and behind his ears. Curious. When I inquired about the scars, Karajan appeared not to have heard me, and went on talking about something else. When the subject came up between us later he said that he had hit his head on a tree, opening a wound that had healed unevenly, necessitating cosmetic surgical work on his face.

Karajan had explained that the film project was a two-fold culmination for him. On one hand, it capped a long fascination and involvement with film. Just as he had sought out the best sportsmen to help him learn the intricacies of skiing, driving, sailing, in the mid-1960s he had induced the French filmmaker Henri Clouzot to make a film about the Berlin Philharmonic. Naturally, Karajan worked closely with the master on this project. In Haeusserman's book, there is a photograph of Karajan standing with Clouzot on the camera platform looking more the part than Clouzot. The collar of his knit shirt is turned up, his sleeves are pushed up, and his dark glasses are black wraparound. After this project, Karajan says that Clouzot told him, "you don't need me any more."

Buoyed by Clouzot's blessing, Karajan forged ahead. Over the years, he has made many films, most of them with Unitel, a Munich-based company that specializes in films for television. From 1970 to 1982, Karajan did twenty films for Unitel. Most were symphonic films, although he did three or four operas as well. The one Unitel film I watched was *Das Rheingold*, the first of the four operas that comprise Wagner's *Ring of the Nibelung*. It was a filmed performance of the opera that Karajan made in 1980. Even in large size in the private screening room in Munich's Unitel offices, with heavy black curtains drawn, the beginning of the film was difficult to discern for its darkness. It would have been impossible on TV. Then came the Rhinemaidens, bare-breasted and sexy in their fishtail costumes, "swimming" around their mountain of gold. Sexy maidens or no, this scene became quickly tiresome as it went on and on, despite the ingenious radio-controlled carousel that was developed to suspend the maidens in mid-air. A gentleman at the screening told me that once during the filming, Karajan decided to fly this machine, and came perilously close to driving one of the maidens breasts-first into the layer of colored, broken glass that was being used to produce a glittering light effect from below.

The *Das Rheingold* film was a very literal rendition of the opera; literal without spectacle, which made for very slow going. There were too many shots from the back of singers' heads, and too many moonscape tableaux. The staging was uninspired, with familiar signatures. When, in Scene Three, Alberich turns himself into a dragon, the others in the scene recoil in horror and point at him. And there were too many close-ups of singers singing. Like weight lifting, operatic singing is a one-hundred-percent physical effort. Like weight lifting, it is a little grotesque. The face of the handsomest or most beautiful singer is not a pretty thing in full voice. Opera singers should not be photographed close-up while singing. At best, their necks swell, their mouths contort around tongue-twisting syllables, their eyes bulge, and they show too many teeth. At worst, they make weight lifters look good. Watching an epiglottis at work does not promote proper music appreciation. In the theater, even from the first row, there is some distance between viewer and singer, and that is how opera is best seen.

Rheingold opened in a Munich theater in 1980 and closed after three days. It was Karajan's last film with Unitel. There are several versions of how the final rift with Unitel came about. Mainly it seems that expenses were reaching epic proportions, and the film quality wasn't that good.

Karajan, on the other hand, wanted the same control over his films that he had arranged for his opera productions. It wasn't long after splitting with Unitel that Karajan began Telemondial, his own film company. It was to be a film version of the Easter Festival, a one-man show that would afford him the chance to do what he wanted, how and when he wanted to do it. He engaged Märkle to handle production, Runne to do the editing. He hired film crews as he needed them. Then he signed the Berlin Philharmonic to an exclusive film contract. His plan was to re-record, on film, all the works of "his" core repertoire: Tchaikovsky, Brahms, Bruckner, Beethoven, Mahler, etc.

He had several reasons for putting these works on the record once again. First, there was a technological advance. Through his friends at Sony, Karajan had closely followed the development of the video disc. Now it was emerging, and not a moment too soon. He was impressed by its fidelity—a quantum leap over tape—and its indestructability. He had done his original work on 78 rpm. When the LP came along, he went into a recording frenzy to upgrade his work on the new medium. He did much of his work again on stereo, and with the advent of the compact laser disc, he had started over once again. The video disc combined the advanced fidelity of laser tracking with the sharpest and most vivid visual image to date. Karajan was convinced that video disc was the way of the future. Not only that, video discs were very expensive to duplicate, which would make life difficult for the pirates. Karajan was slightly obsessed by how easy it was to pirate tapes and recordings—even video cassettes. The video disc would put a stop to that.

He would film operas, too: *Rosenkavalier*, *Falstaff*, *Carmen*, *Don Carlos*, and *Otello*. He had expressed his regret at not being able to put all the great operas on film. It was upsetting to him that there was no filmed record of his many productions. But he knew that was impossible. He would settle for the great symphonic works, in itself a project of gigantic proportions, and would begin with the nine symphonies of Beethoven. It would be the fourth time he had recorded the Beethoven symphonies. Over the years, Beethoven had been his best seller. "Making this review of my music," he said, "is like a religion for me."

Karajan said he had discovered, after years of study, how best to put symphonic works on film, and this provided an underlying impetus for redoing his core repertoire. "What we need to do is to get across, on film, the musical idea," Karajan said. "We don't do this so much with the orchestra. But on the film, the viewer should never lose me. This is not just to show me. He should miss me if I am not there, but when I am there he shouldn't necessarily see me." If Karajan's rationale was obscure, a little hard to follow, the nature of the product being put together in the basement was quite clear: Karajan was making films of himself conducting great symphonic works.

He was proceeding on a grand scale. He began with twelve shots of each symphony: three cameras shot each of four run-throughs of the work. There were two rehearsals, during which he would stop every ten minutes for the cameras to reload, and two performances. For each run-through there were also three cameras running sporadically on solo instruments. So, for each symphony, he accumulated about 60,000 feet of raw footage to work with. That's a twelve-to-one ratio of raw to finished film, an impressive figure even by big-studio standards. I suggested to Runne that the people who made Star Wars weren't up to that ratio. "That's right," she said with a grin. "We're bigger than Star Wars."

Karajan said that each film was costing in the $300,000 range, an exorbitant amount for a forty-five-minute film, given the static nature of the subject. The orchestra had to be hired, and three camera crews, with film and processing, but there were no actors to pay, no location logistics, no scenery, staging, or special effects. One wondered where all that money was going.

Incidental shots of solo instruments would consume perhaps five minutes of each film. Instruments, not faces. One might see a player's mouth, or his hands, but not his face. And some instruments were banned. The bassoon, for instance. Karajan said he thought it looked silly, "like a pipe." The flute, on the other hand, he liked. I asked him why no faces of the orchestra. "Because they are ugly," he snapped, with a gruffness that reminded one of the ongoing battle he was having with the Berlin Philharmonic. "You will see faces," he said, coiling to strike, "but they will be out of focus. This will complete the fantasy that the instrument makes music by itself." Surely, this was not a fantasy the players would enjoy. "The players have to cope with me. I'll take them as I want. Some are not photogenic."

Aside from these five minutes of views of instruments being played, Karajan would occupy the screen. It was a curious approach to film— akin to filming a sports event by shooting mainly the coach's face and reactions, and a few key plays—one, it seemed, of dubious marketability; useful, mainly, for students of the art. But as Runne said, "You would need only one camera for a film for students." In the concert hall, one does see the conductor all the time, if only out of the corner of one eye. In most halls, except the Berliner Philharmonic, where half the audience sits facing the conductor, concertgoers can see only the conductor's back, which is perhaps a blessing. Taking the conductor face on, in the intense, limited parameters of film, could be a mistake.

Taking many conductors from the back, in the concert hall, is often too much of a distraction. Perhaps the St. Vitus's dance some of these fellows go through is indispensable for communicating their wishes. Perhaps the orchestra before them would be lost without such gyrations. But on several occasions I have been forced to close my eyes to remove the unpleasant vision that was jumping around between me and the music. Sarah Caldwell, artistic director of the Boston Opera Company, is a woman of such girth that a screen is always placed between her and the audience when she conducts. This is a marvelous idea, one that more conductors should consider adopting.

On the other hand, Karajan's podium movements are spare, clean, unobtrusive. In many passages there is a good visual tie-in between the sound and his presence. In many shots, the viewer is in the orchestra, being conducted, which is an interesting notion. Time will tell if viewers of music on film have a desire to be "conducted" through an entire symphonic work, or if, in fact, there is much of a real demand for symphonic music played on film. "I will be astonished if the films are not a success," Karajan says. "But if not, they are there. If, in three hundred years, people want to know about Karajan the films will tell them. My God, what I wouldn't give to see Nikisch conduct."

There is a great similarity among these films, as one might expect. It would take a rare viewer—probably an accomplished conductor— to tell the difference between Bruckner and Beethoven with the sound turned off. And the work, the cutting and editing, as I observed over several long evenings, is terribly tedious. Karajan never seems to tire of it. He often presses on into the night. One Wednesday evening Runne mentioned that she would like to end fairly early to make a dinner engagement. At 8:30, Karajan suggested they begin another reel. It seemed like a spiteful gesture, but Runne didn't seem to mind. Like all those who have worked many years for Karajan—Busse, Salzburger, Schneider-Siemssen, Mattoni, and the rest—she expects a fair amount of abuse. Working with the great man, working in the glow of prominence, fame, and power seems to make it worthwhile. And Runne, like the rest, had long ago been seduced by the many-faceted crystal of his charm; the little-boy-lost look that underlies even his most outrageous demands, needs, and outbursts. Like the rest, Runne's perception was complete. "He knew I had an engagement. That's why he kept me so long. It was his way of reminding me what was most important. When he finally finished, he said we would have worked longer if you hadn't been there. But the real reason he stopped when he did was to watch *Dynasty* on TV.

"He is difficult. It is necessary to wear gloves with him. If you are hard with him, he will be hurt. And he never forgets."

One wondered what would be the result if Runne just took the film and edited it. "He would hate it," she said. "I did that once. It cost me two months' work." She shrugged. "It is his toy. It is a monument that he makes. It is interesting for him, because he is making something for eternity. Other directors make films just for the money. Soap operas, and lousy films for television. Not Karajan. And he is an interesting man. I learn about music from him. Working to make a monument is more important than making a soap opera."

It is consistent that Karajan would supervise the construction of his own monument. It is not a job he would trust to someone else. He has the money, and what better way to spend it? What could be a more appropriate chore for a seventy-five-year-old workaholic with an extraordinary ego than to document his best work on film? There is something else to be said for the project: he will never complete it. He knows this of course, and it keeps him going.

Not long after Karajan's operation we were walking on the farm road near his house in Anif. The light rain that was falling had not kept him from his exercise regimen. The doctors had told him he must exercise, and he had taken the advice to heart. He had on his navy blue Admiral's Cup hat, a down jacket, his jogging pants, and his green and yellow running sneakers. If he makes it to ninety, he'll still dress like a sportsman. Every twenty steps he would stop to rest from the effort it took for him to walk. This day he tapped his knees, saying they were taking a beating from the new motion of walking. "But the main thing is," he said, his eyes burning, "that I must not stop."

*   *   *

One day Karajan had said to come to the house at noon. Runne and I arrived at the same time to find the big silver 500 SEL Mercedes sedan ready at the front door. Karajan asked if I had ever been to the Berghof, Hitler's residence on the Obersalzberg, a mountain just across the German border to the west of Salzburg, above a town called Berchtesgaden. "I will show you," he said, and we piled into the luxurious car that Karajan described as a sanitorium on wheels for his nerves. The car was equipped with a great stereo that Karajan said he rarely listened to. "If I drive fast, having the music on is dangerous," he said.

It was a short drive. Obersalzberg is only six or seven miles from Karajan's house. On the way we got a different view of the Untersberg, and Karajan pointed out a spot on the mountain where he had nearly been in trouble as a boy. "We bivouacked in a shelter during a thunderstorm. In the mountains, even shoes with studs on them attract storms. One must throw away everything metal."

At the entrance to the Obersalzberg, Karajan turned the big car sharply and punched the accelerator. He drove hard up the winding mountain road, roaring past other cars, braking sharply on the corners. "Now we go to where Hitler used to be," he said. Halfway up the wide, well-paved road with its precisely laid stone embankments and guard walls—built in the late 1930s by Hitler's camp labor—Karajan slowed and indicated an opening in the foliage through which the Eagle's Nest could be seen. Today, this aptly named stone structure, perched on a rock ledge at an altitude of approximately 5400 feet, is a tourist attraction and restaurant. In 1939, it was built under the direction of Martin Borman as a meeting place and lodge for officials and high-ranking friends of the Third Reich. It can be reached only by an elevator from the parking lot. It was considered a major feat of engineering when it was built.

Further up, Karajan stopped to show us the location of the Berghof. "It was all destroyed, so there is no memorial to Hitler," Karajan explained, indicating a sunlit, overgrown knoll. "But here is where his house was. It's all flat now." He drove on. "I haven't been here for a long time," he said, half to himself.

On the next rise was a cluster of long, cement buildings with walls a foot thick, which had been constructed as barracks for the troops on Obersalzberg. Now called the General Walker Hotel, the renovated barracks house American Army personnel and their families on holiday. Opposite the parking lot over the next hill, where Karajan parked the Mercedes, is the entrance to the underground bunker complex Hitler had built as a fallback position from a similar bunker in Berlin. It was a gorgeous autumn day. The covering of heavy frost on the trees seemed out of place in the bright sunshine. Only a few wispy clouds disturbed the blue of the sky. We walked among tourists who had come to gape at some of Hitler's possessions on display in a small museum, tour the damp, claustrophobic tunnels of the bunker that still reek with fear and death, and to enjoy the spectacle of mighty mountains that rise on all sides. We leaned on the split-rail fence overlooking the side of the Untersberg that Karajan rarely sees. He pointed out Rossfeld Mountain, where he had come as a boy to ski with his parents. He spoke of the climber, Reinhold Messner, who has set several altitude records without using oxygen and has written books about his adventures. "He is not a daredevil," Karajan said. "He does it because he must. He is always well prepared, beautifully trained." And he pointed out the gap to the right of the Untersberg through which one could see the end of a runway at the Salzburg airport. "When you have good nerves, you come over the Eagle's Nest clearing it by ten meters, hit the middle of that gap, and you are lined up perfectly for the runway." Karajan said his knees, back, and hips were feeling miserable.

He drove very slowly back down the mountain road. His mind was still on skiing. "When I learned to ski, skiing meant climbing six hours a day. When I trained for Mt. Blanc, I skied Val d'Isère, which was five hours up. We went to Mt. Blanc the end of March. I love that region. Chamonix to Mt. Blanc. Willi Bogner once skied fourteen straight days there and didn't have time to ski all the available runs. We took two guides, one a trainee, and climbed for twenty-two hours. We spent the night in a cabin. We were up at 2 A.M. because we had to be on the top before ten. We didn't do the last eighty meters because of the wind. We could have been blown off. There was eighty kilometers of wind. The temperature was twenty-five degrees below. Our first run was to the hut, where we had warm drinks. By 2 P.M. the sun had broken through and there were spring conditions. We made it down in twenty-seven minutes skiing time, which they said was the fastest run ever made with a guide. It was the guide's seventy-third trip, and he said the conditions were the best he had ever seen. Every time I fly over Mt. Blanc I still don't believe I have been there. I did this at fifty-seven years. I was in the best form I had ever been in."

Karajan drove for a few minutes in silence. "One thing I have still not got over," Karajan said quietly: "That I cannot ski anymore." He slapped the steering wheel as he spoke each word, underlining his frustration. "I can't imagine after skiing for sixty-five years that I can no longer do it. If I see someone skiing, I am nearly crying."

We passed back across the border into Austria and Karajan stepped
on the gas. He loves to accelerate for short bursts, taking the car up
around 100 mph and then letting it slow down. He did this several
times on the straight road that led into Anif. We were stopped by a
red traffic light. People in the car next to us got our attention and
pointed urgently at our right front wheel. I had smelled something
burning, and now we could see wisps of smoke curling up from the
wheel well. We were only a mile from the house, so Karajan drove
slowly to the gate. Josef opened it for us. Karajan spoke harshly to
Josef in German, telling him about the smoke, the smell, and telling
him to check it out. As we entered the house, Josef was already under
the car. Runne and I suspected that Karajan had driven back with the
emergency brake on. But Josef would find the problem.

Back in the cellar workroom, Karajan inquired about my trip to
Berlin the previous week. I had told him I was going, and had asked
him for names of orchestra members to speak with, but he had offered
none. Now he wanted to know whom I had seen. He greeted each
name I mentioned with a disparaging grunt. To my mention of one
particular player, he said, "He is one of the five best players of his
instrument, and one of the five worst characters. The rest of them are
useless, so silly, most of them. They don't know what they play
beyond the notes. In auditions, their reaction to players is embarrass-
ing to me. They know nothing. Then they come to someone like
Sabine Meyer, the clarinetist, who is as much a genius as James Galway, and they can't see it. That was a dark day."

Karajan's initial reaction to the orchestra's resistance of Meyer had
been petulant. If they couldn't see it, he would grab them by the
backs of their necks and show it to them. He had written the letter
in which he acknowledged the orchestra's contractual right to pass on
a candidate, but stating his total disagreement with their judgment,
and informing them of the terms of his punishment: the obligatory
six Berlin subscription cycles a year only—television, recording, tours,
and festival appearances were suspended. He would starve them out.

At that point—the fall of 1983—there was some hope. Meyer was
still playing with the orchestra, which pleased Karajan. But Intendant
Peter Girth was still in place, which didn't please the orchestra. Girth,
whose job is described as intermediary between Karajan, the orchestra,
and the city of Berlin, had blatantly sided with Karajan on the Meyer
matter, and the orchestra wanted his head. The understanding of
many players was that if Meyer was given her year's probationary
stay, Girth would go. Girth's continued presence was a display of
Karajan's loyalty—Girth had, after all, helped Karajan find a way to

keep Meyer. It was also a display of his power, and a slap in the orchestra's face.

As one veteran Berlin Philharmonic player (who must remain nameless) put it, "When you deal with a dictator, you say go to hell, or you go to war, or you talk." This gentleman made the point that in many cases the orchestra had treated Karajan poorly. The extra-curricular schedule of the large chamber orchestra was one example. "Our side has made some heavy blunders, it is true. But he threatens us about the Meyer thing, and if we cave in, it means the annihilation of players' rights that have been the backbone of this orchestra for more than one hundred years. This orchestra was founded in 1881 by fifty people who were unwilling to submit to the dictatorial behavior of conductors and management. They gave themselves democratic bylaws. We cannot simply hand our heritage over just because our music director is a famous and powerful star. He toys with us too much. We wanted a new charter, one in keeping with the times, that would include a voice in programs, choice of soloists, etc. Karajan said to us, 'What do you want? That before I conduct pianissimo I should take a vote?' There is no democracy onstage. But offstage we should enjoy as much democracy as any student in school. He has reached a power that must not be reached again. The only one he puts above himself is Wagner."

As James Galway noted after playing for several years in the orches-tra, the Berlin Philharmonic is "a handful." The players are well paid, admired, highly respected. For orchestral players, their egos are very strong. And Karajan had a hand in creating this situation. Karajan's old acquaintance Dick Bertram, sportsman and yacht broker (now retired), and a master of sales motivational techniques, recalls being surprised at the work Karajan was doing in this area with the Berlin Orchestra in the 1960s. "He was insisting that on the road they stay in the best hotels," Bertram says, "and he urged them to be well dressed. It was his intention to pump them up, strengthen their indi-vidual self-images."

The Berlin Philharmonic is not a homogeneous group. If polled, each player would probably have a slightly different view of the conflict with Karajan and his own formula for resolving the situation. But unity was struck over the question of orchestra rights. On this issue, there was solidarity. Karajan was attempting to tamper with the orchestra's basic structure, and the orchestra was worried. As timpanist-composer Werner Thärichen said, "With new players it is important to have the opinion of the orchestra, because each indivi-dual opinion, when accepted, contributes to the initial *sound* of the orchestra. As I told Karajan, he is a famous man. It is possible he could break our system. So for now we must be very quiet so he doesn't do this; and *we* must take care not to do something that could cause damage. Being a conductor leads to dictatorship. Even young conductors tend toward this. The public and the critics want a star. But Karajan is at odds with today's way."

Bass player Rainer Zepperitz, one of the orchestra's official representatives, was urging similar caution. "The orchestra was the father to Furtwängler," Zepperitz said. "We had to take care of him. Karajan is father to the orchestra. Now, during this trouble, we must continue to do our best. If we have been together twenty-eight years with a great conductor and musician like him, what is one year of trouble? We mustn't cause a break with him. We must ease back, finish out his time. He is a great conductor. We must put up with him. We put up with Furtwängler's madness. We must do the same now."

Over the next year, the situation deteriorated. The fortunes of clarinetist Meyer remained at the center of the problem. As the end of her one-year probationary period came to a close in June of 1984, Karajan privately warned the orchestra that if she were rejected, he would "unleash a scandal." The pressure finally got to Meyer (one wonders how she had lasted a year beneath it), and she resigned. Perhaps she also realized that her chances of approval were slim. Furious, Karajan responded as promised, though no one would have predicted the extreme nature of his revenge. At the last moment, he dismissed the Berlin Philharmonic from a scheduled performance at Salzburg's annual Pfingst-Konzerte series in June. This series commemorates the Pentecost and consists of three concerts on successive evenings at which different conductors lead the Berlin Philharmonic. The Maazel and Ozawa concerts went as planned in 1984. But for his concert, Karajan flew in the Vienna Philharmonic, at his own expense, to take the orchestra's place. He even took the trouble to have the programs reprinted. For the Berlin Philharmonic, it was an insult of the highest magnitude.

It was also a public declaration of open warfare. As nasty as the conflict had been to that point, it had remained a relatively private affair. As well reported as it had been, the struggle raged behind closed doors. Most notably, the private nature of the conflict had allowed Berlin's politicians to adopt a wait-and-see attitude. This was a position they were grateful for: since it was an election year, none of them wanted to touch what was a most delicate situation. The people of Berlin loved their orchestra as Londoners love the Thames, as Brazilians love soccer. And with Karajan, the popular and powerful idol who is credited with having put the orchestra on its high pedestal, only the most foolish politician would have deigned to back one against the other. The newspapers had been carrying daily innuendo, and in Berlin's cafes, it was the number one topic. But now, the nasty business was in the street.

Within a few days of the Pfingst-Konzerte incident, the Berlin Senate dismissed Intendant Peter Girth. Girth went out in anger, threatening legal action over violation of his contract. But as one orchestra member said, with obvious satisfaction, "Girth was biased against the orchestra. He gambled that the orchestra wouldn't be able to withstand the power and pressure of Karajan. And he lost." "Girth made statements he shouldn't have made," Karajan says. "He lost his head, or I would have stuck by him."

On the heels of Girth's dismissal, Berlin Culture Minister Volker Hassemer broke the political silence and, given the Berlin Senate's power over the orchestra, his remarks were ominous. (As Karajan once said, "The Senate can say Bernstein will conduct. They have the right. They would never dare to do this, but they have the right.") "There are voices in the city that are a lot less patient with Karajan than we are," Volker said. "Those who love Karajan also love the orchestra. His action in Salzburg was a break of the marriage."

The expected hue and cry went up. Some German music critics— of all people—warned that if Karajan departed, it would lead to the provincialization of the city's rich musical life. The orchestra was chastised for its "hubris." Some orchestra players responded by suggesting the Berlin Senate find a way to terminate Karajan's life contract. The Berlin newspapers carried daily bulletins. Television carried panel discussions on the subject that featured critics and musicians. Sentiment was not at all pro-Karajan.

Former Berlin Intendant Wolfgang Stresemann, age eighty, was persuaded to become acting Intendant, and this was a good sign. An intelligent, dignified man who knows Karajan well, Stresemann represented a happier time in the orchestra's history. He was beyond bias, and his vision was clear. If anyone had a chance to negotiate a peaceful solution, it was Stresemann. "This orchestra owes Karajan," he said as he settled behind the familiar desk. "The 'gratitude' is not enough. As a director, he is a genius. On the other hand, Karajan has to ask himself—to use a musical image—how long a violinist can successfully play a violin that is out of tune."

Der Spiegel put Karajan on its cover the week of Girth's dismissal. The headline read, "Disharmony in Berlin: The end of Karajan's high flight." The gist of the story: in three decades, Karajan and the

Berlin have given approximately fourteen hundred concerts and have made more that three hundred record albums. Now this lucrative partnership without precedent is over: the orchestra has withdrawn its vote of confidence.

The withdrawn vote of confidence was threefold. First, in retaliation for the Pfingst-Konzerte dismissal, the orchestra informed Karajan in writing that it would not appear for the concert scheduled with him at the Salzburg Festival on August 24. Second, the Berlin Philharmoniker's (the private orchestra) recording contract with Deutsche Grammophon had expired that summer. Player representatives had begun discussions with CBS records for a contract that could not include Karajan (Karajan's repertoire is so widely published elsewhere that no new Karajan release could compete against discounted re-releases other companies would be sure to counter with). The private orchestra has the right to negotiate its own recording contract, but until now, Karajan had usually been consulted, his wishes respected. The CBS possibility was old business. Some years ago, CBS had made the Berlin an offer. Now the plot was thickened by the fact that Lorin Maazel, who has often been mentioned as a Karajan successor in Berlin, was under contract to CBS. And CBS is the only big label with which Karajan has not recorded.

Karajan's next card was to let it be known that he would be happy to record for CBS. As an associate of Karajan's pointed out, it was strictly a tactical move. He knew CBS wouldn't be interested (because of the repertoire problem), but it was a position that made him appear more reasonable, more agreeable.

During the summer of 1984, the Berlin did make a recording with CBS under the direction of Daniel Barenboim, who has never been particularly well thought of by Karajan.

Third, and most damaging to Karajan, the orchestra threatened to cancel its media contract with Telemondial, Karajan's film company. This last would have been a heavy blow, because it would have meant that Karajan could not complete the nine symphonies of Beethoven, the first of his core repertoire film projects, into which he had already poured a large sum of money. Karajan could have sued the orchestra for violation of contract, and probably have won. But it would have been time consuming, costly, a public scandal, and would have resulted in a shambles.

"We wanted to prove to him," one orchestra member said, "that our rights, our responsibility to the structure of the orchestra, are not for sale. People thought when he canceled our recording schedule, our tours, our festival appearances, that we would give in because our earnings would be decreased. He never thought he would encounter such resistance. He finally saw we were serious."

"They could not say 'we won't play' because I have a contract for life and I would stick to it," Karajan insisted. "If they lost face, then they would play without face!" At the same time, it was evident that he was in a bind. Karajan moved quickly and quietly behind the scenes. He contacted both the Vienna Philharmonic and the Dresden State Orchestra in hopes that they might help him complete the Beethoven film project. But splicing another orchestra into the Berlin footage would have been impossible even if the Vienna or Dresden orchestras had been willing and available, which they were not. To further tempt Dresden, Karajan suggested they perform the Bach B-minor Mass (which he was scheduled to do with the Berlin Philharmonic) at the Berlin Music Festival in September. He held out the possibility of recording the Bach piece, and further work (festivals and recordings) in 1985. But his overtures were for naught. The Dresden had a tour of the U.S.S.R. planned, and was otherwise busy.

Having failed to circumvent the Berlin Philharmonic, Karajan made a move toward reconciliation with a letter he sent to the orchestra on August 24: "The international music world and our public expect that we make music together in Bach's B-minor Mass during this year's Berlin Festival Weeks. Exactly this work, so deeply imbued with humanity and Christianity, should make it easier for us to draw a final line in a spirit of conciliation and to return to our former unity.

"Over the long period of thirty years, which embraces almost my entire professional life and also that of many members of the orchestra, we were able to achieve together such great and lasting performances only because we were at one in the music and respected one another. Recent unfortunate dispositions, human failings, and faults cannot and must not be allowed to darken the effect of a musical triumph and uninterrupted progress esteemed throughout the world.

"I therefore propose to you that in September 1984 during the Berlin Festival Weeks, with which I have been associated as conductor of the Berlin Philharmonic Orchestra since 1953, we take up again the mutual musical work. For the outstanding questions we will then find better solutions in greater peace, objectivity, relaxation, and patience.

"With heartfelt greetings
(signed) Herbert von Karajan"

Der Spiegel published in the September 17, 1984, issue ("A Meal That Nobody Trusts"): "as Karajan's letter made the rounds of the

orchestra, nobody folded his hands in prayerful thanksgiving ...
Bach's Christian inspiration was far less important to the musicians,
Karajan's scolded children, than the fervent wish to 'clean house' with
the Maestro ..."

Its lofty, oratorical tone aside, the letter was important in the overall picture as a gesture from the Maestro that could pave the way
for continuation. Those watching the situation in Berlin knew such
a gesture was necessary, but having observed Karajan's behavior over
the years, no one had much hope for it. Suddenly, there it was. It
didn't take strong glasses to see in it the work of cooler heads—
certainly Stresemann among a few others close to Karajan—who were
desperately seeking to break a destructive deadlock.

As the crafty Stresemann told the *New York Times*, "Karajan sent
this letter because he understood that we meant business. He could
see that we were able to say 'no.' But now we have to say 'yes.' Let's
say the door is open for some kind of *modus vivendi*." Indeed, the
Bach Mass was played in Berlin on September 24, as scheduled, with
Karajan conducting the Berlin Philharmonic. Even though the Bach
Mass required only a half-size orchestra, the performance was a good
sign, despite *Der Spiegel*'s insistence that the relationship between
Maestro and orchestra would never be quite the same.

The Bach Mass performance paved the way for the planned tour
of Japan to take place in October 1984. This trip had been in question
until the last possible moment. The full orchestra was once again
assembled under Karajan's baton for the first time since Easter Festival.
It was the longest they had been apart in 28 years, and those who
heard the Japan concerts spoke in emotionally charged superlatives
about them. The tour went smoothly, happily. Karajan's mood was
reported as mellow, perhaps owing in part to the presence of Eliette,
who (it was reported) cheerfully accompanied her increasingly frail
husband, who had to be helped down from the podium by the concertmaster, and who was barely making 50 steps at a time. Eliette did
not want to go to Japan (she hates most tours—American tours are
the only ones she likes), but she gave in under pressure from orchestra
insiders. She was told Karajan needed her, and he did. So she went
along, and was by all accounts a charming and witty hostess, a perfect
wife: supportive, affectionate, and protective.

The orchestra rallied too. To some observers, the way they played
under Karajan made reconciliation a sure thing. Said a Berlin Philharmonic business associate, "When they came together, it was emotional and dramatic. Emotional on both sides. The orchestra realized
what it had been missing. Karajan is one of the greatest conductors of

the century. With each concert you could feel a warmth that grew. It was touching, moving. It was Karajan's best. He could feel it too."

The mood in the orchestra seemed to be one of pragmatism rather than brotherly love. But then brotherly love has not characterized Karajan's tenure with the Berlin. As Paul Moor wrote in 1957, just two years after Karajan had taken over the orchestra, "He commands respect rather than warmth. On the trans-Atlantic stretch of his tours ... he has made obvious conscious efforts to unbend, even to joke, but there is no real *kontakt*, as the orchestra men put it. His habit of conducting them with closed eyes sums up the relationship; the men are left with the discontented, vaguely rejected feeling that their personal identity is denied them, that all they mean to Karajan is this or that voice in the winds or strings or percussion." When asked to describe the feeling when Karajan and the orchestra came together in Japan, one player simply said, "It was normal. Everything was just ... normal." Others emphasized that peace had been achieved, and that was the important thing. Karajan had agreed to abide by the orchestra's rights. The orchestra had agreed to finish the film project. The business of music would go on.

"We can't go back to the past," one player said. "We must try to wind up this era in a sensible way. Being good musicians, we will not let our differences with our conductor influence our music making. We are professionals. Our responsibility is to fulfill our obligations to audience and employer. We played well in Japan. If the public thinks we are happy, that's fine."

Other players were concerned about Karajan's health. One suggested he shouldn't be so proud, that he should use a cane. Several expressed happiness he was with them again. "They should be happy," one of Karajan's close business associates said: "They will never have it like this again."

Once when I was walking with Karajan near his house in Anif, he stopped to rest and to watch the eagles soaring above their roosts on the rocky ledges of the zoo in Anif. "I love to see birds soaring," he said. "I love the harmony with which they do it. They develop a joy of what they do. They don't soar just to look for food, of this I am sure. They have a joy of flying. They spend the day in the mountains, then they come to the zoo at night, where it is safer. When I am in my sail plane they look furious if I hit an updraft and ascend faster. They hate me." Karajan paused, studied the eagles, chuckled to himself.

"I have thought that in my next life I will maybe be a falcon."

I asked him if he was serious about a next life.

"I am so serious I can't even discuss it," he said, fixing me with his eyes. "I like what Goethe wrote about this. He said, if I have so many things to think, to do, and to meditate upon, and my body refuses to follow me, then nature must give me another one. *Must* give me another. Not maybe."

VIII
Postscript

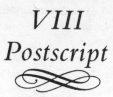

When I heard that Herbert von Karajan had died, I was both surprised and not surprised. For some time I had marveled at how he had persevered against the bad health that plagued him for so many years. At the same time. I knew how he had done it: with the incredible strength of his ferocious will. I had begun to think he was winning his struggle against both the odds and the gods.

When Karajan and the Berlin Philharmonic parted company last April after 35 years, I suspected it would be the beginning of the end for him. Many obsessed business executives lose their starch when retirement finally claims them. With Karajan, it was musical marriage as well as business. As Seiji Ozawa, artistic director of the Boston Symphony and a long-time Karajan admirer and student, told me when I asked him what it was that made the Berlin a great orchestra: "It is Karajan and the Berlin—so many years of the man and the players together is where the greatness lies. The two had become one."

For the last ten years the marriage had been in turmoil. The evolution of musicians' rights did not sit well with the autocratic, paternal Karajan, who considered his players children to whom favors were to be allotted at his whim. But (credit to both sides) even as the battle went on publicly and privately, the music, for the most part, continued to enthrall.

While the musicians' new-found freedom was enraging Karajan, his health was under attack. His affinity to mountain climbing and fast motorcycles had gotten him involved in several spectacular accidents as a youth. He survived them and went on aggressively scuba diving, water skiing, flying, gliding, and snow skiing all his life. He was proud to recall skiing Mt. Blanc at age 54. "At that time I was in the best shape of my life," he told me in 1983, swelling out his chest for emphasis. And there was always a garage full of fast, exotic cars. But while dents in the frame don't hamper the younger man, they become pernicious in old age.

So it was that major surgery for the repair of vertebrae became necessary in 1984. The surgery was "successful" but full recovery required a younger patient. At age 78, Karajan had to learn to walk all over again. He worked at the task with his own outrageous brand of tenacity. He swam, took long, agonizing walks, had massages and physical therapy, and continued to drag himself to the podium where he would plant his feet and conduct long programs with just arms, hands and torso. Those who saw him work in the last three years witnessed the enormity of his ordeal, the measure of his determination. For it was sheer will, not his legs, that carried him through those long evenings at the philharmonic.

After my last meeting with Karajan before publication of my book on his life, I never heard from him. But I kept up with him through friends in Salzburg, and the reports were not good.

That I didn't hear from him was consistent. My recollections of Karajan, whom I was with on and off for nearly three years, are in a series of encounters like unrelated film clips. Our relationship never matured or developed. He came to me with the casual charm and friendliness he affords all sportsmen—sailors, in my case. And he admired what I had written about a man he knew. I'm sure he also thought I could be easily manipulated because I am not a music expert. (Initially, the book we discussed was about music.)

I came to him with great respect for his musical genius. And we got along throughout the three years, including the last anxious meeting when we went over the finished manuscript I had sent him as a courtesy. Even after that difficult session, he suggested I join him for a sail on his boat.

But through it all there was no human progress, nothing given from the heart on his part. We were doing business. He was always on guard, as one should be with a writer in one's midst, I suppose, but there didn't seem to be much carry-over from session to session. I learned to take nothing for granted. Each time I saw him, my approach was to assume it was our first meeting. We would talk for a specified amount of time. At the end of that period, he would dismiss me by slapping his hands on his knees and saying, "Well, that's it. See you tomorrow." I understood something of how his players felt.

Gary Jobson, one of the ranking sailors Karajan employed to help

him organize his 70-foot racing sailboat, retains similar feelings about
his time with the Maestro. "He would send his car for me," Jobson
recalls, "and he was friendly on the boat, but the minute our training
sessions were over, it was as if I didn't exist."

Part of it was Karajan's total self-absorption. Part of it is the price of
interacting with a man of genius, which Karajan surely was. And part
of it was the one-man show Karajan was running *in extremis*. He always
had a major domo, and his loyal secretary Lore Salzburger did the
work of a staff of six. But he trusted practically no one, finalizing all
deals (records, tours, television specials, films) and contracts himself,
and personally selecting everything from singers, soloists, music, costumes, and exact cuts of films being edited, to the breed and color dog
that appears in *Rosenkavalier*. He exercised total control of such an
extensive list of details that one harried Salzburg Festspielhaus official
was heard to mutter during Easter Festival preparations, "I'm surprised
he doesn't sell tickets and show people to their seats."

It was my observation that Karajan kept all these details in his head.
I never once saw him write a note or refer to a notebook. There were
lackeys aplenty with clipboards, but even the Chancellor usually has a
little notebook in his jeans. Not Karajan. Twice he wrote directions for
me and drew maps of how to get places, and he had great difficulty
forming the letters and making the lines. This was after his stroke, true
enough, but his handwriting was scrawled and barely legible. That he
never marked a score, and that he rarely took a score to the podium
for a performance are well-known facts. It wouldn't be unusual for
dyslexia to accompany such powers of mental recall. If Karajan was
dyslexic, it could help explain his abrupt manner and his need to put
people in separate compartments.

Herbert von Karajan never seemed to attain the wisdom or even the
maturity that usually accompanies age. He was the spoiled-brat genius
to the end: endlessly suspicious, amazingly petty, frightfully cold, and
often laughably self-righteous.

I first met Herbert von Karajan in 1981 in St. Tropez aboard *Helisara*,
his 70-foot maxi sailboat. I was on assignment for an American yachting
magazine. Karajan spoke to me then about the possibility of doing a
book with him, saying that he very much admired another book I had
written. It was typical of the way he worked that it took 18 months
and a substantial exchange of letters before the project commenced.

Helisara is a very sophisticated race boat that requires a crew of 25.
It was too much for a man of Karajan's age and sailing ability, nor did
he have the time to campaign it with the other boats in its class.

But he loved sailing the boat, often commenting that no other sport demanded the coordination of so many people at one time. All his life he had commanded the services of the best sportsmen in the world. He skied with Stein Erickson, drove fast cars with Nikki Lauder, and went diving with Jacques Cousteau. Sailing was no different. In addition to Jobson, he hired Dennis Conner, Ted Hood, and Robbie Doyle to help him understands the workings of his maxi. During long afternoons in the Med, he practiced maneuvers for the Corinthian satisfaction of doing them well. He compared sailing the boat to conducting his orchestra.

My interviews with Karajan were held mostly at his villa in St. Tropez during the summer months. I would arrive at 9 a.m. and wait five to ten minutes until he arrived in the living room in a dressing gown. We would get directly to business. I don't usually use a tape machine, but he insisted. Having the machine at work seemed to make him more comfortable. In the afternoons, he would go sailing, and often invite me along. The crew of *Helisara* would moor the boat in the cove in front of his house, and send the rubber dinghy in for the Maestro.

In 1982, I went with him on a race in the Med from Toulon, France, to San Remo, Italy. There was little breeze, and it was very hot and uncomfortable on the boat. Karajan was dressed only in a bathing suit most of the race, and had a great time. When he wasn't steering the boat or napping, he sat in the cockpit regaling the crew with stories and jokes. He also spent time reading the manuals for various electronic instruments on board. Machinery and electronic devices were endlessly fascinating to him.

We won the race, and it was a very happy Herbert von Karajan who greeted the press on the dock in San Remo. As the victorious sailor, he was happy to have the cameras clicking away, and the microphones thrust in his face — quite unlike his attitude about cameras and reporters in the music world. He bantered happily with the paparazzi, then hopped in his car and roared away in a triumphant exit. Those were the days before his bad back caught up with him, and they provided just a glimpse of what a powerhouse the younger conductor/sportsman must have been.

Because I was a sailor, Karajan loved to subject me to his other sporting endeavors. And they were endeavors. Karajan did not play at sports, he worked at them. It was important to him that he perform to perfection, whether on the podium or behind the wheel of a boat, a car, or an airplane. The perfection was his pleasure. When he was driving any of the above, the muscles of his jaw were clenched in concentration, and he wanted no distractions. If someone spoke, he quickly shushed them.

One morning Karajan came by my motel in his new Renault sportscar and took me for a drive up the mountain behind the harbor at St. Tropez. He held the wheel with arms outstretched like a proper race driver, and never missed a shift as we careered up the twisting road at high speed. It was an impressive driving performance for any man, especially a man of 77. At the top, we got out of the car and looked across the Med. He told me he had been to auto racing school. "You can tell how well you are doing," he said with a chuckle, "by how many insects you are killing with the side windows."

He was equally proud of his flying prowess. Before flying with him I had heard the experience could be frightening. It was quite the opposite. Karajan was a good pilot. Once when I flew with him, he made a commendable landing at Munich in a tricky cross-wind. He was very proud of his twin-jet Dessault airplane, and of having passed a tough two-week course given by the manufacturer. "They got me up in the middle of the night," Karajan recalled, "put me in the plane, and told me to land it on the darkened runway."

Karajan was most proud of his sporting accomplishments. The musical accomplishments he considered appropriate to his talents, rightfully his. He expected those triumphs. But it was in the league of sportsmen where he most wanted to belong. He was also proud of his sporting equipment. His plane had the characteristics of a jet fighter, he said. And his cars and boats he considered the best, but with an interesting twist: they became the best because he owned them.

A year or so after my ride in his jet, I flew with him in a helicopter he piloted from his house in Anif to Munich. He had been taking lessons for several months, and handled the difficult coordination problem of flying the machine with aplomb. That day he was on his way to Hanover in northern Germany for his back operation. It pleased him that he was flying himself to the hospital.

After the operation, his pace was slowed. Not so much that he didn't continue to drive, however. Once when I arrived at his house in Anif for an interview, he suggested we go walking. He had a favorite forest several miles from the house, so we climbed into his Porsche. Moments later he was accelerating to 120 mph on the highway.

He entered the forest on an old logging road, and parked in a clearing about a mile in. We began our walk, with Karajan laboriously dragging his unwilling feet along. As we rounded a bend, we came upon a herd of cows, large animals each wearing a big bell around its neck. It was an amusing sight, though not as amusing as the sight of Karajan whacking playfully at one of the animals with his cap to move it from the path.

The film clips go on. There were countless days of rehearsals in the Festhaus in Salzburg with Karajan running his lackeys around unmercifully, stopping the action on stage by making annoying hissing noises through his microphone, repeating the same bad jokes to his entourage, and generally wielding his awesome power like a club. His unpredictable behaviour kept everyone on edge, and with reason. He could change direction as quickly as a bat, and strike with unexpected savagery. There was the afternoon he told his old co-worker Gunther Schneider-Seimsen, the well-known stage director, that Schneider-Seimsen had the eyes of a traitor.

In those days (the early 1980s), the war with the Berlin Philharmonic was hot and escalating. Often he would go off on petulant, vindictive diatribes about the behavior of certain players. "All of them are fools," he said one afternoon, with venomous disdain.

At his home in Anif, he had turned the basement into a professional-quality film editing room. He was in the process of re-recording (some of it for the fifth time) and filming on 16 mm his core repertoire (Brahms, Beethoven, Tchaikovsky, Bruckner). The project was an amazing study in self-aggrandizement. If a symphony ran for 45 minutes, 41 minutes of the finished film featured Karajan in close-up. He wanted to see as little as possible of the other players, as much as possible of himself. "The bassoon is an ugly instrument," he would say, making a cut. "That player is horrible looking, we don't need to see him," he would say with a laugh.

When asked how she could endure this exercise in egomania, Karajan's film editor, Gela Marina Runne, shrugged and said it was better working on a monument than on commercials. She had a point. I'm sure the films will be valuable for conducting students.

Vivid among the moments I remember was the day in Vienna, watching Karajan working with the Vienna Philharmonic at the Musikfreund, recording Brahms German Requiem. Just before he went into the rehearsal, Karajan told me in a whispered aside that he was going to have back surgery. Only a few of us knew at the time, and we were shocked by the news. He had resisted the inevitable surgery for years. We knew it would be a great ordeal for him at his age. Perhaps even fatal.

After a few section rehearsals, Karajan decided to play the entire piece. The tape was started, and it was a lucky thing. All the ingredients were there for magic, and that's what it was. The Requiem went from beginning to end without a hitch. Those of us fortunate enough to be there were left breathless, touched, riveted to our seats. At the end there was silence. Karajan simply put his baton down and left the hall.

Last of all was that nervous day in St. Tropez, sitting with the Maestro as he went through my book manuscript page by page. That's difficult enough with one's editor. With the subject of the book, it is a frightening prospect. Karajan hated confrontation, avoided it whenever possible. Through a third party I had learned he was furious about several sections of the book. I was told these sections *must* be changed. He wanted to solve the problems on paper. I asked for a meeting. He agreed.

Karajan was in his dressing gown, as always. We met at 9 a.m., as always. He sat on one side of the table with his copy of the manuscript. I sat on the other side with my copy. He began turning pages one at a time. He was unhappy about how little space I had given to his third wife, Elliette. He was unhappy I had included remarks from critics of his music. He pointed out that he had sold a hundred million records— wasn't that enough to squash anyone stupid enough to criticize him? And he was insistent that he had joined the Nazi party in 1935, not in 1933 as my research conclusively indicated.

I told him I could not make the changes he wanted. It was evident to me that while he insisted he had joined the Nazi party only to further his career—what he called his God-given mission to make music—he had been a great admirer of Adolf Hitler. His admiration for Hitler's determination was one that would endure. No listing of atrocities and no amount of time or maturity could temper it. Karajan's tenacity included philosophical ideals. He would rather have been shot than apologize for anything he did. But he did want that early date of joining the party erased from the record.

Karajan had driven me up beyond Berchtesgaden to the Eagle's Nest, Hitler's mountaintop fortification across the German border near Salzburg. There had been sadness in his voice as he pointed out the barely visible ruins of Hitler's bunker destroyed by Allied bombs. "There is no monument to him," Karajan said.

Four hours had passed before we turned the final page of the book in Karajan's St. Tropez living room. He had to sense that I would not make the critical changes he wanted. Yet Karajan did not show anger or temper or raise his voice. "Well, we are finished," he said. "We go sailing this afternoon—will you go?" I said I would.

That afternoon I returned to Karajan's villa. The rubber dinghy came in, but only for me. Karajan, I was told, was not feeling well.

For an hour or more *Helisara*'s skipper maneuvered the boat around a short triangular course within sight of Karajan's bedroom window that overlooked the Med. We tacked and jibed, raised and lowered the huge, colorful spinnaker, and made the boat fly through the water. All of us felt the Maestro's critical eye upon us. We knew that the next day he would tell us exactly what we had done wrong.

July 1989

Bibliography

Barwick, James, *The Hangman's Crusade*, Macmillan, London 1980

Berlioz, Hector, *The Conductor*, William Reeves, London 1970

Blyth, Alan (ed.), *Opera on Record*, Hutchinson, London 1979; Harper & Row, New York 1982

Cairns, David, *Responses*, DaCapo Press, New York 1982

Culshaw, John, *Putting the Record Straight*, Viking Press, New York 1982

Fest, Joachim, *Hitler: e. biographie*, Propylean-Verlag, Berlin 1973

Galway, James, *James Galway, An Autobiograpy*, Hodder & Stoughton, London 1979

Greene, Graham, *The Third Man*, Heinemann, London 1950; Penguin Books, New York 1981

Haeusserman, Ernst, *Herbert von Karajan*, Verlag Fritz Molden, Vienna 1978

Haffner, Sebastian, *The Meaning of Hitler*, Weidenfeld & Nicolson, London 1979, Macmillan, New York 1979

Haggin, B. H., *The Toscanini Musicians Knew*, Horizon Press, New York 1980

Haslip, Joan, *The Emperor and the Actress*, Weidenfeld & Nicolson, London 1982; The Dial Press, New York 1982

Leinsdorf, Erich, *The Composer's Advocate*, Yale University Press, New Haven 1981

Manvell, Roger and Fraenkel, Heinrich, *The Goebbels Diaries*, Doubleday, New York 1948

—— *Hitler*, Granada, London 1978

Menuhin, Yehudi, *Unfinished Journey*, Macmillan, London 1977; Knopf, New York 1977

Moor, Paul, "The Operator", *High-Fidelity* (October 1957)

Porter, Andrew (trans.), *The Ring of the Nibelung* (R. Wagner), Faber, London 1977

Prieberg, Fred K., *Musik im N.S.-Staat*, Fischer Taschenbuch Verlag, Frankfurt 1982

Reiss, Curt, *Joseph Goebbels*, Hollis & Carter, London 1949

Rickett, Richard, *Austrian History*, George Prachner Verlag, Vienna 1983

Ross, Nancy Wilson, *The World of Zen*, Vintage Books, New York 1960

Schonberg, Harold C., *The Lives of the Great Composers*, Davis-Poynter, London 1971; W. W. Norton (revised edition), New York 1981

Schwarzkopf, Elisabeth, *On and Off the Record*, Faber, London 1982; Scribners, New York 1982

Stead, Christina, *The Salzburg Tales*, Appleton-Century, New York, 1934

Stresemann, Wolfgang, ... *und abends in die Philharmonie*, Kristall bei Langen Muller, Munich 1981

Suzuki, Shunryu, *Zen Mind, Beginner's Mind*, John Weatherhill, New York 1970

Taylor, Fred (ed.), *The Goebbels Diaries, 1939-1941*, Hamish Hamilton, London 1982; Penguin Books, New York 1984

Watts, Alan, *This Is It*, John Murray, London 1961; Vintage Books, New York 1973

Weitz, John, *Friends in High Places*, Macmillan, New York 1982

Ziemke, Earl F., *The U.S. Army in the Occupation of Germany, 1944-1946*, Center of Military History, United States Army, Washington D.C. 1975

Index